Fighting Spirit
of East Timor

For Kamal
and the people of Timor Lorosae

Fighting Spirit of East Timor

The Life of Martinho da Costa Lopes

by
Rowena Lennox

Pluto Press
Australia

Zed Books
London and New York

First published in 2000 by Pluto Press Australia Limited
Locked Bag 199, Annandale, NSW 2038, Australia

First published outside of Australia by Zed Books
7 Cynthia St, London N1 9JF, UK
Room 400, 175 Fifth Avenue, New York NY10010, USA

Distributed in the USA exclusively by St Martins Press Inc.
175 Fifth Avenue, New York NY10010, USA

Copyright © Rowena Lennox 2000
Cover design by Justin Archer
Index by Neale Towart
Typeset by Chapter 8 Pty Ltd
Printed and bound by McMillan Printing Group

Proceeds from the sale of this book will be donated to the East Timor Relief
Association (ETRA) for their work in Timor Lorosae.

Australian Cataloguing-in-Publication Data
Lennox, Rowena, 1965–
Fighting Spirit of East Timor: the life of Martinho da Costa Lopes
Includes index.
ISBN 1 86403 089 5.
1. Lopes, Martinho da Costa, 1918–1991. 2. Catholic Church — Indonesia — Timor
Timur — Clergy — Biography. 3. Revolutionaries — Indonesia — Timor Timur —
Biography. 4. Timor Timur (Indonesia) — Biography. 5. Timor Timur (Indonesia)
— Politics and government — 20th century. I. Title.
959.8603092

UK Cataloguing-in-Publication Data
A catalogue record card for this book is available from the British Library.
ISBN 1 85649 832 8 hb
ISBN 1 85649 833 6 pb

US Cataloguing-in-Publication Data
Lennox, Rowena, 1965-
Fighting spirit of East Timor: the life of Martinho da Costa Lopes / Rowena Lennox.
p.cm.
Includes bibliographical references and index.
ISBN 1-85649-832-8 (cased) – ISBN1-85649-833-6 (softcover)
1. Lopes, Martinho da Costa, 1918-1991. 2.Timor Timur (Indonesia) – Biography.
3. Catholic Church – Indonesia – Timor Timur – Clergy – Biography. I. Title.
BX4705.L7139 L46 2000
282'.092 – dc21
[B]
00-024637

Contents

III Journeys

Preface

MARTINHO DA COSTA LOPES was the first Timorese leader of the East Timorese Catholic Church. He was born in East Timor in 1918 and educated in the traditional hierarchy of the Catholic education system. Ordained in 1948, he taught in Timor from 1948 to 1957, when he went to Lisbon for four years as a representative on the National Assembly. During the 1960s in East Timor he continued his pastoral and educational roles, and was a representative on the local legislative assembly. He was the editor of the Church newspaper *Seara* from August 1972 until it was closed by the Portuguese secret police in 1973. In July 1975 he was appointed vicar-general of Dili and on 23 October 1977, following the resignation of the bishop, Dom José Ribeiro, he became apostolic administrator of the diocese of Dili.

After the Indonesian invasion of East Timor in

December 1975, Dom Martinho worked tirelessly to protect human rights. He was the first person to speak out publicly within East Timor about the abuses perpetrated by the occupation forces and he brought the situation in Timor to the attention of the Australian Catholic Church. This attracted criticism from the Indonesian government and, under pressure from the Vatican, he resigned from the position of apostolic administrator and left East Timor in May 1983. In subsequent years he travelled extensively, speaking and raising awareness about East Timor. By the late 1980s his health was failing and in December 1990 he fell in the stairwell of his Lisbon apartment. For two weeks he lived on milk and biscuits, until a Timorese family took him in. He died in hospital on 27 February 1991.

I read about Dom Martinho's illness and death during my first visit to Timor in June 1991. With three friends I had travelled from Sydney to Darwin in an old Kingswood station wagon. In Darwin we met with East Timorese activists and were given information about recent events in Timor and the East Timorese diaspora. Three of us flew from Darwin to Kupang in West Timor and two of us took the night bus over the mountains from Kupang to Dili, the capital of East Timor. The sun rose as we descended from the mountains at the border between West and East Timor to the coast. It didn't take long for us to realise we were in an occupied country.

The story of Dom Martinho's last days is one of exile and loneliness. I was initially drawn to it because it offered a way of exploring *agonia*, the time between life and dying. I was also intrigued by East Timor, captivated by its beauty and curious to find out about it before

1975. I wondered whether Dom Martinho took refuge in his memories of a more distant past, the time of Portuguese colonialism.

In November 1991 my friend Kamal Bamadhaj, along with hundreds of others, was killed when Indonesian soldiers opened fire on unarmed civilians near Santa Cruz cemetery, Dili. My commitment to Dom Martinho's story, and the story of the struggle for self-determination in East Timor, was clinched. After I'd started researching Dom Martinho's life — reading about East Timor, interviewing those who knew him, and retracing his footsteps in Portugal, Macau and Timor — I began to see how important he was and is to the history of East Timor.

I have a debt the size of a mountain to the people who helped me compile this biography. To all those who shared their stories about Dom Martinho with me, and suggested others who might have stories to tell, I extend my sincere gratitude. Where possible I've attempted to acknowledge their insights in the notes, and I hope I have not misinterpreted the information I was given. This book belongs to the people of East Timor. I'm deeply grateful to the people who helped me research Dom Martinho's biography even though it was dangerous for them to do so.

Special thanks are due to Father António Alves for taking me under his wing in Timor and Marciano da Silva for interpreting and not giving up. I'd like to thank Pedro Lebre and his family, and Constancia and Cisco and their family for their hospitality. I'm grateful to the priests in Timor who shared their time and their stories with me, and I'd particularly like to thank Dom Martinho's family, Rosa da Costa Lopes, Sebastião da Costa

Lopes and João Lopes, for generously and courageously sharing their photographs and their memories.

I'm grateful to Luisa Pereira and Pat Walsh for sharing their knowledge with me and for steering me in the right direction in the early stages of the research. For translation and interpretation I'd like to thank Nelson Santos, Carlos de Jesus, Paula Pinto, Rocque Rodrigues, Joan Oliveira, Jocelyn Veira and Geoffrey Hull. For explaining aspects of the Catholic Church I'm grateful to Louise Crowe, Sister Kathleen O'Connor, Bishop Hilton Deakin and Father Francisco Fernandes. Thanks are due, too, to the staff at the Portuguese parliamentary archives, especially Abílio Fernandes Magalhães. I'd also like to thank José Alexandre Gusmão, Kirsty Sword, Natacha Meden and Kevin Sherlock for their generous assistance. Thanks are due to the people who put me up and put up with me while I was writing this book, in particular Emma Baulch, without whom I wouldn't have visited Timor in the first place. I'm indebted to the many people who read the manuscript at various stages of its development. I'd like to thank, especially, Louise Murray, Elizabeth Weiss, Carmel Budiardjo, Rick Lunn, Geoffrey Hull, James Goodman and Lyn Lennox, whose encouragement kept me going.

This book would not have been possible without the help and support of Agio Pereira, Ceu Brites, Ines Almeida and the members of the East Timor Relief Association (ETRA) in Sydney, and José Ramos-Horta and the Monsignor Martinho da Costa Lopes Peace and Democracy Foundation in Lisbon. Royalties from the book will be helping ETRA's work in East Timor. I'd also like to thank Tony Moore at Pluto Press for taking on Dom Martinho's story, Jacqueline Kent for editing the manuscript, and Kate Florance and the staff at Pluto for helping to turn the manuscript into a book.

A note on titles and sources

Martinho da Costa Lopes was called by different names throughout his life, and these names appear in the book. When he was a child and a young man at the seminary in Macau he was called Salvador. After his ordination he was called Father Lopes. His younger family members called him Tio Padre (uncle father or priest) and, after he became the leader of the Church in East Timor, Tio Bispo (uncle bishop). His father called him Tinu Kai. *Tinu* is a diminutive form of Martinho and *Kai* means strong or hard in the Timorese language Galolen. After he became apostolic administrator he was given the title Monsignor, abbreviated to Mgr. Although he was never officially named bishop of the diocese of Dili, the people of East Timor regarded him as their bishop and referred to him as the bishop. The text reflects this. Timorese addressed him as 'Ambispu' and Indonesians addressed him as 'Pastor'. In Timor and internationally he became affectionately known as Dom Martinho. *Dom* comes from the medieval Latin title *Domnus* or 'Sir' and is a Portuguese term of respect to prelates and noblemen.

Sources for information and quotes used in the text are given in the notes at the end of the book, with page numbers for reference.

Introduction

WHEN MARTINHO DA COSTA LOPES was trying to raise awareness in the international community about the East Timor situation in the mid 1980s, it seemed that the world did not care. He was slandered by Australian politicians and the press and he paid for his outspokenness by being forced to resign from the position of apostolic administrator of the diocese of Dili and leave Timor. In exile in Lisbon he was spurned by the Catholic Church. Since Dom Martinho's death in 1991, the East Timorese cause has gained much more attention and, because of international pressure, the justice and peace that he had sought for so long for his people could be within reach.

Developments in the international arena and in Indonesia have contributed to the change. The Cold War was a fact of international politics in 1975. Saigon had fallen to the Vietcong that year, despite US efforts to thwart communism in Vietnam. Cambodia and Laos followed.[1] Indonesia under Suharto was extremely anti-communist. Suharto came to power in 1965 and hundreds of thousands of Indonesian 'communists' were murdered in the process. In 1975 the US was committed to honouring its security arrangements in South East Asia and stopping the 'domino effect' of communism. The deep water straits just north of Timor were a stategic link between the Pacific and the Indian oceans, important for US nuclear submarines.[2] In Africa, as the Portuguese empire collapsed, marxist forces gained control in Angola and Mozambique. Australia, Indonesia and the United States did not want a new, unstable left-leaning republic in South East Asia and so, with the tacit support of Australia and the United States, Indonesia invaded East Timor. Jakarta delayed the invasion of Dili on 7 December 1975 until US President Gerald Ford and Secretary of State Henry Kissinger had left Indonesia.[3] They, like Australian leaders at the time, hoped that the Indonesian integration of East Timor would be accomplished quietly.

But it didn't work like that. The invasion was not successful. ABRI (the Indonesian armed forces, renamed TNI after the police split from the armed forces in April 1999) took years to secure the territory, and arguably it was never secured, with ABRI sustaining thousands of casulties throughout the conflict. The East Timorese maintained an armed resistance from the beginning. The brutality and repression practised by the Indonesian armed forces in East Timor, which resulted in the loss of 200,000 East Timorese lives (one-third of the pre-invasion population) by 1990, only served to turn the population against integration. In a tragic irony, the Indonesian regime in East Timor emulated the policies of their former colonial masters the Dutch, claiming that the occupation had been a civilising mission and that the East Timorese were ungrateful.[4]

This book outlines the terrible early years of the occupation. The people of East Timor had to survive systematic detention, rape, torture and murder, the desecration of their culture and the robbing of their lands. In the mountains of East Timor Falintil (the armed wing of the resistance) waged a David-versus-Goliath struggle against ABRI. East Timorese in exile worked on the diplomatic front, lobbying the United Nations and national governments. In the mid 1980s José Ramos-Horta asked the then Australian foreign minster Bill Hayden to convey to Jakarta the message that the East Timorese resistance was willing to negotiate without preconditions under UN auspices. Hayden declined to pass this message on, but Ramos-Horta persevered with UN and Portuguese diplomats. José Alexandre (Xanana) Gusmão, leader of the resistance in East Timor, articulated the principle of dialogue without preconditions in the late 1980s.[5] Despite what at times has seemed like slim hope, this perseverance has borne fruit.

In 1989 the Cold War ended. East and West Germany reunited and the Soviet Union ceased to exist. Communism was no longer the threat that it was perceived to be in 1975. In 1997 the Asian economic 'tigers' collapsed, leaving the region dependent on international bail-out packages. A stable and secure Indonesia remains a priority for the West and instead of using the threat of communism as the justification for its occupation of

East Timor, Jakarta started using a new tactic — the Yugoslavia scenario, or the idea that the unitary Republic of Indonesia could disintegrate into violence.[6] Still, East Timor remained an unresolved problem for the Jakarta government, now more dependent than ever on international capital. Foreign governments have become increasingly critical of Jakarta's record in East Timor.

In early 1991, just a week before Dom Martinho died, Portugal instituted proceedings against Australia at the World Court, arguing that Australia had breached its obligations to both Portugal and the East Timorese by entering into the Timor Gap Treaty with Indonesia to exploit the hydrocarbon resources in the Timor Sea. Four years later the World Court ruled that it could not adjudicate upon the dispute because of the absence of a third party, Indonesia. The foundation of the World Court's jurisdiction is consensual and states can only be judged if they consent to such judgment. Despite the disappointing ruling for supporters of East Timor, the court made it clear that East Timor still had a right to self-determination. The Court 'neither validated Indonesia's invasion nor Australia's subsequent practice in relation to that invasion'.[7]

Many Australians have been disgusted by the Australian government's 1978 recognition of Indonesian *de jure* sovereignty over East Timor, which paved the way for the 1990 Timor Gap Treaty.[8] For others, including both Labor and Liberal politicians and officials in the Department of Foreign Affairs and Trade, the Timor Gap Treaty was a cornerstone in Australia's close relationship with Indonesia, laying the basis for the 1995 Keating–Suharto 'Treaty on Maintaining Security'.

After the events of 1999, the idiocy of basing a close relationship with a powerful neighbour on the illegal and repressive occupation of a third country is widely recognised. The Indonesian government reneged on the security treaty in September 1999.

Canberra has a similarly hypocritical — even nonsensical — stance on East Timorese refugees. In the mid 1990s there were about 15,000 Timor-born people in Australia and about 5000 in Portugal. Despite the Australian government's recognition of Indonesian sovereignty in East Timor, the Department of Immigration maintains that East Timorese asylum seekers are actually Portuguese citizens, and should not be permitted to settle in Australia. Hundreds of young East Timorese, after fleeing persecution in East Timor and Indonesia, have had their lives put on hold in Australia.

The Dili massacre, in which more than 200 people were killed, is regarded as a turning point in international opinion on East Timor. At dawn on 12 November 1991 a funeral procession for a murdered independence supporter gathered at the Motael church on the seafront in Dili and proceeded to the Santa Cruz cemetery. Along the way, the procession turned into a pro-independence demonstration. Indonesian military opened fire on unarmed civilians near the cemetery. During the days following the massacre, more people were rounded up and killed. Unlike other atrocities in East Timor, foreigners witnessed the Dili massacre, the events in the cemetery were filmed and the story reached the outside world relatively quickly.

My friend Kamal Bamadhaj was shot at the Santa Cruz cemetery. He lost so much blood while the Red

Cross driver tried to get through the military roadblocks on the way to the hospital that he died. Kamal's mother, Helen Todd, successfully brought a charge against one of the Indonesian military officers responsible for the massacre while the officer was in the United States serving his 'punishment', which consisted of further military training in the US. While nothing came of it — the officer ignored the summons — he can no longer go to the United States. Indonesia maintained that fewer than fifty people were killed at the Santa Cruz cemetery. In the aftermath, East Timorese activists were jailed while no army members served any sentences.[9]

At the end of 1992 there was another blow to the resistance when Xanana Gusmão, leader of CNRM (National Council of Maubere Resistance, renamed CNRT, the National Council of Timorese Resistance, in 1998), was captured by the Indonesian military. He was sentenced to life imprisonment, which was later commuted to twenty years. Xanana remained a captive in Jakarta when the East Timorese went to the polls in August 1999. Throughout the 1990s the resistance kept up the struggle inside East Timor, in Indonesia and in other parts of the world to ensure that East Timor remained 'gravel in Jakarta's shoe'.[10]

Despite the growing solidarity movement, arms sales to Indonesia, mainly from the United States, the Netherlands, the United Kingdom and Germany, continued throughout the late 1980s and early 1990s. Within two months of the Dili massacre the British government sold a warship to Indonesia.[11] In 1996 peace activists in Britain deactivated the instruments of a Hawk 'trainer' jet, one of a batch of twenty-four destined for Indonesia, at the British Aerospace factory. The activists, accused of criminal damage, defended themselves by saying that their intention was to prevent a greater crime, the crime of genocide, being committed against the East Timorese. The jury acquitted them.[12]

The East Timorese took the lead in trying to send the message that the Indonesian occupation of East Timor was illegal, that genocide was under way and that the right of the East Timorese to self-determination was yet to be exercised. In Jakarta, East Timorese youths started to occupy foreign embassies, initially the US embassy during the APEC (Asia Pacific Economic Co-operation) conference in 1994, and later others. They were seeking asylum and trying to raise awareness about the plight of East Timor. Indonesian democracy activists accompanied the East Timorese, even though they could not expect asylum.[13]

In 1992 the CNRM peace plan was launched by José Ramos-Horta at a meeting of the European Parliament in Brussels.[14] The first phase of this plan was a humanitarian one dealing not with self-determination but with confidence building. This phase focused on achieving an immediate end to all armed activities in East Timor; the reduction of Indonesian troop presence to a maximum of 1000 within six months; the removal of all heavy weapons, tanks, helicopters, combat aircraft and long-range artillery; the immediate and unconditional release of all political prisoners; a reduction by 50 per cent of Indonesian civil servants in East Timor; the stationing in the territory of UN specialised agencies such as UNICEF, UNDP, WHO and FAO; a comprehensive census of the population; the establishment of an independent Human Rights Commission under the Catholic bishop; the lifting of all media control by the army; freedom of political activities; removal of the restriction on teaching Portuguese; and the appointment of a resident representative of the UN secretary-general.

José Ramos-Horta argued that these measures could be implemented without a loss of face for Indonesia. Indeed, not only would the confidence-building measures lead to decreasing resentment for Indonesia in East Timor, they would enhance Indonesia's international reputation.

The second phase of the CNRM peace plan was autonomy lasting from five to ten years. During this phase political parties, including those advocating independence for East Timor, would be legalised; the EU would set up a legation in East Timor headed by a senior Portuguese official; elections would be held for a territorial assembly with the UN to provide technical support and supervision for the process; only Timorese identified as such would be entitled to vote; the assembly would elect a governor for the territory; the assembly and the governor would have a five-year mandate; the territory would be able to enter into trade relations with foreign countries and promulgate its own laws affecting investment, land ownership, property and immigration; remaining Indonesian troops would be withdrawn; the territory would have no army and a UN-trained police force would be placed under the elected governor; there would be a further reduction in Indonesian civil servants; Portugal and Indonesia would normalise relations.

After this period of peace and freedom and in the absence of the Indonesian army, the most hated symbol of the occupation, the East Timorese could decide whether they preferred autonomy or whether they wanted to become independent. The third phase of the plan was self-determination.

Tragically, the agreement signed on 5 May 1999 by Indonesia and Portugal allowed for no period of transition. This agreement was the result of fifteen years' consultation between Indonesia and Portugal under the auspices of the UN secretary-general. The United Nations has played an important role in the search for justice and peace for East Timor and had been defining autonomy as a necessary step on the path to self-determination. The UN special rapporteur on torture, Professor P. H. Kooijmans, was in East Timor at the time of the Dili massacre. He recommended that the powers of the police and armed forces should be curbed by an indendent judiciary, that Indonesia should ratify the UN convention against torture and that an authority to deal with complaints about human rights violations should be established. In 1994 Bacré Waly N'Diaye, UN special rapporteur on summary, extra-judicial or arbitrary executions, called for an end to the impunity of the armed forces.[15] Such calls are still relevant.

Pressure on Jakarta from the United States, Japan and the European Union had been mounting throughout the 1990s. In 1996 the Nobel Peace Prize was awarded to José Ramos-Horta and Bishop Carlos Ximenes Belo, Dom Martinho's successor. The award raised East Timor's profile in the international community and sent a distressing message to some members of the elite in Jakarta.[16] The economic collapse of Indonesia in 1997 and the subsequent bail-out by the IMF increased Indonesia's dependence on an international community that was becoming aware of and outspoken about Jakarta's human rights record. On 21 May 1998, after months of popular protest across Indonesia, President Suharto resigned. He was replaced by a caretaker president, Dr B. J. Habibie.

Meanwhile, in April 1998 East Timorese political representatives from East Timor and the diaspora met in Lisbon and adopted a 'Magna Carta concerning freedoms, rights, duties and guarantees of the People of East Timor'.[17] After peaceful rallies in Dili calling for independence in June and July 1998, President Habibie announced in August his plan of 'special status' for East Timor as a solution to the problem. He agreed to participate in the UN autonomy negotiations on the basis that this would not mean recognition of East Timor's right to self-determination. In East Timor during September and October 1998 there were large-scale offensives aimed at wiping out Falintil. Despite troop withdrawals staged for the international media in Dili, there were more that 21,000 troops on the ground in East Timor in September. In October the Jakarta-appointed governor of East Timor proclaimed that all public servants supporting independence would be sacked.[18]

In November thousands of people in Dili protested against ABRI's closing off of the area of Alas, south of Dili. There were reports of a massacre, with forty-two confirmed dead, forty injured and 200 missing. Colonel Suratman, the ABRI commander in East Timor, claimed publicly in December that he planned to arm pro-integration militias throughout the territory.[19]

In January 1999 President Habibie made a surprising and unsettling offer that set autonomy against self-determination and closed off the possibility of reconciliation and a peaceful transition.[20] He said that if East Timor did not accept special autonomous status, the territory would be given its independence by 1 January 2000. In February Xanana was moved from prison to house arrest in Jakarta.

While Indonesia, Portugal and the UN met in the absence of East Timorese leaders to discuss what was to become the 5 May Agreement, ABRI colluded with the militias and the campaign of intimidation and violence in East Timor escalated. It is interesting to observe how Jakarta tried to depict the conflict as being between pro-integration and pro-independence Timorese, while a Japanese TV crew filmed ABRI soldiers handing guns to militia members[21] and foreign observers reported Indonesian military and police standing by as the militias rampaged. On 6 April militia members massacred civilians in the parish priest's house at Liquiçá. This was followed by violence in Dili and Suai. In rural areas thousands of people were herded into holding centres to be 'persuaded' to vote for autonomy within Indonesia. Despite the visit of General Wiranto, head of the Indonesian armed forces, to Dili on 21 April to oversee the signing of a 'Peace Accord', the militias and ABRI controlled the roads throughout East Timor and prevented human rights and humanitarian organisations' access to the camps where tens of thousands of people were being held without adequate food, shelter, medical supplies or sanitation.[22]

The 5 May Agreement between the Republic of Indonesia and the Portuguese Republic on the question of East Timor provided for a popular consultation with the East Timorese people regarding autonomy for the province. The UN, the East Timorese and CNRT regarded the vote as an act of self-determination, but Jakarta objected to the use of the word 'referendum' and termed the vote a 'consultation'. The vote was scheduled for early August 1999; the people of East Timor would be asked:

> Do you accept the proposed special autonomy for East Timor within the unitary state of the Republic of Indonesia?
> or
> Do you reject the proposed special autonomy for East Timor, leading to East Timor's separation from Indonesia?[23]

The agreement laid out a schedule for an information campaign, voter registration, a political campaign and balloting both within and outside of East Timor. Indonesia and Portugal would be entitled to send an equal number of observers, and Indonesian authorities would ensure a secure environment for a free and fair popular consultation process. They would also be responsible for the security of UN personnel.

There were some serious flaws in the 5 May Agreement, which had devastating consequences on the ground in East Timor. While the UN did not recognise Indonesian sovereignty over East Timor, security was entrusted to the Indonesian military. Portugal had been trying to hold out for an international security presence. The US, too, had wanted peacekeepers in the territory, but Canberra argued against Lisbon and Washington on this issue, instead backing up Jakarta's position regarding the security role of ABRI.[24] Timorese leaders had been left out of the discussions. Xanana remained under house arrest in Jakarta. José Ramos-Horta was not permitted to return to East Timor.[25]

After two postponements because of lack of security in the territory, the ballot took place on 30 August 1999. With the presence of UN observers and foreign media, the heroism of the East Timorese people, who travelled long distances and queued to vote before dawn on the day of the poll, was broadcast to the world — 98.6 per cent of 451,792 registered voters turned out.[26] However, the situation was tense; the militias remained at large and when the results of the ballot were announced a few days later, with an overwhelming majority (78.5 per cent) rejecting autonomy in favour of independence, the terrible rampage began.

Hundreds of thousands of people were forcibly removed and held in camps in West Timor. By 26 September there were 232,672 East Timorese in West Timor according to the East Nusatenggara (the administrative region of Indonesia covering Timor) refugee co-ordination centre in Kupang, West Timor.[27] Humanitarian access to the camps was denied. Other Timorese took refuge in the churches and in the UN compound and the bishop's residence in Dili. However, they weren't safe. Foreigners were evacuated while the militias targeted independence supporters. Many fled to the hills. Many were killed. Militias destroyed property and looted. The Câmara Eclesiástica in Dili was ruined so the Catholic Church's records of births, deaths and marriages no longer exist — that is, independent records of the genocide over the twenty-four years of occupation have been erased. Protestant and Catholic clergy were assaulted and murdered; churches, towns and villages were burned to the ground. With UN sanction, Indonesia responded to the violence by imposing martial law, and bringing in still more soldiers and police.

While many people believed that Habibie's offer of autonomy or independence was made in good faith and that only rogue elements of the Indonesian military supported, armed and trained the militias, it became obvious that Jakarta's object was to remove the question of East Timor permanently from the UN agenda, to destabilise the territory and to make an independent East Timor unviable. The militia violence was strategic. It aimed to frighten foreign media out of East Timor, to contain UNAMET (the United Nations Assistance Mission in East Timor), to punish the East Timorese[28] and to make an example of East Timor for other secessionist movements in Indonesia. As early as April 1999 both the Australian Secret Intelligence Service and the Defence Signals Directorate facility near Darwin had linked the head of the Indonesian armed forces, General Wiranto, with the militias.[29] Yet the Australian government failed to act on this information. The transportation of more than 200,000 people from East Timor to West Timor and other parts of Indonesia required detailed prior planning.[30]

On 12 September 1999 Indonesia was finally forced to accept an international peacekeeping force in East Timor and on 20 September the deployment of Interfet (the International Force for East Timor) began.[31] However, it is possible that Jakarta's attempts to destabilise East Timor will continue despite the UN presence. Without TNI support and backing in West Timor it is unlikely the pro-integration militias will be able to sustain a guerrilla war in East Timor. Ominously, Indonesia opposed the setting up of a UN Human Rights Commission of inquiry into violations in East Timor, and, at the end of September 1999, there was still no evidence that TNI and West Timor authorities were providing security from the militias for refugees in the West Timor camps.[32]

Peace and justice for the new nation of Timor Lorosae are directly linked to democracy in Indonesia. Hopefully, the violence and destruction imposed by the Indonesian armed forces and its lackeys in East Timor, and in other parts of the archipelago, are a sign that the military is in its death throes. On 19 October 1999 a new Indonesian parliament agreed to ratify East Timor's independence. The price the East Timorese have paid for this independence — over the twenty-four years of occupation and during the terrible months before and after the consultation of 30 August 1999 — is extortionate, but I, like many others, believe East Timorese resilience will be triumphant.

Like his people, Dom Martinho paid a high price for his beliefs. Hopes for an independent East Timor seemed distant as he became increasingly ill and depressed in 1990. When he died in 1991 he was the national hero of a forgotten people, an outspoken leader who devoted his life to the service of his community. He had been a central figure in the East Timorese Catholic Church and in the struggle for self-determination, beginning the work that Bishop Belo has continued. At the end of his life, however, Dom Martinho was marginalised by the Church, living on the periphery of his expatriate community. Nevertheless, he was and is well remembered in East Timor, and in 1997 his role was recognised internationally with the establishment of the Mgr Martinho da Costa Lopes Peace and Democracy Foundation in Portugal. The story of Dom Martinho's life is, in some ways, emblematic of the story of his country. *Fighting Spirit of East Timor* aims to contribute to his legacy by tracing the important role of this selfless leader.

EAST TIMOR

I

Poverty and plenty

•1•

Fall

IT WAS THE EVENING OF Wednesday, 5 December 1990. The repetitive arcs of the wipers and drizzle smeared the windscreen of the Renault as Dom Martinho drove up the hill on his way home. If his sight had been stronger and he had looked through the rear view mirror he might have been able to see the shanties and beyond them the wide River Tagus flowing to the sea. The river's motion was imperceptible, unlike the jerky gear changes of the Renault. Ahead he could perhaps just make out the greenish hump of unkempt grass at the top of the hill and, overspanning it, the dome of the Lisbon sky, darkening behind the clouds.

When the Renault's brakes screeched, Dom Martinho might have winced as he had trained his face to wince, impassively, the drooping furrows around his mouth and eyes deepening very slightly. Perhaps one last shudder ran through the car after he had turned off the engine outside his apartment, as if it were saying, 'I could go on, you know. I don't have to stop now.' And then quiet. If he sat for a few moments, out of breath from the drive, collecting himself, he might have heard the shouts of kids playing in the dying light on the vacant land across the road.

Dom Martinho's sight was poor. He had had time to become accustomed to the cataract curtains over his eyes and perhaps he felt slightly more confident in the dusk as he made his way to the apartment building at 109 Rua da Eira, fumbled with the door and searched with his hand for the light switch on the pebble-dash wall.

When his hand found the switch and pressed it, nothing happened. He moved forward in the dark, dark made darker because of his exhaustion. There was only a short flight of stairs down to his basement flat but he was slow and corpulent. There was an ornate light fitting but no light to reflect from his thick glasses, no light to guide him.

Which step did he slip on? Did he wonder whether his fall was part of God's plan, an event that had an intrinsic meaning and purpose, or whether it was just a gratuitous, meaningless piece of bad luck, one of those things? Perhaps his fall happened so quickly he couldn't remember the exact order of events. His flailing arm missing the banister, the palm of his hand slapping the wall as he slid, the jab of pain in his coccyx, dismay weighing down his face, his open mouth merging into the darkness. Dom Martinho was stuck on the stairs, thinking perhaps that the slow trickle from the cut under his eye was just moisture from the rain outside.

The banister was too far away for him to reach. The

wall was too sheer for him to grip. His arms would not raise him and his legs could not bear the weight of his torso to lift him. None of these things would have stopped him from trying to get up, because he was a determined man, but the strain wore him out. If he did call for help, no one heard him.

The blue ceiling and its white cornices were a long way away from the bulk of the old man. The old man was a long way away from the cheeky child he had once been, the boy who had corrected his schoolteachers and run away from home so that he could study. In his middle years he had represented his country, Portuguese Timor, in the metropolitan parliament in Lisbon. Later, after East Timor was invaded and occupied by Indonesia, it felt as if the world had abandoned the Timorese. But he had stuck his neck out. He had talked about a situation that people in Timor had not been permitted to mention. Because of that he had been regarded as an indefatigable troublemaker, and had been forced into exile.

Who was going to help this man who had helped so many people? Dom Martinho had been tireless. In Timor he had carried flour and sugar to hungry widows and orphans, clothing and messages to people in prison. He had offered refuge to those in need. He had tried to ensure the safety of prisoners held by the military authorities. He had compiled lists of those who had gone missing and he had not kept quiet about them, nor about the massacres and military operations.

Perhaps, as he lay on the hard floor tiles at the foot of the cold marble stairs, he thought back to the invasion and sacking of Dili; the gruelling war that followed as the occupation forces tried to control the interior; the starvation and disease of villagers and townspeople forced to flee the army and then forcibly resettled in camps in military-controlled areas; the indiscriminate murder of the young and the old. Perhaps his horror — at the militarisation of his whole society with the compulsory enlistment of civilians in the campaign to flush any resistance to the occupation, at the years of terror as the occupiers sought to silence any dissent — was as strong as ever.

Dom Martinho might have had little recollection of his neighbour helping him to his feet and supporting him while he took the few last steps to his threshold a few hours after his fall. The old bishop sat on the sofa in his cramped basement flat as the rain bore down over Alto de Alges. His back was sore and he could hardly feel his feet. He didn't realise his eye needed bathing. It was predictable, the December darkness and the cold winter rain falling on Lisbon.

At home, in Timor, hot December rain ushered in the wet season. There the rains were a time for rebirth. The rivers swelled. The *aia forfora* bird sang and it was time to plant the rice. At the granary, the oldest woman in the village cupped her hands around the grains. She passed them on to her younger sister, who passed them on to her cousin, who passed them on to another woman, and so on, until the rice had passed through the hands of all the women elders of the clan. These were the hands that had woven and planted and cooked and carried. These were the hands that would ensure the harvest was bountiful, that the chickens and goats were fat. These were the hands too far away to care for Dom Martinho.

• 2 •

Beginnings

MARTINHO DA COSTA LOPES always had something to say. As a child of about eight he sat with a solemn face for the group photograph in front of the Portuguese administrator's residence at Liquiçá, but his serious face belied his enthusiasm, his cheeky chatter. The building was a gracious-looking emblem of the languid colonial administration — curvilinear columns on the entrance patio, curved stairs leading up to it, thick walls. Martinho Lopes sat on the ground in front of the most important Portuguese administrative officials on their chairs, right in the centre, by himself. The Portuguese wore white. Their clothes were pristine, like the white stairs and the white walls of the building. The Timorese, wearing traditional dress — patterned *tais* (cloths wrapped around the waist) and no shirts — stood in rows behind the Portuguese. Martinho, dressed in shorts and a short-sleeved shirt, sat with his knees up to his chest and legs crossed below the knee. Unselfconsciously at the centre of the various hierarchies captured in the photograph, he looked ready for whatever role he was to play.

His parents, António and Isabel da Costa Lopes, had been married in a church. António was from Laleia, a village east of Dili on the north coast of Portuguese Timor, and he worked as a nurse. Isobel was from Bucoli, a village on a hill a little further east than Laleia, between Vemasse and Baucau. They already had one son, Cristóvão, born in 1915. António wanted more children, however, and while he was working in the infirmary at Liquiçá he met Binamo. It seems António travelled regularly in the course of his work for the colonial administration. When Binamo became pregnant, António brought her to live with him at Laleia.

This was in 1918, a time of some stability in Portuguese Timor after three decades of upheaval. The last years of the nineteenth century and the early and middle decades of the twentieth saw a new zeal in Portugal's colonising mission. Agreements made in Europe about Africa reverberated in Portugal's most distant colony. Until the 1890s the Timorese had been responsible for extracting the beeswax, cutting the white sandalwood, growing the coffee and providing the small quantities of maize, horses, buffaloes, beeswax and slaves that made up the exports of Portuguese Timor. Chinese merchants and a few Arab traders were the middlemen in these enterprises. The authority of the traditional local rulers or *liurai*s was absolute and independent of the Portuguese, who had no permanent posts in the interior.

At the Congress of Berlin in 1884–85 Portugal's

dream of an empire that covered the whole of southern Africa from the Atlantic to the Indian Ocean was shattered. During the late nineteenth century European countries, including the most industrially advanced nations of England, France and Germany, scrambled for colonies in Africa. The Congress of Berlin established that for control of an African territory to be legal, its occupation must be effective. Consequently Lisbon enacted legislation regarding tax and labour to ensure that its territories were firmly under colonial control. The subsequent uprisings were not confined to Timor, but occurred throughout most of Portuguese Africa.

In 1887 Lacerda Maia, the new and oppressive governor of Timor, was assassinated in Dili. Under the leadership of Dom Boaventura of Manufahi (a kingdom on the south coast of Timor corresponding with the present-day district of Same), some of the *liurai*s of Timor made a blood pact to resist the Portuguese. When Governor José Celestino da Silva arrived in Timor in 1894 strife was rampant. There were uprisings in many districts, and in some areas agriculture had been abandoned altogether. In 1895, with a force of twenty-eight Europeans and 12,000 other troops, Silva set out to vanquish Dom Boaventura. After several months of bitter fighting Silva claimed victory, even though Manufahi did not surrender until 1900. Silva set about pacifying and developing the territory and Timor was declared an autonomous province; the governor of Timor was no longer under the authority of the administration in Macau, but answered directly to Lisbon.

Silva preferred large plantations to smallholdings and proceeded to 'pacify' the mountain area around Ermera south-west of Dili because it was well-suited to coffee. SAPT (Sociedade Agrícola Pátria e Trabalho), which had been established by Silva in 1897 and became Portuguese Timor's largest agricultural company and import/export agency, moved into the district. The plantations relied on short-term labourers. Employers told the local military commander how many workers they needed — the commander told the local chiefs to supply the workers and the planters paid the chiefs a fixed price per worker.

After 1908, the year that Silva left Timor, some of the plantations were controlled by military garrisons. The military were responsible not only for keeping law and order but for civil and administrative roles. Governor Silva's successor, Eduardo Marques, introduced a head tax. Every Timorese male between the ages of sixteen and sixty had either to produce agricultural products for the market or engage in wage labour.

After the Republicans came to power in Portugal in 1910, Filomeno da Câmara was appointed governor of Timor. Silva's policy of large landholdings was reversed and Câmara gave small concessions to his cronies in the bureaucracy. Câmara granted some land to Timorese in an effort to quash the power of the *liurais*. Although the Republicans had ideals about labour reform, their progress in this area amounted to replacing slave labour with forced labour.

In an attempt to stimulate a free flow of labour the head tax was doubled, but this strategy failed. Tax could be paid by selling produce, and wages were so low that paid employment was not an attractive proposition. Consequently all able-bodied Timorese adults, men and women, were legally obliged to work for wages unless they were chiefs or property owners or were regularly employed. These conditions, combined with prohibitions on cutting sandalwood trees before they were a certain age, the imposition of a tax on every tree cut, and a tax on the slaughter of animals for festivities, as well as new conditions on the registration of coconut trees and live-stock, fomented widespread rebellion across the whole central area of Portuguese Timor, from Oecusse in the west to Baucau and Quelicai in the east to Dili in the north and Same in the south. Another factor that might have contributed to the rebellion was the new Republi-can Portuguese flag. The flag was regarded as a totem or *lulik* by many Timorese and many resented the change in design.

The leader of the Great Rebellion of 1912 was Dom Boaventura, the son of the leader of the 1895 revolt. The centre of the rebellion was Manufahi. On 5 October 1911 a number of *liurais* made another blood pact against the Portuguese; others, such as the *liurai* of Suro–Ainaro, swore to remain loyal to Lisbon. Those who remained loyal to Lisbon preferred the indirect rule of the Portuguese. They feared that, if the Portuguese left Timor, they would be crushed by the Dutch as West Timorese leaders had been.

In December Suai was the first site of the anti-Por-tuguese revolt, followed by other places. In January 1912 the *Pátria*, a gunboat from Macau, arrived in Timor and started to bombard Dom Boaventura's forces on the south coast. In February 1912 rebels looted Government House in Dili. Two Portuguese officers were decapitated and their heads paraded through the capital. After the governor telegraphed for help, reinforcements of one hundred Europeans and two hundred natives were sent to Timor from Mozambique; still the uprising could not be thwarted. More reinforcements were sent from Mozambique but by April conditions were worse. It was August before the Portuguese, with the help of Timorese forces hostile to Dom Boaventura and his followers, finally defeated the rebellion. According to Portuguese accounts thousands of Timorese were killed and wounded in the last great battle of the revolt. Dom Boaventura was put in shackles. People say that he was imprisoned at Aipelo, twenty kilometres from Dili, and that he was buried under the gates of the Santa Cruz cemetery in Dili, so his grave would be trampled by those who went to Mass.

After Dom Boaventura had been defeated the Portuguese strengthened their grip on Timor, setting up administrative posts in the interior and dividing the *liurais' reinos* (kingdoms) into smaller units of administration called *sucos* (princedoms). The Portuguese tried to maintain control with limited numbers and resources by allowing some traditional rulers to retain private armies and by prohibiting movement between districts. In addition, intermarriage between *liurais* was forbidden after 1912.

Governor Câmara tried to force the Timorese to cultivate cash crops. Each family was to grow coffee, coconut trees were planted and sandalwood seedlings were raised in nurseries. However, the coffee plants were placed too close together in unsuitable areas and neglected, and the sandalwood seedlings failed. The Timorese resented the theft of their lands and the destruction of sacred sites for the planting of cash crops.

The colonising mission was an organising mission. In 1914 the long-disputed border between Dutch Timor and Portuguese Timor was finally settled. The forced labour code of 1914 stipulated that all male 'natives' who did not have a cash income had to work for wages for at least three months of the year. If they did not comply, they could be forced to work on public works. Corrupt and underpaid officials told chiefs to round up workers, and then the workers' labour was sold to entrepreneurs.

It was in this stability that Martinho da Costa Lopes was conceived in 1918.

Liquiçá, Binamo's home town, is situated between two rivers on the north coast of Timor about forty kilometres west of Dili. Binamo's bumpy journey east, by foot and by pony, took her from the bougainvillea-lined streets and substantial colonial buildings of Liquiçá over the headland, around the Bay of Tibar, past the salt lake at Tacitolu to Dili. East of Dili the road climbed over the mountains and descended to Hera. The buttress roots of the mangrove trees jutted from the salt flats as she followed the shore of the turquoise sea. On her left the island of Atauro rose from the water like a dream. On her right the ridges were tinged sienna by sunlight. In the district of Manatuto the road was scratched into marble mountains that crashed straight into the water. Near the town of Manatuto the land flattened out and the waves of the quiet north sea, the female sea, formed frills on the grey coral shelf.

It was the dry season, so Binamo and her travelling companions were not obliged to wait for days or weeks at Manatuto in order to cross the Lacló River that divided

Portuguese Timor in two during the wet season, or to travel inland for miles looking for a suitable ford. Near Laleia the land looked dry and barren. The mountains had been replaced by hills. An outcrop of black, rounded rocks marked the village.

Who can remember whether the grotto of Our Lady of Fátima was there when Binamo arrived in 1918? Perhaps the statue of Our Lady came to reside underneath her carved rocky canopy when Father Almeida, a Goan priest, built the church of the Blessed Virgin Mary at Laleia in 1933. Perhaps the shrine was there before the church. The rocky outcrop looked like a sentinel, situated at a bend in the road, overlooking the Laleia River. Perhaps the rocks had had a different significance before the shrine to Our Lady claimed the spot for the Christian faith.

South of the village of Laleia stretched the Laleia River valley. During the wet the Laleia River swelled and broke bridges on its journey from the mountains near Lacluta to the sea. During the dry season the river dried up and became a wide, stony river bed. All or nothing, the rivers of Timor. In the village, circular *palapa* (bamboo) huts with palm-frond thatched roofs looked out over the river. Children, pigs and goats played in the mud.

People rarely spoke affectionately of Laleia. In the dry season it was hot and dusty. In the wet season, which approached as Binamo's pregnancy came to term, it was hot and muddy. Laleia was only about eighty kilometres east of Dili but it felt like a frontier town, even though there had been contact between the locals and the Portuguese for a long time. It was from the east that the village looked cohesive. Below the string of huts along the ridge, rice paddies stretched out in front of the Laleia River. Rice and maize grew at Laleia, as well as eucalyptus trees, coconut and sago palms, mangroves, banyans and bananas. Behind the village the mountains of Manatuto faded into the sky.

In Tetum, the most widely spoken language of East Timor's fifteen or so languages, *lalehan* means heaven, and some say that Laleia means 'heaven'. But heaven is not like this world. When the child of Binamo and António was due to be born, the Portuguese officers called António away to another village, Uatolári, where his wife Isabel was living, leaving Binamo to give birth without António's support, isolated among the Galolen speakers of Laleia. Perhaps Binamo gave birth within earshot of 'the sweet monotonous chant of water/sometimes flowing gently,/sometimes a rushing babble, as though afraid,/hiding amid weeds the colour of hope'.

On Saint Martin's Day, 11 November 1918, Salvador Martinho da Costa Lopes came into this world. Possibly the old wise women put the placenta of the newborn baby into a bag and took it away from the site of the birth to a secret place. Maybe they cursed and threatened any men they met on the journey to frighten them away, as was the custom, because they believed it was bad luck for men to catch sight of the bag.

Binamo died before her baby had been baptised and she was buried in Liquiçá. Isabel da Costa Lopes took in Martinho as a foster child and he publicly acknowledged Isabel as his mother though, five decades after Binamo had died and after Martinho da Costa Lopes had become a priest, he asked the parish priest at Liquiçá to represent him at Binamo's grave. Isabel, too, died before World War II, at Lahane near Dili. The family called him 'Salvador' at home, and he was called 'Salvador' at his elementary school in Liquiçá, and later at school in Soibada and at the seminary in Macau.

When Martinho was very young, António went to Liquiçá to work at the infirmary. His sons Cristóvão and Martinho, and probably Isabel, went with him. At some places on the journey west the mountains seemed to tip the road into the sea. Seen from the pass high above it, Dili emerged from its swamp: a few white buildings around the harbour; a half-hearted lattice of dirt roads petering out into bush that camouflaged brown *palapa* huts. Dili was more than halfway to their destination; the most difficult terrain was behind them. Their journey might have taken months. If they travelled in the wet season they would have had to ford flooding rivers. The journey would have been made longer by their visiting friends and family along the way.

The infirmary at Liquiçá combined modesty and grandeur in Portuguese proportions. It was a single-storeyed building with a coat-of-arms over the door, sheer façades, balustraded verandahs at the front and the back with short columns decorated with the cross of St George, and deeply recessed windows onto the veran-dahs. As a child Martinho would have played in the deep shade of the verandahs and among the oleander trees in the swept-earth yard behind the infirmary. Every day he walked down the hill from the infirmary, past the court of justice — another striking combination of severity and austere decoration — and past the district adminis-trator's house to the primary school, one of the few state primary schools in Portuguese Timor. Down the hill a couple of hundred metres further, the north sea lapped on the ash-coloured beach.

Martinho loved school. Hungry and thirsty for reading and writing and arithmetic, he completed first, second and third grades in record time. It was a small school in a solid, homely building. What he learned at school showed him new worlds, civilisation — the world that, according to the times, was the real one, the world that mattered. So when his father went to work at the hospital in Dili, taking his brother Cristóvão with him, Martinho gladly stayed with his uncle, Feliciano Freitas, in Liquiçá.

It was during the late 1920s that António de Oliveira Salazar came to power in Lisbon, the metropolis of the Portuguese colonial empire. The Portuguese republic was over. Less than two decades before the religious orders had been expelled from Timor. Some lay priests had remained but they were confined to their schools, unable to travel without permission, and they could only teach. In the early 1920s the Canossian sisters came back to Timor but the Salesians and the Jesuits did not return until after World War II. Salazar's ascent marked the beginning of a long-running and cosy liaison between the Church and the government. His fascist Estado Novo policies in faraway Lisbon — patriotic unity of the Portuguese empire, and the close co-operation of the Catholic Church and the state — would have a profound effect on the shape of Martinho's life, not just on the history and geography he learned or even the language he wrote in. But, of course Martinho didn't know that then. All he knew was that he loved history, the history of Portugal. He loved geography, the geography of Portugal. Before he had lost his baby teeth his expansive mind could make that history and geography relevant and meaningful in the hills near Liquiçá or by the water of the Ombai Straits. When Dom José da Costa Nunes, bishop of Macau and Dili, visited from Macau looking for the best and brightest boys in Timor to go to the seminary in Macau when they were old enough and become priests, Martinho was proud to be singled out.

Despite his success at school, life at home was not very good after Feliciano Freitas divorced his first wife and remarried. Perhaps it was Martinho's specialness that his uncle's new wife didn't like: his cleverness, his talking. She gave him all the hard manual work to do. The tasks never ended.

For half the year the sun baked the mountains and the dry earth turned to dust, and for the other half the rains turned the dust to mud and the gullies to rivers. The farmers wondered when the rains would come, and when they would stop. The coffee plantations foundered and prospered. The September winds blew through the leaves of the coconut palms and banana trees and their noise might have brought the clamour of ancient and heroic cavalry assaults to the hills where Martinho Lopes did his chores at dawn.

At the schoolhouse there were books, precious and rare. Reading made Martinho's days bearable. Even the most repetitive little exercise books contained worlds more marvellous than farm routine: burning, clearing, planting, weeding, digging the garden, tending and feeding the stock. Even the most faded and archaic cover promised more than the bleating of a forlorn sheep or the unyielding earth covering a heartily sized yam.

Martinho had been converted. Every day, with the faith of a believer and the audacity of the chosen, he took one of the scarce books from the dark classroom to the hard sunlight of the fields. There was hardly any grass to keep the sheep content, so he broke branches from the trees. While the sheep ate the leaves, he read. His eyes and his child's finger followed the lines of type. His tongue fiddled in the cavity made by a lower loose tooth. It was hanging on by a strand. It felt jagged and his gums bled, but he didn't mind the pain. Pain was a gift, in a way, some kind of test. He could bear pain. Silently, that was the way to do it. He would use pain. It would make him strong.

The end of fourth class, the end of primary school was looming. He was too young to finish primary school and not old enough to go to the seminary. What would he do?

The heat of the sun beat him, the sheep and the hill-side indiscriminately. It glared down on the days in front of him. So many of them, without variation. Martinho knew how hot it would be in the middle of the day, how early he would have to get up to tend the garden and the animals. He knew the seasons and the work they brought. He didn't mind the work. It, too, would make him strong. But he wanted more than earth and yams and sheep and the familiar, distant sky. He wanted more than the indistinct days that animals experience. Perhaps that was why he decided to leave the sheep and the horses and the stupefying labour and his uncle and his uncle's wife, and go to Dili.

His journey was only as miraculous as any journey in

19

Timor was in those days: a small boy travelling on foot and riding a borrowed horse with dozens of kilometres to traverse. That was the way everybody travelled. For Martinho it was an adventure. He knew how to live off the land and when he reached Dili he met Manuel Sarmento, a colleague of his father's. Manuel took him to the island of Atauro, where António was working. Martinho spent time in Atauro and in Dili before he went to live with the priests. Somehow, even though he had finished primary school and there was nowhere for him to go, he ended up at school in Dili for a while.

It was a big school — 120 students — and it was free. Each district could send three students. They played soccer and basketball, and Martinho loved the sports field as much as he loved the history and geography of Portugal. His classmates regarded him as close to perfect at school, top of his class in every subject and a good athlete as well. He liked to prove he was tough. At school in Dili he met Alberto Soares, who was tough, too. One day Martinho broke his arm, or, as Alberto claimed later, Alberto broke Martinho's arm.

In split seconds both boys raced across the patchy grass of the field straining after the same thing, the *toranja* — a Timor grapefruit that served as a football and was often kicked to smithereens by bare feet before the end of a game. The *toranja* was rolling, rolling. Who hit and who pushed and who tripped? Alberto and Martinho neck and neck, chest and chest, thighs intertwined, hard breaths mingling. From the end of someone's foot the *toranja* spurted into the sunlight. One thing was as clear as the sunshine-etched sphere of the *toranja*: it was Martinho who hit the ground. He didn't cry out with pain. He got up by himself, and a teacher came to help him as he walked from the field, his arm twisted beside him.

When Martinho was about eleven years old, Salazar's Colonial Act was introduced. According to the Act, Lisbon administered all Portugal's colonies and constitutional rights for indigenous peoples became dependent on their assimilation into a Portuguese lifestyle. This meant that António da Costa Lopes, with his Christian name, his Portuguese training, his nurse's income, his spectacles, and his Portuguese jacket and shirt, belonged to the minute proportion of Portuguese Timor's population permitted to vote in the Portuguese National Assembly and in the local Legislative Assembly. António was what the regime called an *assimilado* (assimilated native). For his son Martinho, this was unquestionably a good thing. His father didn't pay head tax, he could travel where he wished and he was exempt from bonded labour, even though he was paid less for his work than a European would have been. António, whose wiry hair was already white, and whose generous lips and wide, brown face were so similar to Martinho's, was a Portuguese citizen. Martinho would be a Portuguese citizen, too. It was progress, the way of the future.

At the Seminário de Nossa Senhora de Fátima in Soibada, the mission school in the mountains of central East Timor, Martinho committed himself to his studies. Not for him a farmer's life. He would study language and history, the four corners of the world of knowledge, stories of conquest and Christianity, ancient and marvellous civilisations. He studied world history as well as Latin, Portuguese and French.

At Soibada the earth was moulded into mountains and the sky came down and touched the earth on some days. When Martinho Lopes studied there, no roads led to Soibada. If you travelled from Dili to Manatuto and instead of continuing east to Laleia took the road that veered right, and if you followed that road into the mountains, and if you kept going even when the road had stopped, and if you were with someone who knew the way, and if you were fortunate and the track was in good shape and you had a good horse, you might find Soibada. Near the village of Samoro, it wasn't marked on the maps. During the wet season the tracks became impassable torrents of mud, and even the sure-footed Timor ponies couldn't get through. Some students didn't see their families for years.

It could hardly be regarded as an important centre of civilisation. It wasn't Jerusalem. It wasn't Rome. But, later, when Timorese no longer living in Timor said that word, 'Soibada', those three open-ended syllables expressed all the distance and longing in the world. Everyone remembered Soibada.

The mountains of Timor are sacred: from Matebian in the east, resting place for the dead, to Mundoperdido, to Ramelau, symbol of the short-lived Democratic Republic of East Timor, and Cailaco on the border in the west, they form a spine along the island. They also contribute to Timor's ethnic and linguistic diversity. The Mambai people, one of Timor's many ethnic groups, come from the mountains south of Dili. Their creation story centres on the sacred mountain, Nama Rau, where Mother Earth and Father Heaven had their primordial union. Later — after the birth of the first men and women and after Father Heaven ascended to the sky — Mother Earth moved to a lower mountain, sickened and died. She lay with her head in the south and her feet in the north, left hand toward the west and right hand toward the east. Seven earth mounds came and covered her, but her body did not decay. There were numerous attempts to bury her, and Mother Earth made another journey before her putrescent flesh formed a layer of black earth, covered by four earth mounds to keep her warm and tuck her in. Underneath the black earth was Mother Earth's nourishing white milk, source of fertility.

Some of the buildings of the college at Soibada were under construction when Martinho and his classmates arrived there in 1935. Only the washrooms and the toilets were ready. The students stayed in bamboo buildings and slept on bunks of *lantare*, bamboo split and split again and flattened to form flexible slats.

The priests looked after the boys, the nuns looked after the girls. The boys and the girls never spoke to each other, even though they spent their days in the same classroom. They would enter the classroom from different doors, one from the boys' school and one from the girls'. The boys entered first with their teacher, Father Jaime, nephew of the bishop, Dom José. The boys went to the front of the classroom and remained standing. The girls waited at the door until the boys were all in the classroom and then they went to the back of the classroom. They all remained standing during the prayer. The nuns sat between the girls and the boys. The girls left the classroom first.

As usual, Martinho always had something to say and

he argued with the priests when he thought they were wrong. He simplified Father Jaime's mathematics on the board in front of the class, if necessary. Father Jaime couldn't get angry, because Martinho was correct.

Every minute of the day was accounted for. Wakened at five in the morning, Mass in the chapel at six, prayers to Mary and Jesus for the Pope, the Bishop and the health and wisdom of Salazar. Weekly confession and Ave Marias and Salve Reginas prescribed as penance for their sins. They learned the catechism by heart in Portuguese. 'God is in heaven, on earth and everywhere.' There were only enough books for the older students, not the younger ones, and only the priests possessed Latin breviaries and altar missals. The priests were like fathers to the boys, and if you didn't like the priests you didn't say so. In fact, some students didn't say much for quite a long time, because Tetum and all the other languages of Timor were forbidden. Those who couldn't speak Portuguese spoke their mother tongues discreetly, if at all, to avoid a beating.

The beatings made them even tougher, no doubt. The ferule or *palmatória* was a stick of hard wood a few centimetres thick and about forty centimetres long with a handle and a disc with holes in it so there was no air to cushion the blows. It was used by the priests on the boys' palms when they stole fruit, but it didn't stop them. They picked oranges, mandarins, grapefruit, mangoes, bananas and tamarinds from the forest, or they'd steal the pigs' food.

It was impossible to be too tough, and the best place to be tough was on the sports field. The priests controlled the games — soccer, volleyball, basketball. Martinho liked soccer best. He kept playing even when he got older and fatter.

The priests tried to make life at Soibada disciplined and orderly. The students tended the gardens where maize, pumpkin, sweet potato, manioc (cassava), potato and sago were grown. They fed the animals — a pig, a cow or a goat, perhaps. They worked hard for a monotonous diet of maize, beans and vegetables, which might be just the leaves of the papaya tree. Meat was scarce, and they ate it only once a month, even though they were supposed to have meat and rice once a week. At Christmas some students' families visited and they all feasted or gorged themselves. On the day after Christmas they would be sick.

Every student had a duty, even though Martinho much preferred to play music: the violin, the accordion, the piano or the organ. Like other schools in Portuguese Timor, the seminary was a self-contained village. The students did the hard manual labour, the girls and the nuns sewed all the time. Martinho was cutting the grass one day and, close enough for the girls to hear, he said, 'There's no school today!' One of the girls told the nuns, and the nuns set the girls to sewing. Then they saw the boys going to the classroom with their books. 'That little Vemasse liar!' someone shouted. Vemasse was the village on a hill a little further east than Laliea, and that little Vemasse liar was Martinho.

The girls were surprised when the nuns told them that after four years at Soibada, Salvador Martinho Lopes was going to be a priest. The other boys were thinking about getting married, asking the nuns to intercede on their behalf for a particular girl. Martinho Lopes and Jacob Ximenes, also from Laleia, the brightest of their year, would continue their studies for the priesthood in Macau. The girls thought Martinho was too cheeky to be a priest. When he walked he talked to the air in those days.

•3•

Macau

A COUPLE OF MONTHS after his twentieth birthday, Martinho Lopes (or Salvador, as he was known then) left Dili with Jacob Ximenes on a boat bound for Macau. They were off to study at the Seminário de São José. They didn't cry when they left Dili, even though one of Martinho's relatives wept. For the young seminarians it was a great opportunity — better then staying in Timor and getting married.

For two years they studied at the minor seminary before entering the major seminary. Martinho topped his first-year classes in philosophy, physics and chemistry, and mathematics. Seminarians — the courses were the same in all Catholic seminaries around the world — learned philosophy in Latin: mainly St Thomas and Aristotle. They also learned how to refute the errors of Voltaire, Kant, marxism and even existentialism during their second year. They learned the history of the Portuguese discoveries, too. That was apt because the students at the Seminário de São José came from the north of Portugal, the Azores, China, Macau and Malaya as well as Timor. About half the seventy students were Chinese and the Portuguese speakers could study their language. After the first few months they all understood Latin.

Seminarians sang dirty songs and shouted, and played hard whenever they got the chance, but the seminary was a strict establishment. Seminarians wore their cassocks all the time except in bed. They were long black cassocks, a kind of penance in the humid climate of Macau when they played football and volleyball in the concrete yard. They wore out their shoes every three weeks on the concrete, but the seminary paid for new ones. The oldest tree in Macau, a gnarled banyan, stood in the yard of the major seminary. Its green foliage followed no particular shape, sprouting from its cavernous trunk as well as from its branches, and people said its roots stretched all the way to China.

For Martinho academic success was merely the foam on the crest of a much bigger wave. In 1940 the Vatican and the Salazar regime signed the Concordat and Missionary Agreement, under which Catholic missions were to receive an income from the state. The missions were responsible for educating indigenous peoples and for implementing government policy. Dili became a diocese and the Dili cathedral was to have its own bishop — Martinho's former teacher, Dom Jaime Garcia Goulart. The cathedral was a grand building with two tall spires on either side of its many-windowed façade in the centre of Dili. Its bells could be heard all over town.

Officially, seminarians were not permitted to read newspapers or listen to the radio but eventually no amount of censorship and isolation could hide the fact that there was a war on. Chinese from China and Europeans from colonies occupied by Japan took refuge in neutral Macau. The Portuguese government looked after the Portuguese citizens — the governor even swapped a cannon with the Japanese for food. The students from the seminary wrote out ration cards for rice, oil, vegetables and tinned foods for the people. Food was smuggled in from God knew where by God knew whom, but many — particularly Chinese refugees — went short.

Writing the ration cards was one of Martinho's few opportunities to see the streets of Macau, the world outside the seminary walls. On Thursdays, their day off, the seminarians visited another church, but all they saw was the road between their seminary and their destination. The Cantonese fishermen casting and hauling their nets from the sea wall, the women sitting on the ground in the shade mending nets, the children crouched quietly beside them, the sails of the junks silhouetted against the low sun, were all part of another world.

Until World War II reached Timor, the seminarians wrote to their families once a week, mundane news about their studies or the rowing races in the summer holidays. On the streets of Macau the Chinese sold and the Portuguese bought. However, during the war, the vendors had less and less to sell. They were running out of matches and clothes, pots and crockery, pickles and fish, sweets and tea. During August, from the tranquil courtyard of the seminary if the breeze was blowing the right way, Martinho could smell the incense the Chinese offered to the hungry spirits, those who had died violently or at sea, those who lacked a proper burial. It was like the smell of sandalwood trees burning in the bush-fires during the dry season in Timor. No air smelt as sweet as the air of Timor.

The best part of seminary life was the music. Every day for at least half an hour after lunch Martinho played woodwind instruments, the organ, the piano, any instrument. His musical instruction would have started at Soibada, if not before. He took Timorese songs to Macau. In Macau he read music and he could also play by ear: Gregorian chants, Spanish songs, Bach, Mozart, Beethoven, Verdi, classical and Renaissance polyphonic church music. When the maestro was away, Martinho took over conducting the seminary's thirty-four-piece orchestra. Martinho Lopes was competitive, and he was also a born performer. Music was his world; no matter how hard they tried, no one could match him when it came to playing the piano.

There were plenty of opportunities to perform. There were concerts for graduation, concerts for the anniversary of the bishop, any occasion was good reason for a concert in the auditorium. When their teacher, Father Texeira, appointed a seminarian to prepare a speech each Saturday, Martinho Lopes set to the task with gusto. His speech went up to the moon with its images. He was full of fervour, full of life.

By the time Martinho entered his final three years of theology in Macau, Timor was embroiled in the war. While he learned about the Creation, the Incarnation and the Resurrection in Latin, while he read the Bible in

Portuguese, and while he thought about the battles of the Roman empire, the pages of Timor's history were accruing.

The convergence of spies in Timor in the early 1940s was inconsistent with the level of economic activity in such an undeveloped backwater. In early 1941 both the Australian airline QANTAS and the Japanese company Air Nippon set up offices with support staff. By 1941 a Japanese shipping company owned 40 per cent of SAPT, the Portuguese agricultural company, and the Japanese ships that came to Timor were staffed by highly qualified naval personnel. In 1941 Charles Archer, a British visitor to Portuguese Timor, recommended that sending French-language newspapers from Sydney and Chinese-language newspapers from Singapore would be the best way to encourage pro-Allied sentiments. British observers saw the Timorese as politically passive, with little fighting capacity.

But then Timor became a strategic flashpoint in the Pacific war. The first action the Allies took after the Japanese bombing of Pearl Harbor was the invasion of Timor. Despite Portugal's neutrality about 400 Allied (mostly Australian) troops landed in Timor early in 1942. Their presence precipitated the full-scale Japanese occupation of the island by a force of 20,000 soldiers. With the help of sympathetic Timorese, the Allied troops conducted a guerrilla war against the Japanese in an effort to halt the Japanese advance towards Australia. However, after a year the Allied troops were evacuated and the Japanese were in control. Portuguese sovereignty shrank to a zone around Liquiçá and the hospital at Lahane near Dili, and there was no communication between Macau and Timor. With the withdrawal of the Allied troops the Timorese were left to suffer the consequences of the assistance they had given to Japan's enemies. Carnage — repression, reprisals and hardship — engulfed the island.

The headquarters of the Church moved from Dili to the mountains at Ossu to Soibada before Dom Jaime Goulart finally gave the order for the priests and nuns to leave. Word had spread of the Japanese order to their Timorese allies to kill all remaining Europeans. The clergy were evacuated from Betano to Australia on 16 December 1942 and Dom Jaime was consecrated Bishop of Dili in Sydney on 28 October 1945 before they returned to Timor.

Dom Jaime took responsibility for the flight of the priests, even though Vatican policy was for the priests to stay with the people to minister to their spiritual needs. When Dom Jaime reported to Rome he said, 'I'm the guilty one. Punish me.' That was typical of Dom Jaime. Whether religious or not, everyone loved him. He was a good bishop. In 1952, after his ordination, Martinho Lopes dedicated a sonnet to his former teacher: 'in the celestial Eden, pearls/Of great brilliance encrust your crown.' Years later when he was asked why so many of Timor's independence leaders had been taught by him, Dom Jaime replied, 'I simply opened their eyes.'

Martinho Lopes and Jacob Ximenes returned to Dili on 1 September 1946. They were shocked at what they saw. The gentle arc of Dili harbour enfolded them, the mountains stood where they always had. But where was Dili? Had the ship brought them to the right port? Slender trunks of palm trees crisscrossed empty space. Their foliage fluttered in the wind like fingers waving in the air above where the town would have been. It had been obliterated by Allied bombs. The cathedral was a ruin.

Their friends and relatives were waiting on the beach — the passenger wharf had been destroyed and there had never been a cargo wharf. When Martinho came ashore on the lifeboat, António was there to meet him. Everybody heard António's prosaic greeting to his son; it was reported all over the island. 'Tinu Kai, what's this?' António da Costa Lopes said. 'I sent you to study so you'd get an education, so you could be an important person, and now you're going to become a priest?' Nothing his father said dissuaded Martinho.

The privations in Macau, where the Japanese had respected Portuguese neutrality, had been mild compared with what had happened in Timor during World War II. Livestock was almost completely wiped out. Farms had been abandoned. Food shortages continued for many years after the war and the reconstruction of the most rudimentary infrastructure took decades.

Martinho's brother Cristóvão, had been working as a postman at Luro during the war. At the end of the war he was sent to the island of Atauro, which was used as a prison by the Portuguese, for allegedly helping the Japanese. He died on Atauro; nobody knows when, and no grave marks the site where he was buried. Martinho's uncle Feliciano Freitas was imprisoned during the occupation and he died too. Cristóvão's young children — Rosa, Sebastião and Cristóvão — lived with António. From then on they were Martinho's children, too.

•4•

Rebuilding

AFTER HIS RETURN to Timor from Macau, Martinho had worked as a trainee teacher at the São Francisco Xavier School and the high school in Dili. In 1947, the year before their ordination, Martinho Lopes and Jacob Ximenes took part in a pilgrimage to Portugal made up of Timorese, Angolans, Mozambicans, Cape Verdeans and Goans. They spilled down the gangplank of the boat in the Algarve with priests from the four corners of Christendom. In Lisbon all their knowledge of Portuguese history and geography fell into place. Portugal, unlike Timor, had been unharmed by World War II. The metropolis was grander than any place they had ever encountered.

In Lisbon Martinho found the civilisation his future students might assimilate if they were persevering and diligent. Here was the land the Romans had cultivated with grapes and olives and oranges, the land the Cru-

saders had fought for. It was from here that the naviga-
tors Gil Eanes, Bartolomeu Dias, Vasco da Gama, Pedro
Alvares Cabral, Afonso de Albuquerque and Fernão de
Magalhães had set forth on their epic voyages of discov-
ery. Here was the source of the missionary zeal that had
made Dominican friars come to Timor in search of sandalwood and souls.

The official history of Timor had started in Lisbon
and was kept in Lisbon, but in 1947 there were no Timorese in Lisbon. Martinho Lopes and Jacob Ximenes
organised a conference about Timorese customs. Many
of those on the pilgrimage brought their national dress
with them.

After three months in Portugal Martinho and Jacob
returned to Timor. They were ordained in Timor on 18
April 1948. Father Lopes adjusted to life in the outside
world after all those years in the seminary by working
hard. His seminary education had not prepared him for
the way that most people in Timor lived and thought
and talked. All his knowledge of the Scriptures made no
difference when he was communicating with the villagers about their stock or their crops or the hunting
conditions in the wide Maliana valley. Only what his
father and Feliciano Freitas had taught him about
gardens and livestock was important now. Food production, daily needs — not Roman sieges and moral theology. He continued to do the work of three men long after
he had stopped missing the days of study in Macau.

When he first went to the district of Bobonaro, the
Colégio Infante Sagres was situated in the town of
Bobonaro. It had been there since the liberation from
the Japanese, but the surrounding land could not

sustain the school's 400 students, boys drawn from the districts of Bobonaro and Covalima. Father Alberto da Conceição decided to move the school to Maliana. They moved on Roodmas (Holy Cross Day), 14 September 1948, a holy day that symbolised the triumph of the Cross over death.

The students carried their personal belongings; the horses were loaded with food. Packhorses, racing horses, riding horses, all joined the snake that had its head in Maliana and its tail in Bobonaro. It was a feast day for the boys. Father Lopes accompanied Father Afonso, a priest from Portugal, and his sister Beatriz, a primary school teacher. As they rode they watched the dark forms of the boys and the horses disappear in the long yellow grass and emerge again, only to be lost among the trunks of the trees. The *régulos* (traditional rulers of the area) welcomed the establishment of a mission school at Maliana, and a small bamboo house was waiting to accommodate Father Lopes. By the end of 1949 the Colégio de Maliana had moved to its final location on the slopes of Mount Loelaco. Moving, rebuilding, starting again from the ashes of war — it was like that all over Timor after the Japanese occupation.

From a plateau on another mountain, which Father Lopes called 'the gigantic, watchful hulk of Cailaco', the newly built Colégio Infante Sagres could be seen. In Father Lopes' view the college was 'conceived along thoroughly modern lines in which the grandeur of art combines most admirably with simplicity, elegance and good taste'. The Maliana mission residence was situated on a hill above the plateau, 'enveloped in a fine mist like a white seagull bobbing serenely on the wave'. The mission residence looked down over the Maliana plain, 'as though in rapture'.

Maliana was a good place to be in the hard years after the war, but not for ten years would there be ample food or what might be called good conditions. There was always sufficient water and irrigation for rice, corn, coconuts, papayas, mangoes, potatoes and cattle. The best tobacco in Timor grew in the district of Bobonaro near the border with Dutch Timor. Deer, buffalo, boar and field rats could be hunted. In the rivers and creeks were fish, eels, crocodiles and prawns. Bobonaro had few Catholics then — less than 2000 in a population of almost 49,000 — but Father Lopes was responsible for them. This meant long journeys over non-existent roads to say Mass, hear confessions, preside over funerals and weddings, visit the sick and bless the children.

On top of his pastoral work was the task of organising the boarders and preparing lessons for his students. He was a strict teacher, but he tried to be kind to the young boys starting school, awestruck to be so far away from their families and tongue-tied as they constantly tried to speak Portuguese. They were lively, those youngsters, laughing, joking, turning somersaults. Later, some of the students had trouble remembering what had been good about life in the mission schools, but Father Lopes thought that order and discipline could do them no harm.

The boys were wakened early and they were working in the fields by 5 am before the heat of the day descended on the valley. First there was Mass, then there was gymnastics. The boys, dressed in white and arranged in straight rows on the playing field, moved

uniformly in time to the marches Father Lopes com-
posed. One student, Simão Barreto, jumped when an
ant bit him one morning. He was whipped for that. After
gymnastics there was school — Latin, Portuguese,
mathematics, science, music, history — before football.
Every evening before dinner the boys recited the rosary
and by 8.30 pm they were ready to sleep.

Some said that Maliana became a very good school
while Father Lopes worked there, that it rivalled in
excellence the mission schools at Soibada and Ossu. The
young boys were only eight or nine years old, homesick
and nervous. Father Lopes made them laugh with games
and sweets and biscuits. Some of the cocky ones thought
they could speak Portuguese properly when they arrived.
They weren't so cocky after the other boys nicknamed
them with the first mistake they made in Portuguese.

Father Lopes had a good horse in Maliana, a gift from
a local *liurai*. The priest cut a fine figure in his long
boots, white riding trousers, doctor's smock and cork
Portuguese policeman's hat. One afternoon he headed
down from his house to the administrator's residence to
telephone Dom Jaime in Dili. His horse was full of
beans, he looked after her well. Off she went, through
the scrub, hooves pounding on the orange earth in a
mesmerising rhythm. The tall yellow grass whipped
past, and all of a sudden Martinho Lopes was flying.
Perhaps his horse had shied at the low branch of a kapok
tree. His flight was very brief. His right arm out in front
of him to brace his fall, he hit the dirt with a thud. *Crack*
went his arm. Broken. His horse stopped when he fell,
and he remounted, clumsily. They went to the *posto* (Portuguese administrative post) where he was treated.

Not many people in Bobonaro, or in other parts of Portuguese Timor for that matter, were aware of the war of independence being fought at that time in the Dutch East Indies. The Indonesian independence movement had been active since the early years of the twentieth century. In the 1920s a young student called Sukarno had argued that the Islamic, marxist and nationalist movements in Indonesia should unite to fight capitalism and imperialism. In 1928 the National Youth Congress proclaimed Indonesia to be 'one nation, one language, one motherland'. The national anthem 'Indonesia Raya' was adopted and the *lingua franca*, Malay, was renamed Bahasa Indonesia. The congress drew on the fifteenth-century Javanese kingdom of Majapahit for national symbols. Majapahit's red and white were chosen as the national colours, the *garuda*, a mythical hawk-like bird, was chosen as the national emblem and the motto 'Unity in diversity' (*Bhinneka Tunggul Ika*) was taken from a poem of the Majapahit era.

Muhammed Yamin, a pioneer of modern Indonesian literature and a participant in the Indonesian independence struggle, thought that the unity of history was important in nation-building. As he saw it, the history of Indonesia was not a history of Java, Sumatra, Borneo or Celebes (Sulawesi) but one single development, from pre-colonial independence to colonialism and back to independence. The nation was more like a spirit than a body.

Throughout the 1930s the struggle between Indonesian nationalists and Dutch colonial authorities had hardened. Sukarno was imprisoned. While the Dutch continued to extract wealth, they imposed a police state in their East Indies colonies. When the Japanese arrived in Java and Sumatra during World War II, many Indonesians viewed them as liberators. Within six months the Dutch population was interred in prison camps, and the Japanese allowed the red and white flag to be flown and 'Indonesia Raya' to be sung, both of which had been banned under the Dutch. Towards the end of the war the Japanese military authorities set up the Investigating Committee for the Preparation of Independence (Badan Penjelidik Usaha Persiapan Kemerdekaan).

It was before this committee that Sukarno delivered his Pancasila speech on 1 June 1945. The principles of Pancasila — faith in one God, humanity, nationalism, representative government and social justice — were to be the bedrock of an independent Indonesia. At this meeting the territorial definition of the new nation was discussed: thirty-nine members of the committee, including Sukarno and Yamin, voted for an Indonesia that included former territories of the Netherlands East Indies and North Borneo, Brunei, Sarawak, Portuguese Timor, Malaya, New Guinea and surrounding islands. Nineteen voted for just the former territory of the Netherlands East Indies, six for the former territory of the Netherlands East Indies combined with Malaya and omitting New Guinea. As it happened, the first plan was put on hold and the second plan was accepted.

It took four years for the nationalists to win the war for independence against the Dutch and on 27 December 1949 the Federation of Indonesian States came into being. The Federation's support came from Java and parts of Sumatra, as well as other parts of the archipelago, including West Timor. The Japanese had not permitted Indonesian nationalists to organise in eastern

Indonesia and there was no strong nationalist presence there. The Ambonese (Ambon is an island of the Central Moluccas north-north-east of Timor) fought on the Dutch side during the war of independence and in 1949 leaders of the Moluccan revolt moved with a large part of the population to the Netherlands. Guerrilla movements existed in West Java, Aceh, South Sulawesi and Kalimantan from 1950 to 1962. In 1950 the weak federation became the highly centralised and Java-dominated Republic of Indonesia.

In 1957 Indonesian territory was further defined by the Wawasan Nusantara (Archipelago Principle), which treated the whole archipelago as a single entity, not as a set of islands — each with its own territorial sea, as had been the situation under the Dutch. The water between the islands was seen as a linking device, not a divisive one. By 1960 the Wawasan Nusantara became national law and consequently Portuguese Timor was something of an anomaly, half of a single island breaking the unity of the archipelago.

One part of the Netherlands East Indies that the Dutch did not give up in 1949 was West Papua, the western half of the island of Papua New Guinea. In 1962 the so-called New York Agreement was struck between the Indonesians and the Dutch. An act of self-determination in West Papua would be carried out under Indonesian control, with the United Nations providing advice, assistance and participation. Despite protests in West Papua, administration of the territory was handed over to Indonesia in 1963. Indonesian military involvement in West Papua had started before the New York Agreement, commanded by Major-General Suharto with Ali Murtopo's assistance for intelligence. Once Indonesia gained control, Papuan political parties were banned, Papuan cultural artefacts were burned and Indonesia appointed a regional assembly.

During the late 1950s, under an increasingly authoritarian system of government called 'guided democracy', Sukarno tried to tread the line between the right-wing military and the Communist Party. He pursued an aggressive foreign policy and was insensitive to regional differences, spending vast sums on national monuments while the Indonesian economy deteriorated. In the early 1960s Sukarno embarked on a policy of *konfrontasi* (confrontation) against the federation of Malaysia, regarded by Jakarta as a British colonial instrument where United Kingdom and other Commonwealth troops could be stationed. When in 1965 Malaysia gained a seat on the UN Security Council, Indonesia withdrew from the UN.

Later in 1965 Major-General Suharto came to power after an alleged attempted coup by the Indonesian Communist Party (the PKI). Under Suharto's New Order (Orde Baru) regime the PKI was outlawed; hundreds of thousands of 'communists' and ethnic Chinese were slaughtered. The focus of the New Order was stability and economic development. Indonesian rejoined the UN. The army, known as ABRI (Angkatan Bersenjata Republik Indonesia), subsequently had two functions (Dwi Fungsi) in civil as well as military arenas. The army was the largest political organisation in the country. Under Suharto, the 'floating mass', the population, were encouraged to participate in economic development, but not politics.

Suharto co-operated with the UN on putting into place

the New York Agreement in West Papua and an 'Act of Free Choice' under UN auspices was conducted in 1969. This was not a one-person-one-vote referendum because, according to the Indonesians (or rather the Javanese), the West Papuans were too primitive to vote. The Act was conducted by consensus. After Ali Murtopo's threats — West Papuans should emigrate to another Pacific island if they did not want to be part of Indonesia, those who voted against Indonesia would be shot, after having their tongues torn out — a council of 1025 members agreed to stay with Indonesia. In 1999 West Papua is off the UN agenda, but still the Free Papua Movement (OPM) continues its struggle while the Jakarta government suppresses dissension and extracts raw materials.

Unlike the Netherlands East Indies, there was not the same impetus towards independence in Portuguese Timor after World War II. The Japanese occupation of Timor had been so brutal that the indigenous inhabitants of Portuguese Timor welcomed the return of the Portuguese. The Japanese had not set up nationalist organisations in the eastern islands, nor had they managed to turn the Timorese against the Portuguese. The people wanted stability, not a return to war. Nevertheless, when the Portuguese colonial government reestablished itself in Timor they controlled people's movements between districts and there was a closer surveillance of the border, especially after Indonesia gained its independence.

Maliana, only a few kilometres from the border, was overlooked by the mountains of Dutch Timor and in 1951 Father Lopes was aware of the sentinel nature of the mountain border posts. During the preparations for

Indonesian independence there was a commission made up of representatives from three countries. The Indonesians had selected Belgium, the Dutch had selected the United States and both had chosen Australia. Representatives from the commission used to drive over from Atambua, a town in West Timor, and spend weekends with Father Lopes in Maliana. They gave the boys sweets.

People in Portuguese Timor paid little attention to Indonesian independence. Other matters were far more important; for example, the visit of the journeying statue of Our Lady of Fátima to the mission of Bobonaro on 23 and 24 July 1951. In an article published in *Seara*, the bulletin of the Catholic diocese of Dili, in September–October 1951, Father Lopes described the festivities on the day the Queen of Heaven in effigy visited Maliana. The Pilgrim Virgin travelled all over Portuguese Timor, by plane and jeep, travelling along 'endless roads that, sometimes straight, cut across the plains shaded by palms lashed by a hot tropical sun, and sometimes meandering and circuitous, winding in capricious sinuosity around the steep slopes, enjoying the vast panorama, taking everything in — people and things — in the blue sweetness of her divine gaze'. Arches made from bamboo, foliage, saplings, greenery and other paraphernalia lined the road from the Maliana airfield to the church. The night before the Pilgrim Virgin arrived, wooden stakes were lit in the shape of a huge cross which shone in the dark 'as though held aloft by the hand of some invisible deity'.

On the day of her arrival church bells started ringing at dawn and the crowds began to gather. At 7.30 am the image of the Queen and Patroness of Portugal was met at the airfield by Father Francisco dos Santos Afonso, the superior of the Bobonaro mission; the administrator of Bobonaro; Lieutenant Loureiro of the Native Army unit of Angola (Companhia Indígena de Angola); and Second Lieutenant Martins of the Border Police Patrol (Pelotão de Polícia de Fronteira or PPF). Father Afonso had enlisted the support of the civil and military authorities to make sure the feast day would have the requisite pomp and ceremony. A sea of people lined the road as the image of the Virgin travelled by jeep to the college. The chiefs wore festive robes and steel breastplates glittering with large moons of gold and silver on their bare chests. Around their heads they wrapped brightly coloured cloths from which emerged long feathers that swayed in the wind. Their sword blades shone as they presented them. The women, too, wore bright colours and their finest gold or silver clasps. Old men, children, everyone made the air vibrate with their singing, 'Hail noble Patroness', as the Pilgrim Virgin, guarded by PPF cavalry, was carried to the site of the religious ceremony.

Father Afonso spoke to the congregation in Portuguese and Tetum, exhorting the Queen of Heaven to welcome all Christians, to protect Catholic homes, to convert unbelievers and to include each and every one in her maternal blessing.

Father Lopes wrote of the effect that the visit of the statue of the Pilgrim Virgin had on the people of Bobonaro in the language of Portuguese Catholicism. He was astounded to see that 'souls distanced from the sacraments, living in an ignoble quagmire of vice ... were now repenting and humbly falling on their knees to confess and emerging from the confessional with cheeks made rosy by the blood of Christ, fully regenerated by the salutary waters of sincere remorse, going home with gladdened hearts and eyes gleaming with the peace and serenity of a clear conscience as had not happened to them in a long while'. He recorded that 1870 confessions and 2645 holy communions had been made during the Pilgrim Virgin's two-day visit.

Throughout the night the faithful and the PPF watched the image of the Virgin while they said the rosary. Father Lopes couldn't describe the way the singing of the college choir lent solemnity to the next morning's Mass; it was something that had to be experienced, he said. No doubt for Father Lopes, it was right and proper for the people to be more interested in the Marian cult than in the newly independent state seven kilometres away.

Very few people in Portuguese Timor would have had any access to information about Indonesian independence. Would it have made any difference if they had taken any notice, if they could have taken any notice? In September 1975 would they have been prepared when Indonesian soldiers, not dressed in uniform and bearing weapons that could not be identified as coming from a particular source, made incursions into Bobonaro? Was there any way they could have known how dangerous the missions of Bobonaro — Maliana, Cailaco, Atabae, Batugadé and Balibó — would become? Did Mount Tapo issue any warning? Was there any augury in the way the shaft of noon sunlight hit the black water at Corluli Bau Sai?

Corluli Bau Sai was a sacred place, an oasis of rainforest on the Maliana plain where the Kausmata Creek joined an underground spring. Tall *kiar* trees, their domes visible from the mission residence on the plateau, spread their canopy over the water. Palms grew in their shade and vines snaked their way through the foliage. It was always cool there and the sunlight splashed gold on the deep green pools in the afternoon. The water flowed, but imperceptibly, coming out of the ground and disappearing into the forest as silently as the snakes slithered from the branches of the *kiar* trees. Corluli Bau Sai was a silent place that made some people afraid. God dwelt there because, although some said he lives very far away, he speaks where there is silence. People prayed there and left their sacrifices in the caverns of the buttress roots of the totemic *kiar* tree. Bees made their dripping hives high up where the branches caught the sun.

Catholicism and animism existed harmoniously in Portuguese Timor. Both involved veneration of the dead, and Maromak, the animist supreme being and source of all temporal and spiritual good, was not dissimilar from the Christian God. Even when Timorese people had been baptised, they still wanted to attend the animist *estilo* ceremonies for the dead, though most priests discouraged this, promoting instead the *kore-metan* and other Catholic rites. Animist rituals venerated certain *lulik* (totemic) objects and the souls of the ancestors. Flags, drums, papers, rocks or trees might be invested with sacred qualities and they became *lulik*s. There were *lulik*s in the bush all over Timor — a pile of stones to which a traveller might make an offering for a safe journey, some old wood from a boat revered as a powerful ancestor. *Lulik*s might protect a fruitful tree from thieves.

Father Lopes took his students to Corluli Bau Sai for picnics. When they emerged at the end of the afternoon with *kiar* seeds for making cakes, it was as though they had been in another world, so different was the oasis from the blazing heat of the plain. But the boys were mischievous. Corluli Bau Sai was teeming with wildlife — fish and animals — and the boys played up. They went fishing and caught game there. In the wet season of 1949–50 the local custodians of Corluli Bau Sai complained to the colonial administration about the boys' taking away fish and small animals, showing no respect for the sacred place. Father Lopes went to Dili to face the subsequent inquiry, even though the traditional custodians' anger was directed at the boys and not the priest. When Father Lopes returned to Maliana after the inquiry he was no different.

In 1951 Father Lopes was transferred to Dili, where he was appointed teacher, accountant and head of training at the seminary at Dare.

The seminary, strung out along a ridge in the hills behind Dili, had been destroyed by Japanese soldiers during World War II and it was destroyed again by the Indonesian soldiers in the 1975 invasion. When Father Lopes worked there in the 1950s the playing fields were for volleyball, not firing squads. Tall, thick-trunked, vine-wrapped *santuku* trees grew out of the gully. In October, after the school year started, the coffee plants flowered. Then came the coffee beans, green then red. Banana trees, kapok trees: all was verdant. One felt elevated at Dare, high up there on the ridge under the canopy of the *santuku* trees. From the road to Dare you could see the hospital at Lahane, Dili and the sea.

At Dare Father Lopes set the routine for the future leaders of East Timor. They had all been to the seminary at Dare. While Father Jacob Ximenes, who taught at Dare as well, was tall and angular, Father Lopes became as rotund as a pumpkin. He had stopped riding by then, and drove a very old Land Rover.

Life at the seminary in Dare was even more ordered than it had been at the college in Maliana. Sometimes Father Lopes was the priest who woke the forty seminarians, walking through the dormitories, clapping his hands and saying *'Deo gratias'* (thanks be to God) at about five in the morning. An hour of meditation was followed by Mass and communion was received on an empty stomach before breakfast. Then some students cleaned the dormitories while others practised the organ or piano. This was all before classes started at eight or nine. Latin, Greek, Portuguese geography and history, mathematics, physics — Father Lopes taught them all. Lunch was at noon and after lunch, while some students cleaned up, others had music lessons. Of course Father Lopes taught music and conducted the choir. After lunch the students walked in the gardens of the seminary for half an hour, then slept with their heads on the desks of the big study room. Classes went from two until five in the afternoon and after classes there were games: football, volleyball, basketball. After bathing it was time to say the rosary, then came half an hour's study, then dinner. They were full days.

Father Lopes was in charge of the food at Dare. It wasn't very good. 'What doesn't kill you makes you fit' was his philosophy. The boys ate in silence while one student read from the Bible. Christ was the head of the house, the unseen guest at every meal, the listener to every conversation. Father Lopes walked around the tables with his hands behind his back. He cleared his throat when the boys' plates were empty, as if to say, 'Now you like it!' Only after one of the priests said '*Deo gratias*' were the students allowed to talk. After dinner they walked for half an hour and at 9 pm there were last prayers in the chapel for twenty minutes. After last prayers there was silence.

Father Lopes was awake to the students' tricks. Sometimes they would feign sickness to avoid working in the garden. He gathered the 'sick' students together and offered them a rice cake. It was from America, he told them. It could cure any diseases. If you were sick it made you well, but if you were well, beware — it was dangerous. That fixed them.

In 1953, while Father Lopes was working at Dare, the Organic Law of Overseas Territories was passed in Lisbon. Timor and other Portuguese possessions were no longer colonies but overseas provinces with their own organs of government, part of the larger organism of the Portuguese nation. The council of ministers in Lisbon appointed the governor and there were to be local councils of government. Legal distinctions between *indígenas* (unassimilated natives) and *não indígenas* (whites, *mestizos* and assimilated natives) were no longer applicable, and the first of Portuguese Timor's five-year plans was launched.

The great five-year development plans relied on an age-old practice, conscripted labour: every adult male was required to work for the administration for one month a year, for which they were paid. Local chiefs supplied a specified number of men to the administrators. Some people paid their way out of the obligation. If the chief had it in for you, you'd have to work for more than a month. If he liked you, you might escape the labour gangs. If you refused to go, the administration brought you in by force, gave you a lesson, and made you work without pay.

During 1954 Father Lopes spent a few months as acting attorney of missions and missionaries. He worked in the Câmara Eclesiástica opposite the port in Dili, the hub of Church organisation in Portuguese Timor. All the important offices were housed in the two-storeyed building and the adjacent single-storeyed wing: the bishop's, the vicar-general's, the attorney's, the secretary's. The priests sat in cane chairs on the wide colonnade that linked the main building to the single-storeyed wing and talked while water bubbled in the cement fountain. In a glass-doored cabinet in the foyer of the main building were the postboxes for all the missions of Portuguese Timor in alphabetical order, the visible network of the Church infrastructure. In the 1950s who would have predicted that the Church, an arm of the Portuguese state, would by the 1980s be regarded by the Indonesian state as a subversive organisation? When Martinho da Costa Lopes was the leader of the Catholic Church in East Timor in the early 1980s, the parishes — Ainaro, Alas, Baucau, Balide, Becora, Bobonaro, Dare, Ermera, Fuiloro, Liquiçá, Maliana, Manatuto, Motael, Ossu, Oecusse, Same, Soibada, Suai, Uatolári — were mostly staffed by one priest each and a few nuns. A couple of parishes had two priests, some had none.

Through the louvre windows in his office at the

Câmara Eclesiástica Father Lopes could see across to the port, where labourers worked in primitive conditions. Men unloaded thirty-kilogram bags of cement and carried them on their backs from the boats to the warehouse. This was the cement that was going to rebuild Dili — paved roads, municipal buildings, improvements at the port — but who would rebuild the workers' lungs, eyes, backs, and limbs? Father Lopes could hardly see the men through the haze of grey dust. He much preferred to write to the papers about the conditions for those workers than to get to the bottom of the paperwork on his desk — documentation for weddings, baptisms, confirmations and funerals, invoices, letters and payslips. He advocated better working conditions, more forklifts, safer methods. He could have got into trouble if he hadn't been so nimble with his words, so indispensable to that venerable partner and collaborator of the state, the Catholic Church.

Was that why he was moved to Baucau, Portuguese Timor's second biggest town on the north coast east of Dili, as assistant vicar at the beginning of the dry season in 1954? On the way east it wasn't unusual to see teams of men breaking boulders with sledgehammers. A couple of men might be whipping the labourers with short, thick ropes. Lashes flying left and right like snakes left purple welts on bare backs. And then another man came to beat the whippers with a sprout of birches if the workers slacked. What kind of development was this?

Father Lopes was in Baucau for just over a year. The mother he had known, Isabel, came from near Baucau. She had died before World War II, in Lahane near Dili, but he still had family everywhere there. In 1954 Baucau was a well-kept town and life at the mission was peaceful. The mission school only went up to grade four so if the children wanted to continue their education they had to go to Ossu. For the whole school year, for one-and-a-half hours every afternoon from about three o'clock, Father Lopes prepared the girls for their first holy communion. They were so young, not even eight years old. They learned the Ten Commandments and their prayers — Our Father, Hail Mary — and which things young children ought to recognise as sins — not to pinch or hurt their friends, not to answer back to their parents. The kids used to come and ask Father Lopes' servant for ice. They climbed the tamarind tree. When Father Lopes asked, 'Did you climb the tamarind tree?' no one answered. 'God can see you everywhere,' Father Lopes told them.

One of Father Lopes' pupils, Elvira, was awake all night before her first holy communion. She was so excited. The ceremony, with ten boys and ten girls, was on the morning of 13 May 1955, the feast of the first apparition at Fátima. Afterwards there was tea at the church. In the afternoon, dressed as an angel, Elvira participated in the procession for Our Lady through the streets of Baucau.

Father Lopes played the accordion and taught Portuguese folk dances to the children. When they were good, they would all walk down the hill for a picnic on the seafront. Elvira and her sister Natércia and their cousin Saturnina were often left behind on the long walk back up the hill. Father Lopes walked at the back with them. They dawdled, talking, distracted by leaves and insects and jokes, precariously carrying the shells they had collected between them in their scarves. One afternoon they dropped their shells and Father Lopes helped pick them up.

At the end of that dry season in 1955 Father Lopes moved back to Dare, in time for the school year to start in October. For the next two years it was the ordered life of the seminary, where he founded and edited a journal with the Latin title, *Avete Juvenes* — the first of its kind in Timor.

•5•

Faith and empire

THE PALÁCIO DE SÃO BENTO in Lisbon took up a whole
block with its grand authoritarian uniformity. Its steps
stretched out in front of it like the mantle of a Renaissance
prince. At the base of the steps two white lions on
pedestals growled at the jumble of many-coloured, dis-
coloured houses crammed on the hill facing the *palácio*.
Black stains ran from under the lions' snarling mouths
down their manes. At the top of the steps soldiers guarded
the arched entrances to the parliament; behind the soldiers sat four huge eyeless statues.

In November 1957 Father Lopes, representative of
Portugal's most distant colony of Timor, ascended the
stairs and walked slowly along the red carpet, rolled out
especially for the first meeting of the National Assembly, in his freshly polished shoes. He had just turned
thirty-nine and, if not for his priest's dress, he would
have appeared to be an oriental gentleman. He was

shorter than most of the other representatives, but he was broad and strong-looking. Being from Timor, he was darker, too. Underneath the long grey coat that gave him protection from the chilly autumn he wore a suit, and underneath his suit jacket a light-coloured waist-coat and his hard white clerical collar, which he always wore when he travelled. The face that looked out above that collar was even-featured and open. With his friends and family he was quick to break into an infectious smile, his head tilted slightly back, his eyes crinkling with merriment and his mouth open, but he was a long way away from his friends and family on this important day. In the photograph for the parliamentary report his dark eyes looked into the distance; the line of his flared nostrils matched the line of his mouth, which was solemnly closed.

Unlike other representatives walking along the red carpet that day, who had paragraphs about their engineering achievements or their books on economics in their descriptions in the parliamentary report for 1957, only the briefest sentence described the representative for Portuguese Timor: 'Martinho da Costa Lopes, born in Timor, 11 November 1918. Missionary.'

Father Lopes was elected in November 1957 with 1892 votes to be the representative of the only political party permitted at the time, the government party, for a four-year term on the seventh *legislatura* of the National Assembly. Just the year before, Portugal had finally been admitted to the United Nations. The funds for Timor's first five-year development plan, which began in 1953, were allocated to the reconstruction of Dili and to the development of agriculture and livestock resources. It was in 1963, ten years after the enactment of the Organic Law of Portuguese Overseas Territories, that Portuguese Timor was formally declared an overseas province and the local Legislative Council was established in Dili in 1964. Despite the changes in terminology that the law brought about, the Salazar corporatist regime continued its repressive censorship and curtailment of political freedoms in Portugal as well as in the countries that made up the Portuguese empire: Angola, Mozambique, Guinea Bissau, Cape Verde, Goa, Macau, and Timor — all in the name of the Fatherland's historic civilising role.

Less than 2 per cent of the population of Timor were eligible to rubber stamp the choice of Martinho da Costa Lopes as the delegate to the National Assembly in Portugal. As he boarded the plane in Baucau, site of the main airport, at the beginning of the wet season, water buffalo were churning up the rice fields with their hooves in preparation for planting. Fertilisers, and even ploughs, were not used in Portuguese Timor at that time.

There were about 60,000 Catholics in a population of less than half a million people in Timor. Dili, the biggest town, had a population of about 7000. More than three-quarters of the people of Timor lived in traditional hamlets. It was a desperately poor place, still reeling from the devastation of World War II. Slash-and-burn agriculture was the main form of cultivation. The people subsisted on maize, rice, sweet potatoes and manioc, and supplemented their diet with hunting. Sticks and dibbles, not ploughs and fertilisers, were used in farming. Coffee and small amounts of copra and rubber were exported, and the labour for such enterprises was sometimes conscripted, even though by the late 1950s this practice was officially illegal.

The Palácio de São Bento was a megalith with offices of state and corridors of rule. Nothing like it existed in Macau, let alone Timor. The Salão das Sessões, where the representatives spoke and listened to each other and Dr Salazar, was magnificent. In the later years of his term on the assembly, after he had travelled enough to know, Father Lopes was convinced that the architecture in Lisbon was unsurpassed in the civilised world. In the Salão das Sessões statues representing the constitution, law, jurisprudence, eloquence, justice and diplomacy looked down on the assembly. Representatives could gaze upon the republic, embodied as a woman, behind the president's seat. Roses and coats-of-arms adorned the domed ceiling, and lions breathed garlands of flowers around the partition that divided the viewing gallery from the assembly. In the Sala dos Passos Perdidos outside the Salão das Sessões, statesmen of centuries past gathered on the painted wall panels. Bronze lions stalked each other from the doorway lintels.

Father Lopes' first speech to the assembly in Lisbon, so carefully thought out, was aimed at demonstrating his true patriotism to both Portugal and to that distant island, 'the land that was Portugal in the Far East'. When his voice filled the Salão das Sessões it was as warm and rich as the pink and yellow columns of Italian marble, *pedra mármore*, that supported the architectural splendour, but the content of his speech reached beyond the physical space contained by walls and ceiling.

He paid homage to the government and transmitted his feelings of gratitude and admiration for 'Salazar's politics of truth as opposed to the politics of lies and errors'. He spoke of strengthening the links of fraternal love that united all Portuguese around the sacred altar of the Fatherland, the cohesive and united Portuguese nation. He then spoke of the work to be done for school-age youth and the anonymous masses in that far plot of Portuguese ground so that the image of the Fatherland was engraved upon its soul. The Catholic missions needed moral and material support. The post-World War II reconstruction of Timor was in its early stages. Dili still had no port and no electricity-generating plant. Private initiative needed to be developed, locals needed to be trained to improve agriculture. The Timorese needed access to education. There were buildings to be built, bridges to construct, roads to improve, and for this Timor needed substantial aid from the government of the nation. Father Lopes appealed to the honour and just aspirations at stake because the work of the Portuguese, as Salazar said, was not that of a passer-by who looked and then walked on, or of the explorer who sought to get rich quick and then left, but the work of one who took the image of the Fatherland in his heart, engraving it wherever he went.

He made that speech in what seemed like mid-winter, on 14 December 1957. However, the winter continued. The layers of clothes he wore made him look even rounder that he already was. By February the cold still hadn't abated. It seemed that the winter would never end. He moved to an apartment near Campo Pequeno. He had come to take electricity, running water and street lights for granted. There were so many streets to choose from in Lisbon, so many apartments. He sent home a photograph. The apartments, the paved streets, the mosaic pavements, the cars — it was difficult for his family in Timor to imagine Lisbon. He immersed himself in studies of law and his real love, music. When the spring came he wrote a request in his careful, curly handwriting, with its flamboyant ascenders and descenders, elegantly signed, on official notepaper to the Secretary of the Assembly for a return ticket to Timor.

He delivered his second address to the assembly on 17 April 1958. He spoke of faith and empire — faith preceding empire as the first rays of the Church's sun lit the pagan world. He spoke of mariners and missionaries, carriers of Portugal's historic mission. He asked the intelligent men of the government to encourage interest in and affection for the overseas missions in school and university students. The missionaries worked hard and, despite the fact that the government had promised that missionaries would be entitled to receive retirement pensions, the pension had been revoked, except in the case of prelates. He asked the government to right this wrong.

In the European summer of 1958, before he returned to Timor, he moved again, to a ground-floor apartment near the Cemitério dos Prazeres. It was an old part of town, on the route of the number 28 tram that went right past the Palácio de São Bento. If he was feeling energetic he could walk to the National Assembly, but more often than not it was probably too hot to climb the hills and he caught the tram, lurching with it as it ricocheted cheerfully through the narrow cobbled streets with centimetres to spare between the tram window and the old buildings.

It was a long journey back to Timor, even by air. He had

become accustomed to Portuguese food, soup and custard tarts and wine, and the *rabi-rabi* (bitter papaya and squash leaves) served in his father's house didn't seem to satisfy him any more. When he looked around Dili, when he travelled in the countryside, all he could see was work to be done. Nevertheless, nothing would have compared with the sight of the mountains of Timor and the joy he drew from the simple faith of the people there.

His first address to the National Assembly at the beginning of the second year of his four-year term was a lament on the death of Pope Pius XII. A few weeks later, on 29 October 1958, he delivered his most important speech. This dealt with the national development plan. All the people of Timor, he told the assembly, were jubilant about the allocation of 220 million escudos (about £2,750,000 sterling or US$7,700,000 at the time) for the reconstruction of the province. The fact that Timor always appeared last on the lists of overseas provinces — the least input, the least exports, the least development, the least significance — didn't stop Father Lopes expounding at length about how the money should be spent.

Timor's needs were many. The land needed to be reforested to halt the soil erosion caused by rain and logging. Agriculture, fisheries and industry needed to be modernised to combat malnutrition and to increase production. Timor's small industries — dairy, soap, soft drinks, pottery — needed a boost, and new industries such as tourism needed to be developed.

His vision didn't stop there. Roads and bridges needed to be improved and he even talked about the possibility of railways. Timor needed an international airport in Dili rather than Baucau. Unskilled workers needed to be paid more. According to Father Lopes, the natives were underpaid because they didn't work hard. They didn't work hard because they were underpaid. How could one demand better work from people who couldn't feed themselves properly? The vicious cycle had to be broken. The image imprinted in his mind of the workers at Dili harbour fuelled his speech to the assembly. The vast sum could go a long way in Timor. A sewerage system needed to be implemented, and water and electricity supplied. Timor needed more than the money; it needed trained technical personnel.

Schools and hospitals needed to be built. There were ten million escudos for public health. There were another ten million for education, a significant amount, which, he said, should make the government think about one alarming truth regarding the state of secondary education in Timor: after four hundred years of Portuguese civilisation and culture, Timor had yet to produce one indigenous lawyer, engineer, doctor or university graduate.

His closing comments reiterated that he was a Christian and a patriot. Portugal had brought together the most heterogeneous of peoples, he said, had made them brothers in Christ and given them the soul of the Fatherland.

A few days after he delivered that speech Father Lopes moved again, this time to the centre of Lisbon, near Rotunda and the Parque Eduardo VII. There were no parks or monuments of that scale in Timor. Where did the energy to build them come from? People in Timor worked to to satisfy their basic needs.

Father Lopes was quiet in the assembly for quite a few months after his speech on Timor's development until a new governor, Themudo Barata, was appointed in June 1959. Governor Barata was an engineer, younger than governors usually were. Someone out of the ordinary was needed to implement the development plan. Father Lopes spoke to the assembly about the difficulty of governing an overseas province and the qualities a governor needed.

Later in June he had a chance to exercise his new legal knowledge in his comments on the changes to the constitution. What he said was predictable. He wanted more of a voice for Timor. He also wanted God included in the preamble to article 1 of draft law number 23, despite the fact that there had been objections from the Corporative Council on the grounds that there was a lack of religious unity among the Portuguese throughout the world. Father Lopes pointed out that according to article 45 of the Constitution it could be deduced that the Catholic religion was the religion of the Portuguese nation, and from there it followed logically that the Catholic God was the God of the Portuguese nation.

In the district of Viqueque in the east of Portuguese Timor, there was an anti-Portuguese uprising in early June 1959. Conditions were notoriously bad in Viqueque. Even though whipping and the use of the *palmatória* had been outlawed three years before, these practices continued there. People had to work for paltry wages. The administration had cut the wages offered to local labourers by the Australian-owned Timor Oil Company to less than one-third of what the company had offered. Fourteen secessionist exiles from the Permesta movement in Sulawesi, Indonesia, were granted asylum in Portuguese Timor and it is claimed they fomented the uprisings at Uatolári and Uato Carabau. Telephone lines were cut and there were riots and sporadic attacks. The reprisals were harsh. Hundreds of Timorese were killed and dozens were exiled to Mozambique, Angola and Portugal. Some came to Dili for questioning. Father Lopes, who arrived back in Timor for the regular northern-summer recess a few weeks after the uprising, was able to plead for clemency for them.

Back in Lisbon in the northern autumn, Father Lopes wrote to Governor Barata to thank him for his 'humane and Christian role in the events in Timor'. Governor Barata had arrived in Dili a few weeks after the uprising, too. In his letter Father Lopes requested information about oil exploration for a future speech in parliament, and statistics on demographic movements.

His flight from Timor back to Portugal after the recess took days. With QANTAS Father Lopes stopped in Jakarta, Singapore, Bangkok, Calcutta, Karachi, Cairo, Athens and Rome, where he changed to a Pan Am flight, stopping over in Nice and Barcelona before arriving in Lisbon. He liked the service on board, even though he couldn't sleep properly. What he liked best was flying over the clouds — so far away from the world, closer to heaven.

He found Lisbon as stylish and sumptuous as ever, with the new Metro just about to open. In parliament plans for Timor's development continued at a slow pace, but elsewhere things were changing.

He never did speak about oil exploration in parliament, although he, like many, believed there was tremendous potential for oil in Timor. There had been no allowance for cartography, geographical surveying, soil surveying or mining in Portugal's latest five-year plan for Timor.

While the regime in Portugal managed meticulous scrutiny and documentation of its citizens, Lisbon was a city shaped by inertia and endless delays. In January 1960 Father Lopes pointed out to the assembly that there had still been no review of the pension entitlement for missionaries, which he had brought up in his second address to the assembly almost two years earlier. He also pointed out unfair differences in conditions for civil servants working in Africa and Timor, and the dangerous crisis looming because there were too few missionaries in Timor to cope with the growing number of Catholics.

The authorities regarded Timor as a drain on Lisbon's purse. In April 1960 Father Lopes talked about the general accounts of the state for 1958. The accounts for Timor would improve, he said, only if there were increased exports of local products to offset the imports necessary for reconstruction. He urged the development of the new agricultural products of copra and rubber, while not neglecting coffee, so that the economy would not be dependent on one crop. He also implored the government to support bridge and harbour construction, to improve pavements and road surfaces, to build an electricity-generating plant in Dili and to re-establish the weekly flight between Dili and Darwin.

The next day, invited to speak to the assembly on an anniversary of the life of Henry the Navigator, he gave a rhetorical outpouring on the Infante of Sagres and the Portuguese discoveries. He could go on for hours about

Henry the Navigator. Prince Henry left no progeny but Father Lopes claimed that the Portuguese discoveries, 'the valuable and beautiful fruits of his intellectual creativity', were the legitimate sons of the Prince of Sagres. According to Father Lopes, Portugal's possessions in the five parts of the world 'constituted her greatest glory'. There was patriotic applause at the end of his speech.

The irritating delays must be overcome, he wrote to Governor Barata. He wanted to increase the velocity of development. The province and its problems were in the minds of the government and Salazar, and the growing interest was a good sign, he wrote. His letter was carefully typed and signed in his flowing handwriting. He had moved again by that time, to an apartment near Rua Pascoal de Melo. Another black and white photo of another quiet street with a huge car parked in it and good gutters was sent back to his family in Timor. They couldn't keep up with him!

The 1960 recess of two months allowed him hardly any time at all in Timor. Transport was so slow there. The Church's vehicles were often in use and it was hard to move around. He asked Governor Barata for the use of a jeep so he could travel quickly to any part of the province. It was his last chance to report back to Lisbon on the state of affairs in Timor.

Before Christmas 1960 Father Lopes defended Portugal against the 'insidious slander' expressed at the United Nations. Even though he advocated development for Timor, and opportunities for the Timorese, at this time he saw himself as a Portuguese patriot. For him the Portuguese colonies were the crowning glory of the Portuguese nation. He was speaking as a political representative in a repressive fascist regime. Critics of Portugal did not understand the humane and Christian methods the Fatherland used to civilise people, he said.

In the spring of 1961 Father Lopes reported to the assembly the patriotic demonstration staged in Dili outside the governor's residence. At the demonstration people expressed their indignation about what Father Lopes described as 'the acts of banditry perpetrated by hordes of savages in the pay of Communism'. He was referring to recent events in Angola, where the forces of the Popular Movement for the Liberation of Angola (MPLA) had attacked the prisons in Luanda. Long-running wars in the Portuguese colonies in Africa were eventually to bring about the fall of the fascist regime in Lisbon, but that took many years.

Father Lopes' last speech at the National Assembly on 6 April 1961 reiterated the non-racist and heavenly mission of Portuguese colonialism. 'Portugal did not leave the native in dire poverty, or exterminate aborigines with guns, as certain so-called civilised nations did … on the contrary, imbued with principles that consider every human to be God's adoptive child and inheritor of celestial glory, Portugal generously held out its hand and spread Western and Christian civilisation.' As Father Lopes saw it then, the Portuguese nation was indivisible: 'Just as in the human body, when one member is afflicted, the whole organism is affected. So the tears and sorrows of Angola are also the tears and sorrows of Timor, Macau, India, in fact, all of Portugal.'

• 6 •

Could the centre hold?

JUST AS VERY FEW people in Portuguese Timor knew
about Indonesian independence in 1949, very few knew
the details of the revolt in Angola when Father Lopes
returned from Lisbon in 1961, even though the event
made headlines in other parts of the world. During the
late 1950s Lisbon had decided to open up the African
colonies to foreign capital. Huge companies — Gulf,
Firestone and Anglo-American — moved into Angola
and Mozambique so the unrest in Angola was watched
in business circles. Nevertheless, censorship in Portugal
and the colonies was strict and non state-sanctioned
political activity was forbidden.

On his return to Timor Father Lopes became the
superior of the mission at Suai close to the south coast
and near the potentially oil-rich, wild, 'male' Timor Sea.
It was at Suai that in August 1912 a cannonship from
Macau finally quashed the last major uprising in Timor

before the 1959 revolt. Precipitated by events in Europe and Africa, the Great Rebellion of 1912 had been the culmination of thirty years of insurrection on the part of the fiercely independent mountain *liurais*.

After the quashing of the 1912 rebellion Portuguese colonial 'progress' continued throughout the decades of the twentieth century, despite the fact that the regime appeared to be apathetic and neglectful to many foreign observers. The policies of Salazar's Estado Novo ensured that the Catholic Church played a pivotal role in Portugal's colonising mission and Martinho da Costa Lopes was part of this role. Abuses of power, undeveloped economies geared to produce cash crops, arrogant assumptions about civilised standards of behaviour — these stories are not confined to Portuguese colonialism. The remarkable thing is the longevity of the Portuguese colonial empire.

Perhaps Father Lopes was optimistic about cultural development and material progress when he moved back to Dili as the director of Colégio Bispo Medeiros in 1963. The effects of the development plans were visible and there were signs of progress all around the capital. Dili now had an electricity supply, some sealed roads were being built and a sealed airstrip at Baucau was under construction. Themudo Barata was replaced as governor by Alberto Correia and in 1964, more than ten years after the Organic Law of Overseas Territories was passed in Lisbon, Timor was finally officially declared an overseas province.

Bispo Medeiros was tucked into the hills behind Dili, not far from António Lopes' house at Lahane. From the road to Bispo Medeiros you could see Lahane's hospital. The school's main building was two-storeyed, with a verandah around it and a two-pronged set of curved stairs from the verandah to the road. The boys sat on the square wooden seats with a small writing desk attached as a right arm to the chair. The bright tropical light was filtered by dusty louvres. Outside, slender palm tree trunks emerged from the tangle of jungle and bush. In the classroom Father Lopes did his best to teach his students Portuguese and Latin, but they didn't always see the relevance of what they were being taught. Some students preferred to run away and hide in the graveyard rather than learn Portuguese. The classrooms were arranged around a central courtyard, the all-important basketball court.

Father Lopes returned to politics as a representative on the newly formed Legislative Council in 1964. There he mixed with everybody who was anybody. Council members advised and assisted the governor, mobilised public support for policies from Lisbon and canvassed public opinion.

Things were moving. The wharf in Dili was finally completed in 1964. In the same year war broke out in Mozambique and, while the colonial regime managed to keep a 'curtain of silence' across events for about a year, a full-scale guerrilla war was reported in a series of articles in the London *Evening Standard* in 1965. The struggle in Mozambique was referred to as 'the forgotten war' throughout the 1960s because Portugal was seen as a small player in world affairs. Nevertheless, business interests were watching Africa and the Portuguese colonies of Mozambique, Angola and Guinea Bissau occupied key positions on the Cape route from Europe to Asia. This route became important when the Suez Canal couldn't take the new large tankers and instability wracked Aden and Cairo.

Movement of information throughout the Portuguese colonies was controlled, but the practice of removing troublemakers and sending them to other parts of the empire meant that ideas of dissent were spreading.

In 1965 Father Lopes was appointed superior of the new mission at Liquiçá. Father Monteiro, the parish priest at Ermera, had asked Dom Jaime to divide the parish, and so the parish of Liquiçá came into being. The church at Liquiçá wasn't inaugurated until January 1967. It was a brand new church, a striking building with its bell tower on one side of its modern façade. Just as the church at Liquiçá was completed, Dom Jaime announced his retirement and Dom José Joaquim Ribeiro became the new bishop of the diocese of Dili.

It was a good life at Liquiçá, there by the quiet north sea. Father Lopes drove to Dili for the Legislative Council meetings along a road that was much better than it had been when he was a child. The population of the parish was small and the number of Christians was even fewer. He taught the catechism on the beach and rested in the afternoon, while the sun shone into his house through the blue glass louvres. He grew huge in Liquiçá; his white soutane billowed out around him. At the church retreats, held every year during the dry season, the priests arranged themselves in order of their ordination — the longer they had been priests the closer they sat to the bishop. Father Lopes, however, preferred to sit at the end of the table. That way, after everybody had taken their share of the food, he could polish off whatever came his way.

In the late 1960s Father Lopes became superior of the mission and principal of the Santa Teresinha boys' school at Ossu. Ossu, close to Mount Mundoperdido in the east, was rich in the same way as Soibada was — with lush vegetation and cool at night. Natural gas came out of the ground nearby, sign of the wealth of that sacred place. All the best things in Timor could be found at Ossu though the *samodo*, Timor's only venomous snake, lurked in the branches of the trees.

By the late 1960s Salazar had had a stroke and had been replaced by his long-serving colleague Marcelo Caetano. Even then, abuses of power regarding labour continued in Timor. Timor's relationship with Portugal, Portugal's relationship with Timor was an arrangement intended to benefit both parties, according to Marcelo Caetano. The Europeans were the leaders in transforming backward regions and the natives were the beneficiaries of the transformation, preparing for a future as 'civilised people'.

Faithful to the status quo of the time, Father Lopes maintained it wasn't the system that was corrupt; greedy and lazy individuals were the problem. Take the incident with the administrator in Viqueque.

Every Sunday Father Lopes went to celebrate Mass at Viqueque. It wasn't far from Ossu by car — less than an hour if the road was in good condition. It was a pretty drive, the trunks of the trees that lined the track were whitewashed and made stripes of shade on the road. But there was something wrong in Viqueque. The people were sullen; there was resentment in their faces but no one came to tell him what was the matter.

On Sundays he ate a lunch of white rice and pork,

then returned to Ossu to sleep it off. The food was good at the mission in Ossu, too. The priests had the best cooks and when Father Lopes told the Portuguese army captain that the mission needed Portuguese sausages and wine, the captain obliged. The army wanted to have a good relationship with the people and the best place to start was with the priests. Father Lopes, Father Francisco Fernandes and Father Ivo Dinis Rocha sat down to lunch every day punctually at noon.

'Have you had enough?' Father Lopes asked the two other priests after they had finished eating. He looked around at the empty plates. 'I think we need some more,' he pronounced, and then, '*Reforco*! [Reinforcement!]' he bellowed.

The boy was sent to the Chinese shop for more bread. Father Lopes disappeared into his room and emerged with cans of sardines from Portugal and beef from Australia. He opened the cans forcefully and, once they were open, he spread his substantial arms out, palms upward. 'Eat!' he exhorted the two younger priests. That's the way he did everything, wholeheartedly, directly.

It was during the siesta one day that the people from Viqueque came. Father Lopes' snores echoed around the spaces of the priests' house but on the dot of two he emerged. His hair was neatly brilliantined into place, his white soutane was smoothed over his shirt and trousers. He sat down with the villagers from Viqueque where they wouldn't be overheard. The foliage of the *jambua* (grapefruit) tree made flickering patterns of light and shade through the gappy blocks that made up the wall of the reception room, while the spokesperson from Viqueque spoke in the traditional Tetum way, saying everything twice and altering the words the second time.

'Every day we work in the rice paddies. Every day, each of us, in the fields for hours and hours. The administrator forces us to work. He demands we work in the rice paddies. No one minds working in the rice paddies. We work hard. When there's work to be done, we have to do it. But we are not slaves. We don't receive any pay for our work. No money for our labour, and no time to tend to our own gardens to feed our families.'

'The whole town must work for nothing in this way?'

'Yes!'

'How long has this situation been going on?'

'For seasons — it started a few years ago. Only he's getting worse now. We don't see how it will end.'

'Father, will you help us?'

'Yes. I'll do what I can.'

Soon after that conversation Father Lopes was in Dili and while he was having a cup of coffee with the governor, he mentioned the situation in Viqueque. He didn't go through the bishop, as other priests might have. Having been a politician himself, Father Lopes thought his own intervention would be just as effective as the bishop's. When he went to see the attorney of the republic, the people's watchdog, he was sure the people of Viqueque had a good case. His role in the whole affair ended there. The attorney of the republic examined the case and the administrator was prosecuted. It was the first and the last time a Portuguese administrator ended up in jail. When Father Francisco Fernandes and Father Lopes went to visit the former administrator of Viqueque in prison, he received only Father Francisco. He knew Father Lopes had started the proceedings.

Father Lopes also wanted to sort out some family affairs while he was in Dili. He went to see his father in the house at Lahane just down the hill from the hospital. Father Lopes was puffed from walking up the track to the house. António was out the front in the well-kept garden, looking as fit as ever. Here in the square, lattice-fronted, corrugated-iron-roofed house was Martinho da Costa Lopes' other life. In this house his niece Rosa and his nephews Sebastião and Cristóvão had lived with António and his third wife Luisa. One of Rosa's children, João, also lived here with António. In this house *raba-raba* was served more often than Portuguese sardines. In this house Father Lopes never spoke about his work. He played with the children and followed the football, happy if Sporting defeated Benfica in Lisbon. He played music, too, and lay down after lunch for a two-hour sleep.

On this day, his visit wasn't purely social. He wiped the sweat from his shiny brow with his handkerchief.

'Where's João?' he asked António, looking around. 'I need to talk to you about him.'

Fourteen-year-old João was a skinny kid with a friendly face. João's Tio Padre would have beamed when he saw João. António sent João off on some errand and the boy disappeared into the shadows of the house.

'He's going well,' António said. 'He does well at school. He's happy.'

'Yes. I wanted to talk to you about his education.'

'He's getting a good education.'

'I wanted to talk to you about his future.'

'Yes?' said António.

Father Lopes said what he had to say firmly — after all, he was paying for João's education.

'It's time he went to the seminary.'

'The seminary?' António looked angry.

Father Lopes took a few steps backwards. He was fast on his feet, despite his bulk. He turned his head to check for obstacles on the dirt path and turned back. 'Yes,' he answered, facing his father squarely.

'No!' roared António. He'd found a stick in the garden and as he took a few steps toward his son he raised it in the air. 'The priests took you and look at you now! You got fat. You've got no children.' António broke into a run.

The priest wasn't facing his father any more. He was off down the little track to the road where the parish car was parked.

'No!' shouted António after him. 'The priests aren't going to take João away, like they took you. He can stay here. He can have a family if he wants.' All he could see was his son's broad back retreating down the path. Martinho Lopes didn't answer his father and later he made no objections when João enrolled at the polytechnic.

Not long after that, when he was working in Dili, Father Lopes visited his family at Lahane every Thursday. They were friendly gatherings with António and Luisa, Rosa and her five kids, Sebastião and his five kids, and sometimes Cristóvão. They joked and talked about whatever pleased them. Father Lopes held the babies and watched the children grow up. One Thursday Rosa came up to him. She was cross.

'Look what I found.' No one's face could look quite as stern as Rosa's when she was cross. She held out the torn page of an exercise book.

It was a love letter, very passionate, very ardent, promising the earth. And it was signed by João. The boy was getting carried away! He was only fifteen years old.

Father Lopes chose a quiet moment to talk to João.

'Did you write this?' he asked, showing João the letter.

João blushed crimson to the top of his big ears and nodded.

'Why?' asked Father Lopes.

'I wanted to learn more, get more experience. I'm getting old.'

Father Lopes delivered two slaps to João's hot cheeks — one hand for each slap, simultaneously on both sides of his face. Then he became gentle again.

'You're too green to get married now,' he said, sitting down beside João. 'You're not old enough. You'll enjoy it more later. You have to study first. Then you have to get a job, earn some money, buy a car even! Enjoy yourself first!'

João laughed. His Tio Padre laughed. 'Then you'll enjoy getting married.'

Work as a teacher and a priest was more controllable than family life, no matter how much work there was to do. There were 200 students boarding at the school in Ossu. As usual, the nuns looked after the girls and the priests looked after the boys. Mass, mathematics, music. Stories from far away: Jerusalem, Rome, Lisbon. And, of course, football.

As the superior, Father Lopes was in charge of the documents, the money and the administration of the mission. Father Francisco and Father Ivo visited the other missions by horse and by motorbike to celebrate Mass in Portuguese. Sometimes the route was more direct on foot. The pastoral work was demanding, but the distances were the really tiring part. All three priests baptised babies and adults. The people were mostly animists. Less than one-third of them were Catholics. They worshipped Maromak, who wasn't so different from the Christian God, and left offerings at nearby *luliks* in the bush to cover all sorts of contingencies. Even if they hardly spoke or understood Portuguese, they were ready to try Christianity, especially after a run of bad luck. The catechism was normally taught in Tetum. A new God and a Christian name might bring a change of fortune. Consequently the priests were busy.

At Ossu Father Lopes and Father Francisco used to watch the *pontapé*, called *hafetu* in Tetum, every so often. Pontapé was an elegant sport, like kickboxing but less crude, in which the blows were struck with the feet. A man could not kick his opponent when he was down and the contestant who succeeded in kicking his opponent's head was the winner.

Father Lopes continued to play music, especially the piano accordion. He conducted the choir and taught people songs in Tetum. He didn't regard singing folk songs as a subversive act, but who knows? Had the Portuguese secret police, PIDE, been there in the remote mountains of Ossu they might have had some objections. On the coast in Manatuto, PIDE — now officially called Direcção Geral de Segurança (DGS), even though everyone still referred to the organisation as PIDE — trained their microscopes on the União soccer club. Made up of students from the missions of the parish of Manatuto, it was a dangerous club because it promoted 'barefoot' Timorese culture.

On Father Lopes' good radio equipment, the priests at Ossu listened to news from around the world: the

BBC, the Voice of America, Portuguese radio. So they knew more than most people about the wars in Angola, Mozambique and Guinea Bissau. PIDE tried to keep those things under wraps, but the news could not be contained, especially when political dissidents from Africa arrived in Timor. The Portuguese empire was under siege, and even a barefoot soccer game was too potent a sign of defiance for the Portuguese state.

II

Silent mouths, speaking mouths

•7•

Awakening

WHEN FATHER LOPES took up his appointment as chancellor and canonist (or canon lawyer) of the diocese of Dili in 1972 there were still more catechists than doctors in Portuguese Timor, but times were changing. Long-haired hippies flew from Australia to Timor with the Australian-government-owned airline TAA and slept on the beach. Some of the children of Father Lopes' contemporaries were meeting to discuss politics, even though in Portugal and throughout the Portuguese colonies it was treasonable to do so. They were watching the struggles in Africa inspired by independence leaders Eduardo Mondlane in Mozambique and Amilcar Cabral in Guinea Bissau.

The colonial wars dragged on. The sons of poor Portuguese families spent years fighting in the African colonies — mandatory military service was increased to four years — and the soldiers and their families gained nothing from the sacrifices. Despite the grand civilising role Portugal claimed for itself and the sumptuous buildings in Lisbon that had so impressed Father Lopes, Portugal remained a poor country on the edge of Europe. Adult illiteracy ran at 40 per cent and it had the highest infant mortality rate in Europe. Shanty dwellings housed nearly one-fifth of Lisbon's population and the villages in the countryside lacked medical services and electricity. Under the Estado Novo, Portugal had been politically and culturally isolated from Europe for a large part of the twentieth century.

In 1972, under Salazar's successor Marcelo Caetano, new legislation was enacted to give the Portuguese colonies some autonomy while keeping the Portuguese nation united. Angola and Mozambique were now called states, but the wars there continued. People in Timor grumbled and gossiped about the Chinese, who ran nearly all the businesses in Dili and the villages, about their bosses, about the governor and his policies, taxes and the cost of living. Some wished the Portuguese would go away. Still, ideas of liberation were only discussed in secret and Timor was a peaceful place compared with Angola, Mozambique and Guinea Bissau.

In Father Lopes' eyes the governor, Colonel Fernando Alves Aldeia, was doing his best, building on the development that had begun in the 1960s, trying to establish an infrastructure: water pipes to remote villages, schools and medical facilities, coffee seedlings, roads. The governor tried to dispense with the bureaucracy. 'What do you need?' he asked when he visited Maliana or Ermera, and after a pause the surprised villagers answered, 'Coffee plants.'

'How many?' Governor Alves Aldeia asked. A calculation was done on the spot and, before anyone knew it, the coffee plants were there.

In September of the year of his return to Dili, Father Lopes became editor of the fortnightly diocesan newspaper *Seara*. He was proud of *Seara*. He published articles about transport, which was always important: aeroplanes in Portugal, railways in Mozambique; lessons from sacred literature; marxism and Christianity; information on religious conferences, religious appointments, pastoral visits.

The emerging leaders from both sides of the political spectrum — Nicolau Lobato, José Ramos-Horta, Francisco Xavier do Amaral, Mari Alkatiri, Francisco Borja da Costa, Domingos de Oliveira, Manuel Carrascalão — appeared in the pages of *Seara*. Father Lopes threw the anonymous articles in the wastepaper bin, arguing that if the authors could not take responsibility for their words, their work deserved no better fate. He accepted pseudonyms — such were the times — as long as he knew who the authors really were.

He wrote his own articles and announcements. The words came easily, jokes, descriptions, debate. Heroes were in the making. He applauded heroism in his account of Portuguese and Timorese resistance to the Japanese occupation — a page from the history of Timor and a page from the history of Portugal, the two inextricably linked.

Revolution was in the air. In his article 'The year of revolution in the schools' Father Lopes assessed the standard of education and the priorities for a government with limited funds. Governor Aldeia had proclaimed that the 1972–73 school year was revolutionary:

they were going to take education to every corner of Timor. The goal was 100 per cent schooling in Timor, achievable by 1980. However, such growth would require increased state spending. While some argued in favour of quantity over quality, Father Lopes' article concluded that it was better to have fewer well-equipped schools than many ill-equipped ones.

People were generally optimistic. Father Lopes upbraided the cynics, the old men of Restelo, for not believing that Alves Aldeia's government would be given the funds to develop Timor.

Change was in the air, too. On Bishop Ribeiro's anniversary Father Lopes publicly wished him a firm hand to guide the boat of the diocese of Dili through any storms that might come.

Father Lopes was permitted to fill *Seara* with articles expressing the spirit of the times for only six months. Despite the relatively free hand granted to the Church publication, *Seara* was closed down by DGS, the secret police, on 24 March 1973. Which article caused the final offence? José Ramos-Horta's 'Maubere'? The word *maubere* was a man's given name, and it was used in Tetum to refer to anyone who was poor and ignorant. The Portuguese and many Timorese used the word as an insult. Some young socialists reappropriated it and used it with pride and solidarity to show the importance of the poorer classes as the real people. Father Lopes tried to rewrite Horta's article; he tried to tone it down by adding 'Jesus was poor too', but it didn't work. The last issue of *Seara* appeared with a notice from Dom José, the bishop, that the publication would be ceasing temporarily 'for convenience'. No explanations were given.

The African wars finally took their toll on Lisbon in 1974. In October 1973 two hundred Portuguese army officers who had all done a tour of duty in Africa formed themselves into the MFA (Movimento das Forcas Armadas or the Armed Forces Movement). By the end of the year they had drafted a program calling for independence for the Portuguese colonies and complete democracy in Portugal.

In Lisbon on 25 April 1974 the young officers from the MFA occupied broadcasting stations and key government installations. On 15 May a provisional government, with General António Spinola as president, was formed. All political parties apart from the fascists were allowed and socialists and communists were in cabinet. The secret police were dissolved and the days of censorship were over. By 24 July the MFA government had adopted a constitutional amendment that recognised the Portuguese territories' right to self-determination.

Portugal's so-called Carnation Revolution was completely unexpected in Timor. Just two days before the coup, Governor Alves Aldeia had made some criticisms of the Armed Forces Movement and Bishop Ribeiro was not in favour of the revolution in Portugal. In Timor some people were afraid, others were jubilant. But everyone was politicised. From a situation of strict censorship and suppression of any kind of political activity, the inhabitants of Portuguese Timor found themselves permitted to think not only about politics but the future of their province. By May three political associations or unions had formed and, Portuguese Timor being the way it was, Father Lopes knew people in all of them.

They were not called parties because the legislation

allowing parties had not been enacted yet but together they expressed the differing aspirations and interests of East Timor's people. UDT (União Democratica Timorense), made up of the more conservative and prosperous elements of the population, favoured ongoing association with Portugal. Fretilin (Frente Revolutionaria de Timor-Leste Independente), which until September 1974 called itself ASDT (Associacao Social Democrata Timorense), was based on the universal doctrines of socialism and democracy. Its members — mostly young, sometimes Lisbon-educated professionals working in the Portuguese administration — were committed to independence, but saw the process of decolonisation as lasting for eight to ten years.

Members of both UDT and Fretilin were drawn from the Timorese elites, the families of *liurais*; Father Lopes had taught them at the Catholic missions. José Ramos-Horta, a member of Fretilin, and João and Mario Carrascalão, members of UDT, were the sons of Portuguese *deportados*, men exiled to Timor for their political activities. The policies of the two major parties were not static. By the end of 1974 Fretilin had formulated a program of social development based on co-operatives, and there were policies on health, education, social justice, culture, internal administration and national defence. The aims were economic self-reliance, the overturning of colonial structures and the involvement of Timorese. At first UDT called for progressive autonomy within a Portuguese federation, but by September 1974 federation with Portugal was seen as an intermediary stage to independence. UDT rhetoric became more anti-colonialist by 1975, but the leadership remained anti-communist.

The third party, Apodeti, favoured integration with Indonesia, with autonomous status. Its members were drawn from conservative tribal leaders, the Muslim community, some Timorese Catholics and Timorese who identified with Indonesia because they had family there or because they were politically (not necessarily culturally) anti-Portuguese. Apodeti members used anti-Portuguese rhetoric and sought to exploit tribal rivalries in certain areas — Atsabe, Maubisse, Viqueque and the Arab quarter of Dili — to further their political ambitions. From the outset Apodeti did not co-operate with the Portuguese administration.

In June the Portuguese administration announced Timor's options: continuing links with Portugal, integration with Indonesia or independence. That month Fretilin's José Ramos-Horta travelled to Jakarta and later Indonesia's foreign minister Adam Malik sent him a written assurance that Indonesia respected the people in Timor's right to independence. Perhaps Adam Malik's magnanimity stemmed from a belief that Portugal would remain in Timor for some time to come; perhaps it was an act of cynical duplicity.

Between Governor Alves Aldeia's departure from Timor in July 1974 and Governor Mario Lemos Pires' arrival in November, there was a move to the left in Portugal. In September President Spinola, with his caution about decolonisation and his ideas about a Lusitanian commonwealth, was replaced by a government committed to dismantling the empire and restructuring Portuguese society.

Upheaval in Portugal didn't help the process of orderly decolonisation, and neither did the neighbours. In early

September the prime minister of Australia, Gough Whitlam, and the soon-to-be Australian ambassador to Indonesia, Richard Woolcott, met the president of Indonesia, Suharto, in central Java. Whitlam told Suharto that, after an act of self-determination, the integration of Portuguese Timor into Indonesia would be favourable for stability and security in the region. This was a bewildering stance as Whitlam's Labor government supported self-determination for the Portuguese colonies in Africa; indeed, as far back as 1963 Whitlam had been making noises about the Portuguese colonies' right to self-determination. Perhaps for Whitlam, as for subsequent Australian prime ministers, the relationship with Indonesia was more important than Portuguese Timor's self-determination. Whitlam might have argued that the province's incorporation into the post-colonial state of Indonesia was a form of decolonisation. There were parallels of progressive incorporation into a post-colonial state: the Portuguese colony of Goa had been peacefully absorbed by India in 1961. West Papuan aspirations toward self-determination seemed to have disappeared after its integration into Indonesia in 1969. Perhaps Whitlam thought the same thing would happen in Timor.

Almeida Santos, the Portuguese minister for inter-territorial co-ordination, visited Timor in October and spoke at huge rallies where ancient Portuguese flags were displayed. Flags had long been venerated in Portuguese Timor. People had to stop and salute the Portuguese flag when they saw it. When they passed an administration building flying the flag they had to take their hats off or, if they were riding, dismount and lead their horses. People would not walk across the shadow of a flag; they walked around it. To Santos the flags indicated that the people of Timor wanted to maintain their ties with the metropolis. To Fretilin members the veneration of the flag was an outmoded superstition.

While Santos was in Timor, Ali Murtopo, the Indonesian general and deputy chief of the state intelligence co-ordinating body, was in Lisbon for secret talks with the Portuguese government. No agreements were reached, but Almeida Santos received a telegram from Portugal cautioning him not to posit independence as an option.

In the same month Ali Murtopo's brainchild Operasi Komodo (Operation Iguana), was given the go-ahead in Jakarta. Others associated with the operation were the generals Murdani and Sugama and Admiral Sudomo. They had the special operations unit, Opsus, and the Centre for Strategic and International Studies to help them achieve their ends. Operasi Komodo was designed to secure the integration of Portuguese Timor into Indonesia by subversive methods.

While the Indonesian press printed stories about Chinese Maoists involved in Timorese affairs, Fretilin were planning a program of reconstruction and development to eliminate illiteracy and promote Timorese culture and religious freedom. Work in literacy and agriculture began immediately.

Governor Lemos Pires took office on 18 November. He had arrived in Timor with a group of officers who were to administer the territory and set up a decolonisation commission. Two controversial majors arrived with the new governor: Jonatas, who was eventually in charge of mass media, and Mota, who became responsible for political affairs. The governor unsuccessfully asked Australia to reopen the Australian consulate in Dili, which had operated in the early 1960s, and the new administration set to the task of calling for complaints against former colonial officials in order to conduct hearings and recommend arrest if necessary. Apparently no complaints were received, even though more than a dozen secret police were working in Timor. Without allegations against the secret police, the MFA administration could not prosecute, but it did advise them to leave the territory. This unwillingness to inform on Portuguese officials indicated to some MFA officers that the nationalism forged in Africa through the independence wars had not developed in Timor. Indeed, Timor was a different case from the African colonies — it was more remote and it was next door to a brutally anti-communist power. Ironically, Xavier do Amaral, leader of Fretilin, predicted that Timor would be the only Portuguese colony to gain its independence peacefully. The recognised political parties were given one hour a week to broadcast on the government radio station. There were more than 4000 radios in Timor, many of them listened to by a number of families. In January 1975 the MFA began a campaign of *consciencialização política* (political awareness) and 'dynamisation' groups travelled around East Timor to prepare the people for local elections.

In Maubisse, for instance, Apodeti arrived to campaign in the morning and people threw stones at them. After that, UDT representatives spoke and the people clapped. Fretilin arrived two hours late, because they had been campaigning elsewhere. Instead of going home to eat, the people waited. The Fretilin representatives arrived in a jeep and when a woman offered Xavier do Amaral an umbrella he graciously declined: 'No, you are here because of us.' To the people waiting, his voice expressed the hope of the early months of 1975. It boomed through loudspeakers, larger than life, from where his diminutive figure stood.

'You made the roads, but do you have a car?' shouted Xavier do Amaral. 'You built the houses, but do you have a house? It's time you, the Maubere people, worked for yourselves, made something for yourselves!'

The people cheered. 'Viva Fretilin!' Banners waved aloft: 'Only one force: the people. Only one guide: Fretilin. Only one goal: independence.'

'Do you like bread and butter?' Xavier asked humbly, as though he was speaking personally to each member of the crowd.

'Yes,' came the answer from many mouths at once.

'Well, why don't you eat bread and butter then?'

'We don't have the money to buy it,' someone shouted.

'Why don't you have any money?' He paused for a moment, seemingly as bewildered as his audience about why this should be so. 'I know you work hard but you don't have any money.' The people became excited when Xavier spoke.

As soon as the people of Portuguese Timor were allowed to speak freely, or to listen freely for that matter, propaganda began blaring into Portuguese Timor from Indonesian-controlled Radio Kupang in West Timor. At the end of February 1975 Apodeti's broadcasts, which opened with the sound of machine-gun fire, were suspended from the government station in Dili for inciting violence. During and after the forty-five-day suspension the Radio Kupang broadcasts became a more important vehicle of Operasi Komodo, referring to UDT as neo-fascists and Fretilin as communists.

Wary of Indonesian intentions, UDT and Fretilin formed a coalition in January 1975. Portugal encouraged the coalition, which repudiated Apodeti, rejected integration with Indonesia and recognised Portugal as the only mouthpiece for decolonisation. The coalition renamed Portuguese Timor 'East Timor' and referred to its citizens as 'Timorese'. The two parties and the administration agreed about the plans for independence, proposing a transitional government led by a representative of the Portuguese government. Cabinet positions were to be shared equally by Fretilin, UDT and the Portuguese. The transition would last for a minimum of three and a maximum of eight years.

Bishop Ribeiro addressed the new situation in a pastoral letter issued on 25 January 1975. He said that the priests and missionary personnel were pleased to see new opportunities opening up and that he and the priests were looking forward to the future. They wanted a Timor that was progressive, just, peaceful and Catholic. He warned against materialistic and atheistic communisim and socialistic marxism and said that the Church forbade Catholics to vote for communists or socialists. All Timorese, whether Catholic, Muslim or animist, had a common belief in God, he said. According to Ribeiro, the Timorese were not as sophisticated as Europeans, and not ready for the dialogue and influences that he saw being introduced to the province by Fretilin members. Fretilin had advocated the separation of Church and state. Under Fretilin, the Catholic Church would no longer have its special status as the civilising arm of the state; it would be on par with other religions, animism and Islam.

The propaganda from the western side of the border continued. According to Radio Kupang, Apodeti was being persecuted and MFA officers were conniving with UDT and Fretilin: a communist plot was being hatched. Timor hit the headlines in Australia in February with reports about an imminent Indonesian invasion. Meanwhile, there were meetings in Lisbon and meetings in London. There were departures and arrivals as Timorese political leaders went abroad to drum up support. And in Atambua, on the Indonesian side of the border, a hundred or so East Timorese were being given military training to fight against parties that opposed a merger with Indonesia.

The Indonesians closed West Timor to journalists in March 1975 and the first round of local elections for *chefes de suco* (village heads) in East Timor took place in the same month. Everyone aged eighteen years and over could vote. The process was simple; voters put a stone into the woven basket that represented their choice of representative. Even though the elections were not run along party lines, most of the elected *chefes* were members or supporters of Fretilin.

The parties worked on personal allegiances as well as political platforms. Some towns were Fretilin, others UDT. Even so, many people had friends and family in both Fretilin and UDT. As Xanana Gusmão, later leader of Fretilin, described it: 'UDT parents, Apodeti uncles, Fretilin children. It was a frightening freedom.' People came down from the mountains to the towns to join a party. There were rallies and chants: 'End Portuguese colonialism!', 'Down with imperialism!' Fretilin had devised anti-colonial textbooks. With the support of sympathetic *liurais* they had set up agricultural co-operatives in Bucoli, Aileu and Bazartete. In other districts, Ermera, Maliana and Maubisse, UDT had a stronger hold.

In February Apodeti sent a telegram to the UN alleging that the Portuguese were oppressing people, that violence and chaos ruled in the interior, and that electoral rights had been cancelled. The Portuguese, Apodeti maintained, wanted to hang on to Timor. Major Mota's refutation of the telegram in the newspaper *A Voz de Timor* pointed out that Apodeti had refused to collaborate in the decolonisation process.

The last thing the leftist government in Portugal wanted was to hang on to Timor. Portuguese working in the colonies were war-weary and homesick. Already Portuguese teachers in Timor had been sent back to Portugal. Officers of the MFA felt they were cleaning up a colonial situation that they had not created and that they were missing out on a chance to help at home; Portugal was moving from crisis to crisis with a deteriorating economy, political factionalism and intrigue. After Cyclone Tracy destroyed Darwin in December 1974, Timor depended on links through Indonesia to maintain contact with the outside world.

Ali Murtopo and the Indonesian ambassadors to Britain, France and Belgium met with Almeida Santos and other senior Portuguese representatives, including Major Mota, in London in March 1975. Neither Portugal nor Indonesia wanted UN involvement in Timor's decolonisation, and Portugal undertook not to obstruct Apodeti's activities, provided Apodeti participated in a transitional government made up of the three parties. Indonesia pressed Portugal to set up a consultative body of high-level Indonesians and Portuguese who would advise the governor about preparing the Timorese for integration. The Portuguese told the Indonesians that the best way to improve their image in East Timor would be to co-operate economically, that Indonesia's threatening broadcasts from Kupang and Atambua had not helped their popularity and that the Timorese would need time to come to terms with integration.

Father Lopes and Bishop Ribeiro had had no experience of Indonesian diplomacy then. The Indonesian delegation that arrived in Dili in April 1975 told Fretilin leaders that they had no ambitions in East Timor and that, theoretically, they supported independence. However, they talked with UDT leaders about the presence of a communist threat. The carousel continued. UDT leaders visited Jakarta and Australia. Confused Fretilin leaders José Ramos-Horta and Alarico Fernandes were put up in smart hotels in Jakarta and paid for by Indonesian officials, but nobody would discuss politics with them.

Even though Fretilin members were aware that the breakup of the coalition would only benefit Apodeti, the shotgun marriage between UDT and Fretilin was strained. Rumours were rife. From March there had been fights between UDT and Fretilin supporters in the market places of Dili, Maubisse and Oecusse. UDT wanted a gradual process of decolonisation but Fretilin were impatient with the slow pace of change. UDT did not look favourably on Fretilin's revolutionary brigades and their policies on education and agriculture.

Nevertheless, great plans were afoot. The MFA government in Portugal recognised the right to independence of the people of Portuguese Timor. By October 1975 a transitional government and consultative assembly were to established. In early May, Governor Lemos Pires presided over talks with the UDT–Fretilin coalition. The Decolonisation Committee did not agree to the coalition's demand for an immediate declaration of legal independence and they did not agree to ban Apodeti as a political party. On the contrary, the MFA government advocated that Apodeti should be encouraged to participate in the next round of talks and that they should be represented in the transitional government, or at least be allowed to participate in the October elections. Fretilin members considered it ridiculous to conduct talks on decolonisation with a group that supported a new coloniser.

Apodeti boycotted their talks with the governor but the Portuguese held separate talks with the party's leaders. Apodeti wanted the UDT–Fretilin coalition to agree to *a priori* acceptance of the principle of integration with Indonesia.

At the end of May two right-wing members of UDT, Francisco Lopes da Cruz and César Augusto da Costa Mousinho, visited Jakarta and Australia. They were influenced by the opinions of conservatives there and UDT withdrew from the coalition. As Timorese students with Maoist tendencies returned from Lisbon, Fretilin moved to the left. Seven bad wolves? Nine bad wolves? How many communists were there in Fretilin? Father Lopes knew them all. Most of them were nationalists. They were young. They were outspoken. They had ideals. They threw themselves into their revolution that year. They left their jobs and joined the revolutionary brigades to work on hygiene and literacy projects, and agricultural co-ops, and to increase the villagers' awareness of local history and culture.

When at the end of May the Portuguese government announced that talks would take place in June in Macau, Fretilin decided not to attend if Apodeti were invited. At the farewell demonstration for their representatives to the summit, UDT supporters were armed and Fretilin supporters threw stones at the trucks carrying the UDT members. In Macau representatives of UDT, Apodeti and Portugal met in the presence of Indonesian observers and debated the use of the word 'independence' (a word Apodeti supporters objected to). The Indonesian observers were largely operatives of Operasi Komodo, invited to the talks by the central Portuguese government, not the Timor Decolonisation Committee. The constitutional law that grew out of the summit allowed for Portuguese sovereignty to terminate at the end of three years. Governor Lemos Pires was expected to continue as high commissioner in the transitional government.

Meanwhile, Fretilin members worked on the ground in Timor to gain support and their leaders went abroad: Nicolau Lobato and Xavier do Amaral were at Mozambique's independence celebrations, Mari Alkatiri was in

Africa and José Ramos-Horta was in Australia. Rejecting anything less than full independence, Fretilin refused to appoint representatives to the proposed Popular Assembly. While Timorese leaders attended talks and conferences, published manifestos and undertook consciousness-raising programs, the undeclared war at the border between East Timor and Indonesia heated up.

July was an eventful month. Father Lopes became vicar-general of the diocese of Dili and President Suharto announced that an independent East Timor was unviable. Bishop Ribeiro joined the Indonesia propaganda machine by confiding to the leaders of UDT and Kota, another smaller political party, reports that twenty-six or twenty-eight North Vietnamese communists posing as Chinese and carrying Portuguese passports had arrived in East Timor via Macau, ready to train Fretilin supporters. This story appeared in the Indonesian press.

It was getting hot. Who could believe what anyone said? Tensions between UDT and Fretilin members worsened. Rumours were rife, and when UDT leaders Domingos de Oliveira and João Carrascalão returned from Bali on 6 August they were convinced Indonesia intended to invade a Fretilin-controlled East Timor.

•8•

Civil war

UDT STAGED THEIR COUP on 11 August, the day the new program was to have begun in the mission schools. Like any military operation it had a certain theatricality even if it was hard for the 'audience' to see it. UDT occupied key installations in Dili — the water station, the airport, the Marconi communication centre — and surrounded the military barracks at Taibesse in Dili. There was a curfew: the only people on the streets were UDT soldiers. UDT demanded the arrest of Fretilin leaders and the removal of Mota and Jonatas. The governor didn't comply; instead, the Decolonisation Committee met and agreed on their approach. They would aim to avoid bloodshed, they would try and make Fretilin and UDT talk and they would not support UDT's attempted elimination of Fretilin leaders.

The administration conveyed these principles to João Carrascalão and attempted to reach the Fretilin leaders, none of whom, except Rogério Lobato, was in Dili. Many Fretilin leaders were in the villages to work on literacy and agriculture programs and some of their families had left the capital on the night before the coup. On 12 August Fretilin replied to the governor's communication with a list of preconditions for negotiations. They wanted UDT disarmed, they wanted Timorese soldiers to control Dili, open communication with the outside world, safe conduct for Fretilin members and release of the political prisoners UDT had already taken. They would only negotiate through the governor.

Father Lopes was living in the priests' accommodation, a long single-storeyed building under curly Portuguese tiles, at the Câmara Eclesiástica. From his office opposite Dili's harbour he would have been able to watch the SS *Macdili* leave on 12 August, bound for Darwin with the wives and children of Portuguese officials, some wealthy Chinese, some Australian aid workers and tourists. Luckily, it wasn't common knowledge that UDT had threatened to mortar bomb the harbour area as they embarked. Luckily, they didn't.

The UDT coup had started in some rural areas before it started in Dili. UDT supporters burned houses and Fretilin members in Hatolia and Same were imprisoned. By 13 August the Dili coup had reverberated throughout other parts of Timor. Captain Lino, a Portuguese officer in Los Palos, was marching for Dili in support of UDT. The police chief in Dili, Maggiolo Gouveia, had also come out openly in support of UDT. There were reports that UDT forces from Baucau had marched on Bucoli, arresting Fretilin members there, and that they were on their way to Vemasse and Laleia. In the mountains the

Fretilin command proclaimed a general armed insurrection against all traitors and enemies of the people.

As the situaton worsened, Lemos Pires' administration practised *apartidarismo*, the MFA policy of non-intervention. The army, in Portugal and in the colonies, was expected to rise above conflicts. Fretilin were angry that the Timorese soldiers in the Portuguese army, who had been confined to barracks, were forced to practise *apartidarismo*, but the administration wished to stay out of foreign wars.

Even though UDT started systematically to detain Fretilin members, Rogério Lobato remained at large in Dili. Instead of trying to organise negotiations, he set to the task of securing the army's support. On 14 August he travelled to Aileu to try and contact his brother Nicolau without success. On 17 August, the day that Mota and Jonatas were flown out from the UDT-held airport to Darwin (for their own safety and to communicate with Lisbon, according to the MFA administration), Rogério cadged a ride to Maubisse in a Portuguese helicopter to bring Xavier do Amaral back to Dili for negotiations. When Rogério arrived in Maubisse he discovered that Xavier had recently left for Aileu. Rogério followed him, travelling for twenty hours on foot through the mountains. In Aileu, Rogério secured the support of the garrison. The Portuguese helicopter that had taken him to Maubisse was captured on 18 August, but no one in Fretilin was trained to fly it. Fretilin now had the radio in Aileu and the support of the armed forces in Aileu and Maubisse.

By 19 August, Rogério had returned to Dili and secured the support of the Taibesse garrison there. On

20 August he radioed Fretilin central command in Aileu to tell them he had arrested Gouveia Maggiolo and that other UDT elements had surrendered. He told them that the Fretilin flag had been raised at the headquarters in Taibesse and the Fretilin anthem 'Foho Ramelau' had been sung. Command of Taibesse guaranteed Fretilin control of food and fuel supplies in the capital. What they needed to do next was to win the airport area, Palapaco, from UDT.

For a week, from 20 to 27 August, the battle for Dili raged. Power supplies were cut and Dili was ringed by fire. G3s and Mausers poked out of windows and the noise of mortar and artillery bombardment was constant. The hospital was declared a neutral zone but, though it wasn't looted and the medical staff could continue their work, the neutral zones were not respected for long. Other neutral zones — the governor's residence, at the waterfront, and the harbour — were guarded by Portuguese paratroopers who had been in Timor only since April. Nevertheless, a grenade found its way into the nearby Câmara Eclesiástica. After that Father José António went to live at Motael, before he left for Atambua, and Father Lopes went to live with Dom José Ribeiro at the bishop's house a few kilometres east along the waterfront in Lecidere. Three other priests who had been living at Câmara Eclesiástica, and some nuns, went to the port.

Bishop Ribeiro accompanied the nuns through the besieged streets to the port. He ignored the fighting when he walked through the streets of Dili, and the combatants respected him. They ceased firing and resumed the battle when he was out of range. Some said Bishop

Ribeiro could have played a mediating role, but he refused to have anything to do with the 'communistic' Fretilin leadership.

When the UDT coup happened Lemos Pires' administration notified Lisbon and a few days later the Portuguese sent a delegation to negotiate peace between the two parties. Major António Soares, the principal mediator, was blocked in Denpasar on 15 August until after his scheduled flight to Timor had left and for two days he waited in Bali. After he was told that he could not travel onward, he returned to Europe via Jakarta. The Portuguese government plane flew from Dili to Kupang on 17 August and waited there for a day. The formal protest that the Portuguese lodged with the Indonesian ambassador in Lisbon hardly helped the situation in Timor.

Father Lopes had seen the streets of Dili deluged in the wet season and bombed beyond recognition after World War II, but he had never known them to be a war zone. He hadn't seen them staked out, pockmarked with bullet holes, or heard the awful explosive sound of the exchange of small arms fire. All over the western part of East Timor fighting raged and the casulties sustained in rural areas, where tribal rivalries were fierce, were greater than those in the capital. There were reports of UDT executions in Hatolia, Same, Baucau and Dili. When Fretilin eventually got the upper hand, they did the same thing. Father Lopes was appalled by the political extremism and the suffering it brought.

Father Lopes wasn't pro-Fretilin. He believed some elements were communist, but it wouldn't be true or impartial to make a general accusation. He didn't approve of the practice of arrest for personal revenge. When the families of UDT or Apodeti supporters or ethnic Chinese came to see him to report arrests, he went to see Rogério, leader of Fretilin's armed forces.

'Rogério! Your men got another one!'

'Who do you mean, Father?'

Father Lopes named the name.

'Where?' Rogério asked.

'Maubara.'

'Father, we're fighting a war! It was a military exercise in Maubara.'

'But he's married. He's got nine kids.'

'We arrested him for a reason.'

'But Rogério! He's never done anything wrong. He's a farmer. He wasn't involved in any fighting or subterfuge.' There were long family memories in Timor. In this war people were seeking vindication for grievances carried from the time of the Japanese occupation. 'Please let him go.'

At the end of August a Norwegian cargo ship, the SS *Lloyd Bakke*, answered Governor Lemos Pires' SOS and took about a thousand people to Darwin. When the SS *Macdili* returned to Dili, the fighting was so fierce that the ship was forced to anchor offshore. At 3.30 am on 27 August the *Macdili* towed Lemos Pires and his government to Atauro on cattle barges. Later, 700 people boarded the steamer from barges. Neither Fretilin nor UDT admitted responsibility for the bombardment of the harbour while the *Lloyd Bakke* and the *Macdili* were loading; no one was clear on the source of the mortar attacks.

CIA reports indicated that Indonesia planned to take advantage of the confused situation and increase its work on behalf of Apodeti. Portugal did not want Indonesia to intervene, which it had offered to do, unless it was as part of an international initiative. Australia, aware that Indonesia was resolved to incorporate East Timor, offered to provide humanitarian relief, but no more. Prime Minister Whitlam maintained that Portugal and the Timorese themselves would have to resolve the problems, with Indonesia occupying an important place.

Although Indonesia had been indirectly responsible for the UDT coup, the outcomes were not what the orchestrators of Operasi Komodo had desired. UDT and Apodeti did not band together to fight Fretilin. Sometimes Apodeti members sided with Fretilin, sometimes they were neutral, and in the interior they fought as a separate force according to tribal loyalties, against Fretilin or UDT. In Dili, Apodeti supporters took refuge in the Indonesian consulate and, soon after the Portuguese administration's departure, some of them were evacuated with the protection of Indonesian paratroopers on the Indonesian destroyer *Monginsidi*.

Dom José, Father Lopes and the other priests stuck it out. By 28 August, Dili was under Fretilin control and the Central Committee met to plan creches for war orphans and to organise food for the displaced. In early September a surrender was negotiated between UDT forces and Fretilin in Baucau. There was still a dusk-to-dawn curfew in Dili and during the curfew the sound of gunfire could be heard.

In the west of East Timor, Fretilin forces chased UDT and the leaders of the other minor parties, Partido Trabalhista and Kota, all the way to the border. There was fighting in Liquiçá, Maubara, Atabae and Balibó. In early September UDT leaders were negotiating with Indonesia for ammunition, food and access to West Timor. They were told by Indonesian officials that assistance was conditional on their signing a petition asking for integration into Indonesia. They signed. On 24 September UDT lost Batugadé to Fretilin and a force of 900 crossed the bridge over the Mota Ain estuary into the Republic of Indonesia. They were disarmed and placed in prison-like refugee camps. Thousands had fled across the border ahead of them, some panicked by the exaggerated radio reports from Atambua. At the border these reports were the only information available during the war. In the camps, conditions were poor with many of the men being forced to work under armed guard. Few foreigners had access to the camps, and the international aid that came to Kupang rarely found its way to the refugees.

The civil war left a couple of thousand casualties and 400 dead in Dili. Father Lopes blamed the Portuguese administration for the turmoil. They had given licence instead of maintaining liberty, they had allowed the rival factions to get arms, and the consequences were terrible. Was it foolish optimism to think that any of the lost opportunities might have made a difference? Apodeti didn't participate in the talks with Governor Lemos Pires in May, Fretilin didn't participate in the Macau talks. The Portuguese delegation never arrived to negotiate the situation between Fretilin and UDT immediately after the coup. Proposed talks between Portugal and the leaders of the three main parties never took place in Darwin.

By the end of September, Fretilin controlled East Timor. They called for Portugal to return and complete the process of decolonisation; the Portuguese flag still flew over the governor's palace. They started to organise the processing of the coffee crop. A few schools started up again. Some shops reopened. Journalists and aid teams flew in from Australia and reported that, although the buildings were pockmarked with bullet holes, the damage was minor.

However, in the western districts of East Timor the Indonesian tactics were ceasing to be subtle. When the UDT coup occurred, eighteen of the twenty-three Portuguese officers stationed at the garrison at Bobonaro left. At the beginning of September the remaining five left, with instructions for the Timorese soldiers to take responsibility for the headquarters. The next night the garrison was attacked. The garrison soldiers were prepared, thinking that UDT or Fretilin might attack but it was the Indonesians who attacked. The garrison at Bobonaro was a strong building, with walls of cement and stone, situated at the foot of a mountain. Its guns were trained on the ridges, the source of the Indonesian attacks for two nights. On the third night the Timorese soldiers from Bobonaro decided not to wait but to attack the Indonesians at the Apodeti village where they had been given protection. The offensive was successful — about thirteen Indonesians were killed and one was taken prisoner. The prisoner told his captors that he was a Javanese corporal in a commando unit; there were two groups of about thirty commandos. The corporal's officers had told him that he was in Indonesia; he had come to kill the communists. The prisoner was sent to Dili.

The Timorese soldiers who defended Bobonaro did not identify themselves as Fretilin or UDT. They saw themselves as patriots, not communists.

The twenty-three Portuguese soldiers from Bobonaro tried to walk to the north coast, hoping to be picked up and taken to the Portuguese administration on Atauro. However, they were captured by UDT and ended up crossing into West Timor with the defeated UDT forces.

In Dili civilians queued at the Fretilin administration at Taibesse for food, fuel and transport allocation. The bank, Banco Nacional Ultramarino, which had been started by Governor Silva in the early years of the twentieth century, had closed with the UDT coup. With the Portuguese administration on Atauro, the Fretilin administration had no access to financial services. Civil servants were paid with rations. In the villages the Portuguese *escudo* continued to circulate, and in the towns Fretilin set up trading posts for barter.

At the border, however, the war continued. Batugadé fell to the Indonesian forces after artillery, naval and air bombardment on 8 October. Balibó and Maliana fell on 16 October. Five journalists who had travelled to Balibó to cover the manoeuvres for Australian television and radio disappeared. For a few days nothing was heard of them, until Radio Australia reported that *Kompas*, the Jakarta daily, had published an interview with Francisco Lopes da Cruz, a pro-Indonesian UDT leader, in which he reported that the bodies of four Europeans had been found with eleven others in a shop in Balibó. A Portuguese news crew, which had pulled out of Balibó on the eve of the attack, escaped the Indonesian border invasion and arrived back in Dili with reports of a stream of cars travelling between Balibó and Maliana. In Kupang the finding of the journalists' bodies was officially acknowledged by a representative of the Australian embassy in Jakarta on 22 October. In Australia, the foreign minister, Don Willesee, was still maintaining on 29 October that no definite information had come to hand. According to the Indonesian version, the journalists had been killed by UDT–Apodeti forces; they were communists and deserved to die. Indonesian press reports maintained that a civil war still raged in Timor. Ali Murtopo denied any Indonesian ambitions in East Timor.

However, very few UDT members took part in the assault on Balibó. Benny 'if you listen to Benny you'll be in a war every day' Murdani was the general in charge of the military operations in this phase of Operasi Komodo. From mid September hundreds of Indonesian troops were brought into West Timor through the small port of Atapupu. Colonel Dading Kalbuadi was the field commander of the attacks, comprising a force of 2000, on Balibó and Maliana, and Major Yunus Yosfiah was in command of the assault on Balibó.

By the end of October the situation in Dili was tense. The civil war had disrupted food production and thousands of people were displaced. Food was starting to run out and an invasion was expected at any moment. Sometimes the residents of Dili could even hear the bombardment around Maliana. On 20 September and again on 25 October Fretilin sought negotiations with the Portuguese, but somehow no agreement was reached for talks between the Fretilin leadership in Dili and the Portuguese administration on Atauro.

Early in November, however, talks took place in Rome

between Portugal's foreign minister, Melo Antunes, and Indonesia's Adam Malik. No Timorese representatives were present and the result of the talks was a twelve-point accord. Portugal was the legitimate sovereign power with responsibility for decolonisation; the UN would not be involved; talks should take place between the Portuguese and all the political parties of Timor. The twenty-three Portuguese soldiers from the Bobonaro garrison and the Timorese refugees in West Timor were also discussed.

The Rome talks served to increase Fretilin's sense of isolation. As far as Fretilin leaders were concerned, the Portuguese authorities should have been negotiating with Fretilin about decolonisation, not with the allegedly pro-Indonesian parties. From the end of October trucks loaded with fuel, food and ammunition started to leave Dili, bound for hideouts in the mountains.

By mid November, when there was no flour and only 100 tonnes of rice left in Dili, a barge from Darwin called the *Alanna Fay*, chartered by the Australian Council for Overseas Aid (ACFOA), arrived in the capital. They unloaded 1 tonne of milk powder, 30 tonnes of rice, 25 tonnes of corn, 4000 metres of cloth, 5 tonnes of flour, 12 tonnes of assorted seed, penicillin and other drugs, and fuel, strictly for the distribution of aid. Two days later the *Alanna Fay* sailed with a cargo of Timorese coffee. Since the end of August Fretilin had organised the processing of the coffee crop. The proceeds of Fretilin's first export sale were deposited in a bank in Darwin because the bank in Dili was locked, awaiting the return of the Portuguese.

In the streets of Dili reconstruction was under way.

Gardeners and painters and street cleaners and carpenters, some of them UDT prisoners, tidied up the buildings and the roads. Close to the Fretilin prison one day Father Lopes talked with a young member of Fretilin, Xanana Gusmão, about the conditions for prisoners. They could talk to each other easily because their fathers were both from Laleia and everybody from Laleia knew each other in Dili. Their fathers had worn the same kind of hat — a Portuguese policeman's hat. Father Lopes asked Xanana to ask Fretilin's central committee to stop torturing UDT prisoners. Xanana himself had been imprisoned by UDT at Palapaco during the coup. He and his fellow prisoners had had to clean the latrines with their bare hands. Xanana, too, was disgusted with the mentality of revenge, the appetite for violence and the obsession with crime that had been fanned by the civil war.

After Balibó Indonesian propaganda continued to paint a picture of civil turmoil in East Timor. Within Timor Radio Kupang, now renamed Radio Ramelau after one of East Timor's sacred mountains, broadcast in Tetum and was able to muffle the broadcasts from Radio Dili. Antara, the Indonesian press agency, sent out spurious reports to the international press of 'anti-Fretilin' assaults on various towns including Maubara, Baucau and Dili.

Bishop Ribeiro still refused to have anything to do with the Fretilin leadership. Some alleged that the bishop himself had contacts with Catholic Apodeti members and that he supported a move by the military police to remove leftist Fretilin leaders in early November. When he refused to say Mass for Fretilin troops,

Fretilin authorities disconnected the power and water to his house for a day.

On 11 November there was a Fretilin demonstration in Dili in support of the MPLA's declaration of Angola's independence. Speeches were conducted entirely in Tetum. Also on that day Whitlam's Labor government in Australia was dismissed. A caretaker government led by Liberal leader Malcolm Fraser took power until the elections scheduled for 13 December. The Indonesian military were to take some decisive steps during this period.

Fighting at the border continued. Balibó had almost been retaken by Fretilin soldiers on 10 November. It was becoming clear to the people in Dili that the Portuguese were not going to return and when the wind was from the west they could hear Indonesian ships bombarding the north coast. It took two weeks for the Indonesian forces to take Atabae, which fell on 28 November after attacks from air and sea. To the Fretilin leadership, who had sent another appeal to the UN Security Council on 24 November, the lack of response from the outside world was a sign that the international community would allow Indonesia to use force to destroy them.

The announcement of the fall of Atabae was not made until after Fretilin's impromptu unilateral declaration of independence. The Democratic Republic of East Timor came into being at a tense ceremony in Henry the Navigator Square in front of the government buildings late in the day on 28 November 1975. The decision to declare independence was by no means unanimous among the Fretilin leadership and the ceremony had a slow, unplanned momentum. Civilians and journalists waiting in the square were not sure what the gathering was for. It was some time before Xavier do Amaral arrived in the Portuguese governor's black Mercedes-Benz. Then the Portuguese flag was taken down from the government building and replaced with the new flag of the Democratic Republic of East Timor, sewn hastily the night before. After a minute's silence for all those who had died in the preceding months, and in all of East Timor's anticolonial wars, Xavier read the declaration of independence. The ceremony took place at about six in the evening; there wasn't much time to celebrate before the curfew.

The next day the ceremonies started in the morning: Xavier was sworn in as president and Rogério read the newly drafted constitution. As the government of a sovereign state, Fretilin felt they could appeal to the UN more effectively. The soldiers who died fighting the Indonesians now belonged to a free and independent people, defending an independent country. Three days later the first cabinet was sworn in at the former governor's residence in the hills on the way to Dare. Futilely hoping the Portuguese would return, the Fretilin leadership hadn't touched the governor's grand villa until that day.

•9•

Invasion

INDONESIA REACTED immediately to Fretilin's declaration of independence. The next day planes dropped leaflets over Atabae. Dated 'Balibó, 26 November', the leaflets proclaimed the integration of East Timor into Indonesia. They were signed by leaders of Apodeti, UDT, Kota and Partido Trabalhista. The meeting between these leaders and Indonesian intelligence officials, as well as foreign minister Adam Malik, took place in Atambua or Bali. Malik expected the Timorese leaders to invite him to Dili soon. 'Diplomacy is finished,' he said. 'The solution to the Timor problem is now in the front line of battle.'

On 2 December Michael Richardson and Jill Jolliffe, two of the three remaining Australian journalists in Dili, were evacuated, leaving Roger East as the last foreign journalist in Dili. On 5 December Indonesian warships bombarding Fretilin troops at the Loes River, only sixty

kilometres west of Dili, could be heard in the capital. A
slow exodus from the city began as people set off on foot
for the mountains carrying as many of their belongings
as they could. Bare feet trod the steep walking tracks up
the hills south of the town. Children's small, smooth-
skinned hands and the ancient, latticed hands of the
elderly with their own landscapes of veins and bones,
grasped the same stones for balance. The tracks curved
and snaked. Safety seemed to lie over the ridge, where
the last dust-covered sole of the last weary foot might
disappear into the bush.

Invasion was imminent, as oppressive as the buildup to
the wet season, except that the day that broke over Dili
on 7 December 1975 was fine. Out of the west came an
ominous, airborne, mechanical rumbling. Father Lopes
looked out of the window of the bishop's house on the
waterfront to see rain different from the kind they'd been
expecting. Dili skies were covered by green parachutes;
five Indonesian military aircraft were flying low and dropping paratroopers. Those paratroopers were laden with
AK-47 rifles, ammunition, food for two days, two water
bottles, shovels, machetes, first aid kits and parts for
heavy weapons, Of course at the time Father Lopes didn't
know what soldiers needed for the first stages of a full-
scale invasion. He saw only that it was raining men,
rockets and cluster bombs. They were burning everything
and everybody. He would not have known that there were
264 Kopassandra commandos and between 170 and 200
men from Battalion 502 dropping on Dili. As they fell,
small arms fire opened up from below — *pop … pop … pop*
— and many paratroopers were shot dead. One plane
banked right over Dili harbour and strangely dropped

thirty men with their guns and their equipment into the water, where they all drowned.

But the soldiers who reached the ground alive started killing anyone they could find. From the bishop's house at Lecidere Father Lopes and Bishop Ribeiro could have seen the landing craft pouring forth their deadly cargo. Countless soldiers in packs. Green caterpillars with heavy boots and big guns. Some wore green berets and some wore red. The priests didn't need to speak Bahasa Indonesia to understand them. They ransacked the shops and looted the houses. They raped women, sometimes in front of their husbands. Troops from Battalion 502 gunned down Timorese and Chinese. Mayhem. No one dared to talk to the Indonesians. They shot people who tried. Even though the Timorese were too frightened to leave their houses, the soldiers broke into houses and shot the inhabitants. They shot the Chinese who offered them food. And of course, they rounded up those who had the flags of political parties pasted on their houses and shot them too.

The Indonesian plan was that the Kopassandra commandos would secure the airport, the docks and the radio station, while the marine corps moved in from the sea with amphibious tanks. The remaining two companies of Battalion 502 would then arrive on small transport planes. But the macabre choreography of invasion did not work out. The Indonesian troops fired everywhere. The green berets from Battalion 502 exchanged fire with the red beret marine corps. Indeed, they were so trigger-happy that they ran out of ammunition because Fretilin had managed to prevent the supply transports from reaching the beach.

Some youths ran to the bishop's house and told Father Lopes and Bishop Ribeiro that the streets were full of people dying. The priests decided to take the wounded to hospital. It took no time at all to fill the bishop's jeep. Father Lopes didn't know how many there were. Two young Timorese, Víctor and João, helped lift the bloody bodies. Father Lopes drove, the bishop sat beside him in the front. Both in their soutanes, they headed towards the hospital at Lahane on the hill behind Dili, but before they had gone more than a few hundred metres they were stopped by Indonesian soldiers. The soldiers didn't understand the bishop's explanation or Father Lopes' gestures. They showed Dom José none of the respect he was accustomed to. None of the occupants of the jeep understood the soldiers' words, but their message was plain. The Indonesians pointed their arms and their guns and shouted, 'Commandant! Commandant!'

While the wounded silently bled, Bishop Ribeiro asked the Indonesian commander, in English, for permission to drive to the hospital. The commander didn't seem to understand the urgency of their mission. He tried to be charming in a sinister way. He toyed with them.

'You go,' he said, indicating the two priests. 'You stay.' He stared at Víctor and João. The boys looked at the bishop, their faces paralysed by fear.

'The boys are helping us,' said Father Lopes.

'We need them to care for the wounded,' said Bishop Ribeiro.

'And to help carry the wounded,' added Father Lopes. A clicking noise came from somewhere at the back of the commander's mouth. That was all.

'Senhor,' Bishop Ribeiro was trying to be polite, persuasive, one anti-communist leader to another. 'The boys are indispensable.' The commander merely stared impassively past the bishop's shoulder towards a group of his soldiers. 'We need the boys at the hospital,' Ribeiro tried again, the thin layer of authority in his voice barely hiding the hysteria he was beginning to feel. The commander clearly didn't care whether the wounded reached the hospital or not. The longer they delayed, the more blood those in the jeep lost. Nothing they said could make the commander change his mind, but the priests couldn't leave Víctor and João there alone. Bishop Ribeiro thought quickly. He told Father Lopes to go with the wounded; he would stay at the commander's headquarters with the boys.

Father Lopes was afraid for his own life, but he drove off alone with the wounded in the back of the car. The familiar streets had become strange. He gripped the steering wheel and tried to concentrate on Avenida Bispo Medeiros straight in front of the jeep's dirty windscreen, disappearing into the shade of the trees that lined it on both sides. The uniform hammer of soldiers' boots on the streets beat a menacing rhythm under the sound of the jeep's engine. Could he hear it, or could he only sense those footsteps changing to a manic clatter when the platoons stormed a shop, or a house, or some terrified civilians trying to run away? Shouts and screams welled up like nightmares in the smoky atmosphere. One of his passengers was asking for absolution.

After the intersection with Rua Jacinto Cândido, the buildings and trees lining Bispo Medeiros became more sparse. To the right some buildings towards the centre of town were burning, their light form lost in smoke. Ahead the tops of the hills became invisible in the no-colour sky. To the left, the sports stadium. The solid Portuguese façade of the market looked somehow aghast. Where were the Portuguese this morning? And then, magically, from the shadows of a bullet-pocked banyan tree, two long-haired young soldiers wearing sunglasses and faded fatigues — Fretilin soldiers — appeared. When they beckoned to him, Father Lopes tried to look around, to check the coast was clear. The jeep swerved as he turned his head and the soldiers ran up to him. They grinned unassailably even though their eyes were tense. Father Lopes had known them since they were kids. He had probably known their fathers as well. Both the youths kissed his hand and their conversation was spoken quickly, quietly, no unnecessary words.

'Where are you going, Father?' They had already seen the jeep's passengers.

'To the hospital.'

'Okay. Hurry. Be careful.'

'Is it safe ahead? There are Indonesian soldiers everywhere.'

'You should be okay. We're defending the hills.'

The priest blessed the youths softly and pressed his foot down on the metal accelerator. The soldiers vanished. The jeep droned up the hill through Balide, the big, pale blue church of Dili's oldest parish on the left, past the bus terminal on the right. No buses to Maubisse, Suai or Ainaro today. On the left the land dropped sharply away into a steep gully. People loaded with plastic containers, sacks of rice and fish tied to sticks across their shoulders wound up the walking tracks through the scrub. The tracks were so steep that even a chicken scratching could start an avalanche. It was dry today. Tomorrow, it might rain, and those people would be trudging through the mud.

The jeep's engine strained with the climb. Father Lopes didn't want to stall here. Ahead a dung-coloured truck loaded with people and cumbersome items kept going straight — to Ainaro, perhaps. Father Lopes turned right at Lahane, the road to the hospital. Children peered from *palapa* huts, too afraid today to greet the bishop's jeep with their usual cries of '*Bensa ami*' (bless us). The jeep climbed the last three switchbacks. His father lived nearby and he'd been travelling this road all his life. Perhaps today was the last time.

The hospital, tucked into a cleft in the balding hills, was invisible until Father Lopes swung the jeep into the forecourt. The Portuguese doctors had left but the Timorese nurses had stayed. It was reassuring — a place where babies had been born (in the red-roofed wing) and where people had been cared for (in the green-roofed wing). Youths ran out from the shade to carry the jeep's passengers inside. Father Lopes talked quietly with one of the nurses on the verandah. People from the *palapa* dwellings near the hospital gathered to listen. They had seen the bombardment, the paratroopers and the fires in Dili. Father Lopes tried to sound calm. Fretilin were fighting the Indonesians in the streets and many people were fleeing. The situation was serious. He had to return to the bishop at army headquarters.

From the hospital's Red Cross radio, Alarico Fernandes had sent a message that was picked up Darwin: 'Indonesian forces have landed in Dili by sea, by sea …

They are flying over Dili dropping out paratroopers ...
Aircraft are dropping out more and more paratroopers
... A lot of people have been killed indiscriminately ...
Women and children are going to be killed by Indone-
sian forces ... we are going to be killed! SOS, we call for
your help, this is an urgent call ...'

The jeep was lighter going down the hill. The were
plumes of smoke rising from Dili as the Chinese shops
burnt. Beyond Dili was the sea, the implacable sea. The
horizon was invisible, the sea and the sky merged. Father
Lopes could hear the gunfire behind the roar of the
jeep's engine. It was the middle of the day and the sun,
like the horizon, had disappeared behind the haze of
smoke.

At army headquarters Bishop Ribeiro was saying his
rosary in the corner. The commander wanted to know
what Father Lopes had seen on the way to Lahane.
Trying to sound concerned for the commander's welfare,
but with great satisfaction, he told the commander,
'Fretilin are everywhere. Beware.'

A midday lull fell. Bishop Ribeiro was distraught. João
and Víctor were standing close to him, trying to fade
into the walls, but their anxiety filled the room. Father
Lopes had a feeling that the commander would have
liked to question him further in a less restrained
manner, when he noticed the Indonesian soldiers eating
their lunch. He was surprised to see that even the officers ate with their fingers. Before the commander could
think up any pretexts for detaining them any longer,
Father Lopes approached him and said: 'Your soldiers
are eating lunch. We are hungry too and we want to go
home and have our lunch.'

The commander smiled. 'Okay,' he said, 'you and the bishop can go home, but the two boys must stay.'

Father Lopes went back to Víctor and João. Their faces were terror-stricken. 'Please, Father, don't leave us here. They will kill us.' Perhaps Father Lopes felt fear in the pit of his stomach as he returned to the commander — fear for the boys, fear he did not show to the commander. He spoke slowly and clearly in the rich orator's voice he had used as a teacher, as a preacher and as a politician. It was a voice that filled the space between the army man and the priest and it brooked no argument. 'We arrived as four people and there must be four of us when we go home. I refuse to leave two people here. If anyone is going to be killed, it is better that we are all killed, all four of us. We two can't go home and leave the two boys here. We refuse to do that.'

The commander continued to play with them. There was more talking, whispered messages as soldiers came and went, delays, covert threats and sly interrogations. Then they were all allowed to leave.

The streets were full of corpses: dead Javanese, dead Timorese. Death everywhere. Father Lopes had never seen anything like it. He thought his time had come too, but for some reason it was not God's will and he had survived.

From their corvettes, the *João Roby* and the *Afonso Cerqueira*, moored off the island of Atauro, which was visible on clear days from the bishop's house in Lecidere, representatives of the Portuguese colonial government watched through binoculars as Dili burned. It was more than three months since they had fled to the island that, ironically, had been a place for political undesirables during colonial times. The crew of the *João Roby* started trying to pull up the anchor at 6 am on the day after the invasion, but it was embedded in coral and they struggled with it all day. At 6 pm they severed the anchor chain with a hacksaw and the corvettes sailed to Darwin where they lingered for a few months, waiting for international pressure to oust Indonesia from Portugal's most distant colony.

The Indonesians claimed they were brothers to the Timorese. They said their soldiers were volunteers, that the invasion was an act of union. They took down the flag. They slapped the bishop. Father Lopes was at a loss to know how brothers could behave like these people. On Dili wharf on the day after the invasion scores of people were executed: men in Portuguese army uniforms, women in dresses, Chinese. Rosa Muki Bonaparte, Isabel Lobato, Francisco Borja da Costa, the journalist Roger East and many, many more. Some bodies fell into the sea, some onto the wharf. Terrified onlookers were forced to tie the bodies of the dead to iron pipes with parachute rope and throw them into the sea. The weighting wasn't always effective and corpses washed up on the foreshore. Fathers saw sons executed, sons fathers. People were mustered at the airport while troops stole their belongings from their homes. To celebrate their victory, the soldiers demanded women, whom they raped repeatedly. When the Timorese men protested, they were killed. Father Lopes was ashamed to see what had happened. How could brothers take all their things, show total disrespect for their women?

While the people of Dili climbed further into the mountains, while women gave birth to babies who couldn't survive the mud and the cold and the constant moving, the Indonesians filled up the metal bellies of their ships with everything they could take. Cars and jeeps from the streets, food from the warehouses, operating and X-ray equipment, the air conditioner from the hospital, ancient gold and even, people said, gold teeth from the graves of Timorese rulers. After only ten days in East Timor, Battalion 502 was recalled to East Java in disgrace.

The way Father Lopes saw it, he survived the orgy of killing by God's grace. He and the bishop were totally cut off from the priests in the other parishes of Dili, let alone elsewhere in the country. So it was only much later that Father Lopes learned the details of the bombardment of Lahane. A nurse, Abel de Araújo, was killed by Indonesians as he brought the wounded down to Dili from the hospital, which was under siege a few days after the landing. Around 15 or 16 December Indonesian soldiers killed the boy who looked after Bispo Medeiros, the mission school at Lahane. They put his body at the door. They were about to kill Father Cunha who was also living there but the soldiers found his identity card in his pocket. Villagers were lined up with their hands on their heads, ready for the worst.

'Do you know these people?' one of the soldiers asked Father Cunha.

'Yes,' he said, 'they are my people.'

'Are they communists?' asked the soldier.

'No. They are Catholics,' the priest replied. And so they were saved.

Father Leão was on his way to Lahane on 15 December when he was intercepted by troops at the river and taken to the church at Balide. On Christmas Eve the seminary at Dare, twelve kilometres inland from Dili, was destroyed. The priests there, Father Ricardo, Father Felgueiras and Father Monteiro, were in the chapel when the bombardment started. They couldn't run. The troops rounded up the priests, the nine seminarians and the fifty or so villagers who had come to Dare. The soldiers put everything outside the seminary before they smashed the windows and burned it down.

On Christmas Day thousands more troops arrived at Liquiçá and Maubara. There was gunfire in the hills behind Dili every night. The invaders claimed they controlled all the land within a twenty-kilometre radius of Dili, but everyone could hear the exchange of fire and explosions around the town. Fretilin guerillas came to Dili dressed as civilians during the day to buy or barter for food and other supplies. The mathematics didn't work. There were 15,000 Indonesian 'volunteers' in the first wave of the invasion, and in the first two months it cost 60,000 Timorese lives to defend the land.

History didn't stop just because tens of thousands of people were out of the picture, of course. The United Nations Security Council called for a removal of Indonesian troops and an act of self-determination. Before the UN envoy had even visited East Timor Adam Malik, Indonesia's foreign minister, announced that the provisional government of East Timor had invited Indonesia to declare sovereignty over the territory. Indonesia maintained that the battle was between Fretilin groups and pro-Indonesian forces. In mid January 1976 Fretilin still controlled most of the interior of East Timor.

It was Easter 1976 before Father Lopes made contact

with Father Leão in Balide, a suburb of Dili. By that time food had become extremely scarce and when good food appeared it was a miracle. Father Lopes sought permission from the military to travel to Balide and he was equipped with bodyguards for the drive. He and the bishop had received some help — Portuguese money — from outside. They spoke privately in Portuguese. 'I just came to see if you were still alive,' Father Lopes said.

Father Lopes and Dom José Ribeiro started going to see the Indonesian commanders about Timorese detainees, Fretilin detainees. Only months before Father Lopes had been going to see the Fretilin commanders about UDT detainees. Even though he wasn't pro-Fretilin he could not turn a blind eye to the wanton cruelty, the gratuitous taking of life.

Despite what Dom José had thought about the Church in East Timor benefiting from integration with Indonesia, he wept every time he heard about what the Indonesians were doing. The Indonesians didn't accept the last Portuguese bishop of Dili because he was white, from Europe. They had taken the ring from his finger. Bishop Ribeiro started calling the Indonesians communists. His health was failing and his nerves were shot to pieces by the time he asked the Vatican to allow him to resign in October 1977. 'We have been deceived,' he whispered into Father Lopes' ear. After the invasion they could never be sure they were alone. The walls had ears. God had spared Father Lopes the knowledge of what was to come. The war had just begun.

• 10 •

Integration

A CHARADE OF POLITICAL life continued in Dili after the invasion. At the end of May 1976, while Fretilin fighters met in Soibada and decided to change their strategy from armed confrontation to guerrilla warfare, a thirty-seven-member Popular Representative Assembly met in Dili for less than two hours and unanimously approved a petition addressed to President Suharto requesting the integration of East Timor into the Republic of Indonesia. In June a forty-four-person delegation presented the petition to Suharto and by July the Indonesian parliament passed a bill that enfolded the East Timorese in the arms of their Indonesian 'brothers'. President Suharto's signature on the Act of Integration effectively ended the 1940 Concordat Agreement. Under Orde Baru, the Catholic Church was no longer the close companion of the state. The bishop was no longer the governor's official friend and adviser, the diocese of Dili was no longer under the jurisdiction of the Portuguese Bishops' Conference. The Vatican decided to administer the diocese directly rather than place it under the jurisdiction of the Indonesian Catholic Bishops' Conference (MAWI). Despite the Act of Integration, Alarico's radio reports from the mountains maintained that Fretilin still controlled 80 per cent of Indonesia's newly acquired twenty-seventh province.

Private lives were invaded. The emotions of war ran high and they ran for a long time, so Indonesian soldiers didn't knock when they came to the door. They came and they took. The businesses that reopened were in Indonesian hands, the goods being sold at greatly inflated prices were stolen. Even though many people were homeless, the military occupied private houses, leaving the old Portuguese military barracks empty.

These were crimes against property, but the more unbearable crimes were against humanity. What power did it give them, this bestiality? What kind of satisfaction did they get from making a girl and a boy who had never met each other before have sex in a *mandi* (bathtub)? What joy was there in watching a husband's face as they raped his wife? Did they prefer broken bodies to whole ones?

In the confessional, out of the confessional, people came to Father Lopes and told him terrible stories. Dom José wept and wept. Perhaps his face grew even paler until it was the same colour as his white soutane, and more crumpled and defeated until it seemed his thin skin would dissolve altogether. How could one human being retain the knowledge of so much atrocity? But Father Lopes retained it, and checked it, and sought further details. He went out to look for people who had been reported killed or raped.

The soldiers demanded women. Young girls bound their breasts to their chests and wore T-shirts and shorts so they looked like boys. Still the soldiers felt their bodies to check. The women cut their hair, stopped washing and wore dirty clothes to make themselves unattractive. Those simple things that had been good about life — a smile, laughter — were gone. Dili was full of big black flies. After the charade of the Act of Integration was over, food became scarcer. Sometimes the stray dogs carried human heads or arms in their mouths. The dogs dug up the graves or fought over bodies washed up on the beach. When things grew worse, there were no longer any dogs. Ghosts must have walked up and down the little concrete path opposite the bishop's house to the sea.

The bishop's house was soon full of young women seeking refuge. The girls were too afraid to sing and the sound of bombs and guns dominated the days and the nights. They ate rice and, exhausted by the oppressive atmosphere, went to bed at four in the afternoon. Father Lopes tried to get meat for them; they saw it very rarely in Dili. He took food to families in need: God knows where he found it. Foreign aid agencies were not admitted into the territory. When aid from the Indonesian Red Cross came, the Timorese were forced to buy it from the military, who controlled its distribution. The Javanese confiscated the coffee crop, sold it and used the money to buy guns from the United States, so people in Timor maintained they had paid for the bullets that killed them. The soldiers buzzed around the bishop's house like the black flies.

Towns were taken, lost and retaken as the Indonesian army moved inland from the north coast: Ermera, Bobonaro, Viqueque. The Indonesian forces had problems around Laclubar. They were afraid of Fretilin. Sometimes whole companies of Indonesian soldiers just gave their guns to Fretilin soldiers and ran away. They were the sensible ones, those who could see there was no reason for them to be fighting this war. Even the Kopassandra troops — meant to be good soldiers, the elite — were fearful if someone shouted, 'Look out! Fretilin is coming!' They weren't fighting for an ideal. If you were fighting for an ideal you were strong enough to fight anyone, absolutely anyone, Father Lopes was sure of it. Fretilin still controlled one-third of East Timor in May 1977. They concentrated on ambushes and surprise attacks on Indonesian-held towns — Baucau, Lospalos, Liquiçá, Bazartete, Ermera — and on feeding the growing number of people living in Fretilin-held areas. One-third of the territory was allegedly controlled by ABRI (the Indonesian armed forces), and one-third by God knew whom.

Martinho da Costa Lopes' father died in the dry season of 1977. When did António da Costa Lopes grow old? He had been so strong but on 17 June he died of old age at Lahane. He had never wanted his son to be a priest. Even though Martinho Lopes inherited his brother Cristóvão's family, António, with the same force of will with which he had sought more children back in 1918, had wanted the son he called Tinu Kai, strong Tinu, to have a family. With a tenacity he'd bequeathed to his younger son, António continued to mistrust the priests. They had taken his son away and turned him

António da Costa Lopes (centre) with Cristovão and
Cristovão's wife Ana Pereira Lopes.

Martinho da Costa Lopes as
a young man.

The seminary orchestra in Macau. Martinho da Costa Lopes is in the back row, third from left.

At the Algarve in 1947. Martinho da Costa Lopes is in the
bottom left of the picture and Dom Jaime Garcia Goulart
is standing on the far right.

Father Lopes presiding at a wedding in Timor.

At the seminary in Dare in the 1950s. Father Lopes is in the centre of the three priests in white. Father Jacob Ximenes is on his left.

Father Lopes (standing on the left) in Portugal during his time
on the National Assembly, 1957–61.

The house at Lahane.

The church at Liquiçá in 1997.

Teaching the catechism on the beach at Liquiçá.

Dom Martinho meeting Pope John Paul II in 1983.

Dom Martinho, still wearing long boots, in Dili in
the early 1980s.

into a different kind of person, one who sang Latin choral music and wrote pastoral poems imbued with the landscape of Portugal, not the mountains of Timor. Perhaps he resented his son for leaving behind his Timorese identity and taking on a Portuguese one. António Lopes died before his son became the first indigenous leader of the Catholic Church in East Timor. He did not see him become an outspoken nationalist and advocate for self-determination.

António had kept his hands in the soil. It was from António that Martinho Lopes learned the useful things he taught to his students: how to tend a garden, how to care for animals, how to live with the land. The Portuguese regime had loved Martinho Lopes; perhaps in his family's eyes he became high class and fat from too much Portuguese soup.

António's death was just one of the terrible severances of the time. There was no one left to call Martinho Lopes Tinu Kai in Galolen, the language of Laleia. Everyone had to learn a new language now. *Kabupaten* instead of *conselhos*. The administrators were called *gubernur, bupati, camat*. The *babinsas* didn't carry arms but they had to know about everything. The *babinsas* called in the Koramil (Komando Rayon Militer or sub-district military command) when they needed help. The despised black god, the *sekwilda* (provincial secretary) was Colonel Sinaga. Hansip (Pertahanan Sipil or civilian militia) was the name given to Timorese watchdogs patrolling the neighbourhoods. The Indonesian authorities also set up two battalions of Timorese soldiers, 744 and 745.

On Indonesia's national day, 17 August, in 1977, President Suharto, with much palaver, offered an amnesty to Fretilin fighters and their supporters. In case anyone misunderstood such a magnanimous gesture, the following month began General Yusuf's extermination and annihilation campaign. It meant aerial bombardment, napalm to burn the *palapa* huts, naval bombardment and massive troop movements to drive the people down from the mountains. The helicopters buzzed over East Timor, more terrifying than any malarial mosquitoes. Their sound overhead could penetrate into the stomachs of those on the ground and leave their bowels vibrating after the helicopters had skittered off into the distance.

There were planes from America, planes from Australia. Father Lopes, who had spent his days in the classroom talking about heroes and ancient sieges, would have never foreseen that he would reel off the names of such items so confidently: OV-10 Broncos, anti-insurgency Nomads. The people were herded into hot tin houses in the lowlands. They weren't permitted to leave these 'resettlement villages' to farm. They became depressed and sick.

When the extermination and annihilation campaign began Dom José finally gave up and went back to Portugal. The Vatican pro nuncio, the Italian Mgr Farano, came to Dili from Jakarta and offered the priests three names from which to choose the new leader. Father Lopes was chosen.

He didn't become bishop, however; the Vatican prevaricated and the diocese of Dili remained a 'vacant seat' in the Vatican's eyes. Following the United Nations' lead, the Vatican refused to recognise the annexation of East Timor but, not wanting to fall out with the Indonesian authorities, they did not press for Indonesia's removal. The Vatican's fence-sitting meant that the role of bishop was a temporary one. Officially East Timor was a separate ecclesiastical province, administered not by Portugal or Indonesia but directly by the Vatican.

Martinho da Costa Lopes was never officially named bishop. He was appointed apostolic administrator, a role that involved most of the duties of a residential bishop, but he could not ordain priests. He was never recognised as a bishop by the Catholic hierarchy in Portugal, though he was given the title 'Monsignor' by the Vatican. He could say whether clergy could come or go, but in 1977 Indonesian authorities banned foreign clergy from working in East Timor. The Church was desperately short-staffed and many missions were without priests. Some priests had gone to the bush with the people; the others functioned as best they could in the occupied zones. Foreign priests were too scared to leave Timor in case they were not allowed back. The mission schools had been closed since the invasion.

The bitter irony of Mgr Lopes performing all the duties of a bishop in a diocese that without the invasion would have had a bishop as its head, but not being recognised as one, parallelled to some extent the predicament of his country. Most nations, with the exception of Guinea Bissau, Angola, Mozambique, China and Vietnam, did not recognise East Timor as a nation. Would António da Costa Lopes have been proud of his son? Would he have been pleased? One day, perhaps, there would be time for pleasure and pride. As the apostolic administrator of the diocese of Dili, Mgr

Lopes needed diplomacy and cunning. He didn't smile. Even though the Indonesians preferred it, he didn't smile.

The Indonesian authorities wanted the Timorese to be silent, but Mgr Lopes had never known how. The girls didn't sing any more, but Mgr Lopes would not let the people who were gone simply disappear. When girls were taken to the army headquarters for questioning, their parents went to the parish priest. The priest came to the bishop, who went to the army headquarters and demanded their release. He had to act instantly, before it was too late. In Dili he saved many people this way, but in the country it was a different story. People were far from the missions, they had no transport and he wasn't able to help in time.

He let it be known that people should come to him. It became a joke. In Dili people used his name with defiance: 'I'll go to the bishop,' they said when the soldiers came around to take their daughters. Mgr Lopes would not shut up about the girls being raped in Comarca prison, about the girls discarded like broken toys after they had been abused. The commander was getting tired of him.

One afternoon there was a soft knocking on his door. When he opened it, there were Ruby and Olinda, two Chinese Timorese girls who had taken refuge at his house, obviously upset. They sat on red vinyl chairs on the verandah where their conversation would not be overheard.

'We don't want to give our country to Indonesia, Ambispu.'

'No, I know,' said Mgr Lopes slowly, shifting back in

his seat. 'Who, in particular, is making you give our country to Indonesia?'

'They selected us to go on television.' Ruby doubled over, covered her face in her hands and wept monsoons onto the painted concrete floor.

'They want us to present a peace map,' explained Olinda.

'What's happened?' asked Mgr Lopes.

'They lined us up,' wailed Ruby.

'They made us stand up. And then they said they'd come and get us tomorrow.'

'Don't let them take us away.' Ruby was distraught beyond comfort.

'No one will take you away,' Mgr Lopes said. Ruby's hunched-over back was heaving. 'I'll go and see the commander. Don't worry, Ruby. No one will take you away.' He motioned to one of the nuns to come and sit with the girls. 'Come and sit inside. You can stay here. I'll go and see the commander. No one will take you away.' He was furious. It was depraved, frightening young children.

Shzweep, shzweep was the sound of the stick broom on concrete the next morning as two middle-aged Indonesian men in plain clothes walked up to the compound where the girls were staying. Mgr Lopes was there to greet them. 'You're the television producers, are you?' he said sarcastically. They smiled but Mgr Lopes continued before they could say anything, 'The girls are not going with you.'

When they started to protest — to try and say in smooth tones what a wonderful opportunity it was — Mgr Lopes held up both his hands. 'If you want to kill, you kill me,' he said. 'The girls are not going with you.' He was so angry. The men could see it. They slunk off and Mgr Lopes waited until they had been gone a while before he went to see the commander. The commander was not surprised to see him.

'I want you to write a sign for me.' Mgr Lopes' Bahasa Indonesia, by necessity, had improved — he had taught himself. The commander was surprised, not having realised Mgr Lopes could understand and speak Bahasa. 'It needs to say, very clearly, "No Indonesians can ask for girls".'

When the sign arrived it was duly attached to the low fence of the bishop's house, but still the soldiers clustered around. At first Olinda dared not go out. She dared not look at them in case they decided they liked the look of her and took her away and raped her. After a while she started thinking they might decide they didn't like the look in her eye, and they might just take her away and rape and kill her anyway. Perhaps at first she was scared and then she was angry.

One night Olinda heard the sound of booted footsteps, treading gingerly. She opened her eyes to see a thin shaft of light from an electric torch pass from the window of the room where she was sleeping to the room where Ruby and half a dozen other girls slept next door. She climbed out the window and crossed the yard silently — the trunk of the mango tree and the little shrubs offered her cover. She didn't have to cross the beam of the torch. God was with her. She didn't even feel embarrassed about tapping quite loudly on Mgr Lopes' window so late at night. She knew how he slept. He didn't mind. He came immediately, his soutane hurriedly thrown over his sleeping clothes. He might as well have slept in his soutane in those days!

'Get out!' Mgr Lopes roared at the soldiers in the room.

The girls, who had been pretending to be asleep, opened their eyes. The soldiers flicked off their torch and jumped over the fence before anyone could identify them.

Olinda visited Dare as part of her unpaid work with the Indonesian Red Cross. She couldn't believe what she saw there: people with bony, thin arms and legs and distended bellies came to the Red Cross for treatment. Their skin had gone strange colours and it had no elasticity — when Olinda pushed the flesh, the depression remained. Rotten flesh just fell off when she tried to bathe their sores. She was shocked. Coming back down the mountain she was sad. When she saw clothes and canned goods from the American Catholic Relief Service go straight from the Indonesian Red Cross to the military quarters, she was angry again.

Another young woman Mgr Lopes tried to help was Maria Gorete Joaquim. Somehow he found out that Intel (Indonesian intelligence) were holding her on the first floor of Santaiho, a warehouse that had once been a Chinese shop. They were worlds apart — the bishop, almost sixty, serious and circumspect, aware of his position and what influence it might wield, and Maria Gorete, still a teenager, spontaneous and easy-going, aware that her body was a toy for her captors — but they had much in common. Maria Gorete couldn't keep things inside herself. Her eyes were brave and they liked to smile. She was in jail because she was suspected of passing on information to the resistance in the bush. Mgr Lopes tried to give her strength. Maria Gorete was being tortured while being held in Santaiho. The Indonesians stripped her, gave her electric shocks and burned her breasts with cigarettes.

'They beat me, Ambispu,' Maria Gorete didn't lower her voice. 'They tell me I'm a savage, a whore.' She frowned. 'But I answer back.' She smiled. 'I ask them how they expect us to like them when they do such things, when the smell of my burning flesh is still in the air, I ask them when they will start behaving like human beings!' She even laughed.

'Be careful, child.' Perhaps for a second, uncharacteristically, Mgr Lopes didn't quite know what to say to this defiant young woman.

'Ambispu, they tempt me.' Maria Gorete had to talk. 'They kick me like a dog and then they say "If you become mine, mine only, you can go free." Can I believe that?'

Mgr Lopes shook his head.

'Ambispu,' she moved closer to him, 'I don't belong to myself any more.'

'Pray, Gorete. Our Lord will help you to stay pure.'

Maria Gorete didn't seem to have heard him. 'They say they'll kill me if I don't give myself to them. Ha!' She laughed again and shouted at the door where she knew they were listening. 'They can only kill me once.' Then she said very softly so only Mgr Lopes could hear, 'But I can make a deal with them.'

'Please, Gorete, be serious.'

'Ambispu, it's okay. It's okay. The officer in charge will protect me.'

'I'll pray for you, Gorete. You may feel as though you are alone, but God is with you.'

'Yes, Ambispu.' She looked very alone.

After many, many inquiries Maria Gorete was allowed out of jail. That's when Lourenço, her old friend, caught up with her. Despite her big smile, her twinkling eyes,

Gorete told Lourenço horror stories about her time in prison, how she had been tortured and raped. She started to cry when she talked about it and Lourenço tried to be gentle with her. Maria Gorete went to parties with the Indonesians. She flirted with the soldiers when they were drunk and passed on what she found out to the resistance. However, she grew tired of pretending. Sometimes she would leave her home and visit Lourenço at six in the morning to avoid the Indonesians who constantly came to her house. They thought she was an easy woman since she'd been in prison.

Maria Gorete got sick of her 'freedom' after a year. She tried to escape from Dili to the bush, but she was caught and arrested. After that she appeared in many places in the company of the Indonesians: in Manatuto, Baucau, Lospalos, there was Maria Gorete. Someone helped her smuggle a letter to her mother. 'I have to humiliate myself many times before the Indonesians, but there is nothing I can do, I am in their power, I do not belong to myself anymore,' she wrote, trying to spare her mother shame about her behaviour. People asked about her and talked about her. While people remembered her, there was more chance she was safe. But gradually they stopped talking about her.

Justino, a teacher, saw Maria Gorete in Baucau not long before she finally 'disappeared'. Gorete had changed. She was quiet now, subdued. She told Justino that she interpreted for the Indonesians, that she was an object for their pleasure and that they raped her whenever they wanted. When she couldn't stand it any more, she told the Indonesians that it was time they killed her. Even though she had been broken, Maria Gorete said

'My body is no longer mine, but my soul will be mine forever'.

Mgr Lopes asked the sisters in Baucau to visit her. After that, some said she was taken to Lospalos. There were stories she'd been taken to another island in Indonesia. Gradually, people talked about her less. No one knows where or how Maria Gorete died. There was a rumour that she had been dropped from a helicopter over Jaco Island, then another that she had been shot near Quelicai. She disappeared when no one talked about her any more. Mgr Lopes heard she had been killed. He didn't forget her; she joined the others on the list of vanished people.

He hated the way the Indonesian military erased people. Try as he might to account for them there were so many, too many, who just ceased to exist, gone from this earth. And it was on this earth that justice would be enacted, Father Lopes knew it. People would pay in this world for the wrongs they committed in this world. Asking questions, demanding to know — it had not stopped with Rogério Lobato in the Fretilin–UDT war. It continued with Indonesian Brigadier-General Dading Kalbuadi, involved with the war against East Timor since Operasi Komodo, who was another matter.

When Mgr Lopes failed to save them he prayed for their souls, safe now with their heavenly father. But nothing could make him forget those vibrant ones who no longer walked the earth. For each one he had saved there had been so many he had not been able to save. Perhaps the Bible's promise of the just prophet gave him strength: 'Here is my servant whom I uphold, my chosen one with whom I am pleased, upon whom I have put my spirit; he shall bring forth justice to the nations, not crying out, not shouting, not making his voice heard in the street. A bruised reed he shall not break, and a smouldering wick he shall not quench, until he establishes justice on the earth.' (Isaiah 42: 1–4)

1978 was a bad year, one of annihilation and extermination. Bombardment. Troops. Guns. Helicopters. Mass slaughters. Mass arrests. Routine and arbitrary torture. And famine, too. Not only people, but hamlets, villages and towns disappeared. Cristóvão Lopes, Mgr Lopes' nephew, died in the bush that year. President Suharto visited Dili and Maliana in July. By November Fretilin had been forced into the east, to the country around Mount Matebian, sacred resting place for the dead. In December Alarico Fernandes surrendered to ABRI and Fretilin's radio transmitter went with him. Soon after, Xavier do Amaral was captured. In late 1977 there had been a split in the Fretilin leadership. Xavier had wanted to negotiate with the Indonesians. Nicolau Lobato assumed leadership and arrested Xavier. On New Year's Eve 1978 Nicolau was killed.

Mgr Lopes offered to say Mass for the repose of the soul of Nicolau Lobato, but the Indonesians never returned his body. General Yusuf, now defence minister, flew straight to Dili to inspect it. Nicolau's corpse was flown to Jakarta and displayed on national television.

The people behind Fretilin lines were running like deer from the air attacks. Throughout 1979 they streamed down from the mountains into the resettlement villages. There, their movements were controlled. They couldn't plant, they couldn't harvest. Food was scarce and conditions were atrocious. The death toll rose.

The priests came back from the bush with the people. Father Luís da Costa had been living with the guerrillas for three years. He'd had no equipment to perform the Mass, but they still prayed. Father Luís taught at the high school in Dili, but he was living with a woman. A priest! Mgr Lopes tried to send him to Ossu but that was the last place Father Luís wanted to go. Did he have to spell it out to Mgr Lopes? 'Ambispu, after my three-year association with Fretilin they think I'm a communist.' The school at Ossu had been made into a military head-quarters. Father Luís didn't think he would live if he ended up in Ossu.

Mgr Lopes couldn't understand why he wouldn't go. When he said, 'I want you to go to Ossu,' Father Luís knew he meant, 'God wants you to go to Ossu.' Still Father Luís refused to go. Despite the times, or perhaps because of them, the commitment to celibacy was as important as ever to Mgr Lopes. Obeying the bishop was tantamount to obeying God. And even Vatican II hadn't overturned the law of celibacy. Luís da Costa was neither obedient nor celibate. He and Mgr Lopes were not close after that; there were no angry words between them, just coldness, a distance belied by their proximity around the table at the yearly retreat.

No one knew what was going on in the mountains: who was in command, how many fighters were left after the end of 1978. Falintil (the armed wing of Fretilin) units had been separated from each other and their communications severed. By the end of 1979 Mgr Lopes started to hear reports about the reorganisation of the resistance. In complete secrecy Xanana Gusmão travelled from one end of East Timor to the other. It was a miraculous journey. With the help of Indonesian friends he passed right by Dili. He ascertained how many fighters were left, and started to regroup.

Even though he refused to integrate the Catholic Church in East Timor with the Indonesian Catholic Church, Mgr Lopes attended the Indonesian Bishops' Conference in Jakarta. He had been sick in Jakarta in 1979, his second time as an observer at the Episcopal Conference. He had been hoping for some support from the Vatican that year, but the Vatican said nothing in public about the real situation. The Indonesian bishops met around a big smooth table. Mgr Lopes tried to concentrate but he felt dizzy. The bishops looked blurry, he was thirsty all the time and his feet tingled. He couldn't trust the Indonesian bishops. When they asked him whether he was all right he was irritable with them. Perhaps someone was poisoning him. He didn't want to think like this. Perhaps he would never return to Timor. Perhaps it was being in Indonesia that made him feel so disorientated. The Indonesian church report estimated that hundreds and thousands of people had been killed since the invasion. He didn't have an ounce of optimism left — he must have left his strength in Timor. Then he collapsed.

When he woke up, he was in hospital. It filled him with horror. Perhaps they were going to inject him with drugs that sent him mad. He had to be calm. If they had wanted to kill him they had had plenty of chances before now. They could have killed him out at the salt lakes at Tacitolu, when he arrived to tell the military to shoot him, not the people they took from Comarca prison in the dead of night. They could have shot him then and there and cooked up some story about where he had gone. Now he could hardly see a thing, but he could smell the hospital around him, and, could he let himself believe it? Could that be a familiar voice? It was Father Leão, talking in Portuguese. 'We've both ended up in here, Vossa Excelência,' he was saying.

'I don't like it,' Mgr Lopes said.

'It's a Catholic hospital. It's not run by the Indonesians. They want to tell you what your diagnosis is.'

Mgr Lopes lay back on his pillows. Being told he had diabetes didn't worry him a bit. He just wanted to return home to recover, and so he did. After a week resting at a Jesuit priest's house, he travelled back to Dili, where he took traditional medicine and let a Timorese nurse treat him occasionally. The doctors in Jakarta told him to be careful of rich food. In Dili he was lucky to have much food at all. When flour or sugar came in from outside he went himself from house to house delivering it to the widows and orphans in need.

Fretilin's regrouping aimed at uniting all Timorese opposed to the Indonesian occupation, but it failed to alleviate the effects of the famine for the civilian population. Late in 1979 Jakarta allowed two international aid agencies into East Timor: the US Catholic Relief Service (CRS) and the International Committee of the Red Cross (ICRC). Dr Pascal Grelléty, medical co-ordinator of the ICRC, was distressed by what he saw. Aid donated to the ICRC — foodstuffs, blankets, soap, medicine — was channelled through Jakarta, it could not go direct to Dili. Emergency aid sat for weeks on Jakarta docks. Almost half the money for the ICRC program was spent on helicopter transport to the remote interior. Sixty thousand of the 'most destitute' people in East Timor were issued with yellow cards and received weekly rations. One-third of these were entitled to extra food because of their malnourished condition. They were issued with blue cards. About 500 red card holders were seriously ill and needed daily medical attention. In their agreement with the Indonesian government the ICRC had not been permitted to visit prisons and while ICRC personnel were aware of executions without trial and disappearances, issues of human rights were considered too political. The times were so tough that the ICRC considered that diplomatic pressure and a campaign to alert the international community regarding human rights abuses might help the Timorese, or it might backfire on them. Their aid program just kept people from starving.

The CRS program, the bigger of the two, was not a Church program but a US government-implemented government-to-government scheme, an aspect of US foreign policy designed to help Jakarta secure the territory. The CRS staff in East Timor, all Indonesian and working through Indonesian-government channels, were able to visit the 'resettlement sites' where more than 300,000 East Timorese lived. CRS complicity with the Indonesian government position extended to its account of the situation. The CRS depicted the crisis in East Timor as a result of civil war, drought and crop failure, omitting to mention that Indonesian military exercises had forced more than half the population from their traditional lands and drastically interrupted food production. Frank Carlin, the CRS director in Jakarta and a former US marine, was permitted to visit Dili from time to time. When the CRS began its operations in September 1979 he said that the general condition and degree of malnutrition in East Timor was the worst he had encountered in his fourteen years' experience. According to the Catholic Church food shortages had lessened the people's resistance to diseases such as malaria, TB, influenza and colds, typhoid, fever, diarrhoea, infections and rheumatism.

No doubt Mgr Lopes was relieved to have visitors from the outside, however tightly their movements were controlled. He and the priests had dealt with the strain of the complete isolation of the territory on a day-by-day basis. In their minds they hadn't behaved heroically; they had just done what was necessary at the time. But it was good to sit and eat and talk in the Hotel Turismo with Dr Pascal and Yvonne, his wife. Perhaps they brought a once-familiar sense of normalcy with them. But normal life was just a veneer and, as well as other forms of aid, Mgr Lopes' time was still taken up with the huge task of defending human rights.

If Mgr Lopes could remember who passed Lourenço's note to him, he didn't say. Lourenço — not the same man who had known Maria Gorete — had been a soldier in the Portuguese army. His message to Mgr Lopes was written in beautiful handwriting in a scramble of Portuguese and Tetum on a piece of paper that was well worn and folded many times by the time it reached the bishop. 'Please help me, Ambispu,' it read. 'Death is snarling at my heels.' Mgr Lopes sent word back that Lourenço could come to his house at any time, day or night, and that with the help of God he would do his best for him.

Mgr Lopes knew it wouldn't be long. He could tell

Lourenço was desperate. Late one night there he was, on the doorstep of the house at Lecidere. The wind came in through the patched walls and the waves crashing on the beach across the road sounded like gunfire while Lourenço told his story. He was twenty-three years old, from Remexio. When a soldier in the Portuguese army, he had been noticed by Fretilin leaders for his courage. They had entrusted him with a Mauser and a few rounds of ammunition and he gave the Bapas (Indonesian army personnel) more than his share of trouble on the outskirts of Remexio. It took them five years to catch him. But they did catch him. He was held in Comarca jail in Dili.

'My death was just a matter of time, Ambispu. Every night the Bapas came and loaded ten or twelve prisoners into a military van. They took them to Tacitolu. Sometimes they machine-gunned them down. Sometimes they stabbed them to death.

'One night they came and took me. There were eleven others. My heart was racing, death was so close and the van was speeding us all closer to it. But, Ambispu, something inside me forced me, some kind of survival instinct made me try to escape. I jumped up and catapulted myself out of the van!' Lourenço's right hand broke away from his left hand. His left hand, clenched fist, sped into the shadows. His right hand cut the air in the trajectory of his leap.

'What did the Bapas do?' asked Mgr Lopes.

'It was so quick they didn't even notice I'd gone! I landed in the bush by the roadside and I stayed absolutely still. There was some machine gun fire. I stayed there in my hiding place until I saw the van on its way back to Dili. I've been on the run for months, hiding in the mountains with friends and relatives. I'm scared for them. I can't go on like this, Ambispu.'

Mgr Lopes made an appointment with the commander and went with Lourenço the next day to the Kodim (Komando Distrik Militer or district military command) headquarters. The bishop told the commander the story of the brave young man who had escaped death in Tacitolu by the skin of his teeth. He asked for justice and clemency for Lourenço. Mgr Lopes refused to leave the office until the commander promised that Lourenço would be spared. Intel (Indonesian intelligence) conducted a long inquiry on Lourenço; he bore it only because he knew that he had the bishop's protection. Finally, he was allowed to go back to the bishop's house at Lecidere, where he chose to live. He stayed there while Mgr Lopes did, and nobody bothered him. Every time Mgr Lopes saw Lourenço his faith was affirmed that, thanks to God, he had been instrumental in saving one precious human life from a violent death.

The next Indonesian army tactic was to pit East Timorese against each other. The Timorese soldiers of battalions 744 and 745 were returned from their training in Bali to fight against Falintil. But there were hundreds of defections from both the battalions and from Hansip, the police force made up of Timorese. In Bazartete in 1980 a company of Indonesian troops, officers and all, handed over their weapons to Fretilin. Their brand new guns were useful — many of the old Portuguese army Mausers and G3s had been captured during the wet season of 1978–79.

Fretilin managed some daring assaults in 1980, even one on Dili. On 10 June they attacked the broadcasting station near Dare and the barracks of Battalion 745 in Becora. Fretilin co-opted civilians to carry the arms they had captured into the bush. After several days, hungry and too afraid to go home, the civilians turned themselves over to Mgr Lopes. The bishop and the priests pleaded with Intel to spare them, but they were shot on the volleyball court of the seminary at Dare and their bodies were thrown into the gully nearby.

Everyone paid dearly in the reprisals that followed the attack on Dare, particularly those who had been in the bush. Hundreds were arrested, a curfew was imposed and a no-man's-land security zone was created on the southern edge of Dili. In July Mgr Lopes wrote of the reprisals in a letter to the archbishop of Jakarta. One case he documented was Norberto's. In the aftermath of the attack on Dare, Father Ricardo, Father Felgueiras and Mgr Lopes had taken Norberto to the military command. Mgr Lopes pressed the commander to protect Norberto, and asked that he would not be beaten or killed. The commander agreed and promised not to mistreat Norbeto.

So what happened then? That very afternoon Norberto was taken to Dare and beaten and tortured by Hansip members until he was near death. Father Carlos administered the last sacrament and the next day Norberto was put to death. They threw his body into the ravine near the seminary. There were more bodies thrown into that ravine. Without permission from the authorities, people were too afraid to retrieve them for burial.

It gave Mgr Lopes some satisfaction to think that the Indonesian soldiers were afraid of the Timorese resistance fighters. The Church's position was one of non-violence. He couldn't promote war — that would be the last thing he would do — but he did support self-defence. It was part of his commitment to protect life. He would do that any way he could — through prayer, through hope, through supporting those in the bush. Mgr Lopes could see that the Indonesian soldiers were just acting on orders. Their superiors, the government of Indonesia, were the true sinners. When the commanders regarded him with suspicion, accused him of aiding Fretilin, Mgr Lopes maintained that his concern was the preservation of life on both sides.

The news of Indonesian casualties didn't help the situation, however. The Indonesians started conscripting Timorese as a kind of human bait. Tens of thousands of civilians were forced to march, unarmed, in front of and behind the armed soldiers. The rationale was that Fretilin guerrillas would kill the Timorese, not the Indonesians. But Fretilin refused to kill the Timorese. The civilian conscripts tried to warn Fretilin. Those at the rear lay down so Fretilin soldiers could shoot the Indonesians. Psychologically the strategy backfired. Even though many Timorese were killed or abandoned or died of starvation as a result of Operasi Keamanan (Operation Security), the civilian population saw that Fretilin were there to protect them, that they would die rather than kill them. The conscripts might have been silent when they came back to the towns, but in their hearts the link with the resistance had been established and grew strong.

When the Indonesians went looking for Fretilin they thought they could find discrete elements in specific places. They soon had to realise that Fretilin were every-where. The whole people were Fretilin; if they wanted to kill off Fretilin they would have to kill off the whole people. Even if ABRI controlled half of the territory by then, they didn't control the population's minds and hearts. The new Vatican pro nuncio in Jakarta, the Spanish Mgr Pablo Puente bought the publicity, however. He accepted the Indonesian annexation of East Timor as a fait accompli. Mgr Lopes and Father Ricardo, the vicar-general, were determined to make him understand the situation.

The Pagar Betis (fence-of-legs) exercises that were part of Operasi Keamanan involved marching all the men between fifteen and fifty years of age in an ever-decreasing circle, closing in around Lacluta in the mountains and flushing out Fretilin fighters. The men were taken away from their villages for the whole of the dry season — June, July, August — so they couldn't prepare the ground for planting. The impact on food production was devastating. It was common for people to collapse by the roadsides, weak from lack of food.

Worried and apprehensive about Operasi Keamanan, Mgr Lopes was surprised when the Korem (Komando Resor Militer or sub-regional military command) sub-commander visited him in Dili in August 1981. He delivered an invitation: the minister of defence, General Yusuf, invited the bishop to a meeting in Baucau. He was sending a helicopter to pick up Mgr Lopes. Mgr Lopes accepted.

The Korem sub-commander accompanied Mgr Lopes and at Baucau airport they were taken to the VIP lounge. General Yusuf, General Ali Murtopo, Brigadier-

General Dading Kalbuadi and another official Mgr Lopes didn't recognise were waiting there. The greetings were formal. Mgr Lopes knew more about these men than he wanted to. He had heard reports that Brigadier-General Dading said that the Timorese were cannibals, that they ate their enemies. Of course it didn't make an iota of difference to Brigadier-General Dading that Mgr Lopes had been born in Timor and had never heard of such practices. These were the men behind the propaganda and the obscene bargains: sacks of corn in return for the heads of Fretilin fighters. Mgr Lopes took in their immaculately pressed, cardboard-looking uniforms, their well-fed faces. He didn't have to chat politely to Brigadier-General Dading, didn't have to hear him reiterate how 'nice' the weather had been on 7 December 1975 — just like the day the Japanese bombed Pearl Harbour, according to Brigadier-General Dading because, as afternoon tea was served, General Yusuf got to the point.

'Pastor,' he began, 'it's said you are going around accusing the military of killing the people of East Timor. Is that right?'

'Yes minister,' Mgr Lopes replied, ignoring the attempt to intimidate him. 'I don't completely understand the attitude of Indonesia's troops. The president of the Republic of Indonesia, General Suharto, has granted an amnesty to all those who come out of the bush and give themselves up, yet his own troops are killing them or making them disappear. By doing so, they are not only disobeying their own president's orders, but, above all, they are violating with impunity fundamental human rights, such as the right to life, freedom and security of person.' Mgr Lopes invoked hierarchies and chains of command that men of such rank could not fail to understand. Still, he believed his ultimate authority was higher than theirs.

General Yusuf wanted to make sure the conversation stayed on firm ground. 'Do you have any proof of what you are saying?'

'Yes, general. Unfortunately, I do have such proof. Some of the names spring to mind right now.

'Leopoldo Joaquim, deputy press secretary in the former Fretilin government gave himself up to the Indonesian military authorities in Ainaro in 1977. He had been granted an amnesty document, signed by President Suharto. He showed me the document himself — I saw it with my own eyes. Apparently, he was free at first but in 1979 Indonesian soldiers went to his home and took him away. His fate and whereabouts are still unknown.' The bishop didn't pause.

'Maria Gorete Joaquim was sixteen years old when she was imprisoned in Santaiho for allegedly being in contact with those in the bush. Later she was released. The following year, Indonesian armed forces took her away and she has disappeared forever.' Was that a look of discomfort on Brigadier-General Dading's face?

'Juvenal Inácio, twenty-five years of age.' Perhaps he looked at these men who had lived for decades longer than Juvenal and wondered how they valued human life. 'His father was Portuguese and his mother was Timorese. He was captured in Bibileu, in the Viqueque region. Minister of finance in the former Fretilin government, he came to Dili in 1979 but a few months later he was taken to Baucau by helicopter and then mysteriously disappeared.' Mgr Lopes went on relentlessly; the names were his *matériel*, all that was left to prove that their bearers had existed. The names were precious, and even compiling the lists of names of those who had been killed had involved tremendous sacrifice.

'João Branco from Lospalos was a former sergeant in the Portuguese army. At first he put up heroic resistance. Then, trusting in the amnesty offered by President Suharto, he surrendered in 1977 along with the forty men under his command. He was living in Dili, but in late 1979 he and his men mysteriously disappeared.'

'They might be somewhere else in Indonesia,' General Yusuf suggested.

'Yes, minister. But of the cases I've just outlined, I'm morally certain that all of them, without exception, were eliminated by the military. However, minister, if you were to bring them here to me, one by one, I assure you that I would change my view.'

The minister for defence said, 'It is also said that you, pastor, do not look kindly on the military operation being carried out by the Indonesian army.'

Mgr Lopes had too much on his mind to state the obvious. 'Only Indonesia's armed forces are responsible before God and the world for the military operation you have just mentioned. However, I will say this: I do not approve of the way in which defenceless civilians — children, women and men from fifteen to fifty years of age, without food or medical assistance or transport — are being forced to take part in the operation.' He might not have wanted to tell these men how to do their job, but he couldn't stop now. 'You must know how much such an operation must cost in terms of food, medicine and transport, but for the people there is nothing. They are dying in the streets from hunger.' Perhaps it was such a way of life for these men that they couldn't even grasp the concept of corruption. 'I am amazed' — the bishop was indefatigable — 'that young boys are taken out of school to take part in these operations.'

'That's not correct, pastor!'

Later, when he thought about it, perhaps Mgr Lopes was astounded that the most minor of his complaints was the one that drew a reaction. 'I think if you check, general, you'll find I'm correct.'

The other generals didn't utter a word.

On his way back to Dili perhaps Mgr Lopes pondered their lack of humanitarianism. Were there so many people in Indonesia they didn't value human life? *Tidak apa apa.* No worries. Killing people just didn't matter. They'd lost their sense of sin, the deluded generals. They thought they could win the war just because they had more sophisticated arms and more soldiers.

•11•

Speaking out

EVERY MORNING AT 5.30 Mgr Lopes celebrated Mass in the little chapel attached to his house at Lecidere. In the brief cool of the tropical morning the small congregation — mostly women, many of them with their heads covered in black lace veils — spontaneously sang hymns in Tetum as the bishop put on his vestments and processed to the front of the chapel. The congregation knew the order of service by heart, but they needed Mgr Lopes to hear their confession, to bless them, to offer the holy sacrament of communion. His voice unified them and gave them strength. On the wall behind him to his right was the statue of Our Lady, her rosary dropping in a gentle swoop. On his left was a statue of Jesus.

What were the words of his sermon? Perhaps he talked about Jesus Christ, beaten and crucified. Perhaps Jesus' humiliated, mutilated body, his permanent scars, expressed for each person in the chapel what they couldn't say of their own experience. In a chapel full of silent desperation, perhaps Mgr Lopes preached a message of tenacious optimism. 'Now we are still in the dark but in the future we will see the light.' Perhaps he quoted Corinthians: 'For God, who commanded the light to shine out of the darkness, has shone in our hearts, to give enlightenment concerning the knowledge of the glory of God, shining in the face of Christ Jesus. But we carry this treasure in vessels of clay to show that the abundance of the power is God's and not ours. In all things we suffer tribulation, but we are not distressed; we are sore pressed, but we are not destitute; we endure persecution, but we are not forsaken; we are cast down, but we do not perish; always bearing about in our body the dying of Jesus, so that the life also of Jesus may be made manifest in our bodily frame.'

When the congregation, local women, children and men, as well as the Canossian sisters from the convent across the road, filed out of the chapel, down the red-tiled stairs, out the gates and into the familiar, precarious streets, they had hope for another day.

The early years of the Indonesian occupation resulted in massive loss of life in East Timor. One-third of the population of around 600,000 died as a result of military operations, displacement, famine and disease. Under such conditions it was hardly surprising that the people were more receptive to the Catholic Church than to the Indonesian government. Throughout Timor's long history of abusive colonialism, the priests had not persecuted the people. For centuries animists had been on cordial terms with the Church, even if they had not converted. For Timorese like Martinho da Costa Lopes, the Church's impact had been cultural.

As a child Martinho Lopes would have had an animist name, but he revealed it to no one. He would have regarded it as inferior to his Christian name and been ashamed of it. People who had a Portuguese name in Timor at that time had been baptised, which meant they could go from place to place without the piece of paper issued by the Portuguese administration showing their name and their reasons for movement. When Mgr Lopes trained as a priest the Mass was celebrated in Latin. Latin belonged to everybody; it was nobody's mother tongue. Until 1969 students in Catholic schools learned enough Latin to make sense of the Mass prayers. After Vatican II, from the mid 1960s, Mass was conducted in Portuguese, not Tetum or any of the other languages of Timor. Probably less than 5 per cent of the East Timorese population were fluent in Portuguese in 1975. Under the Portuguese, non-Christians were precluded from holding government jobs and, in some cases, even from residing in towns. Until 1975 Catholicism had always been the religion of the elite.

But by the early 1980s half the population of East Timor professed to be Catholic. By the early 1990s this proportion had risen to 80 per cent, and it continued to climb. Under the Indonesian code of Pancasila (faith in one god, humanity, nationalism, representative government and social justice) the people had to stipulate a religion, and animism was not one of those on the list. The Catholic Church offered them succour and hope. The priests had been there for everyone and the people turned to the Church to protect not only their dignity but their identity. Many animists were baptised after only a brief period of preparation. Being Catholic separated the people of East Timor from the largely Javanese–Muslim state. In addition, if they were good Catholics, they couldn't be communists. If one can speak of success in such circumstances, at one level the Church had had great success.

Church organisation was a different matter in the nightmare years following the invasion. Some of the mission schools, Bispo Medeiros, Maliana, Soibada and the seminary at Dare, were destroyed or partially destroyed, others were closed down. The priests in the towns were in Indonesian-controlled areas. Others had fled to the bush, only to come down from the mountains with the people in the massive operations of 1978 and 1979. Mgr Lopes had a staff of thirty-two priests, seventeen of them Timorese; five brothers, none of whom was Timorese and thirty-three sisters, of whom fourteen were Timorese. At Liquiçá and Viqueque there were no priests or sisters. The other missions — Dare, Suai, Maliana, Bobonaro, Ainaro, Ermera, Same, Manatuto, Soibada, Lospalos and Uatolári — had only one priest each. There were two priests at Baucau and two at Fatumaca.

Rebuilding the education system was a priority and Catholic teachers from the diocese of Atambua in West Timor came to East Timor. Despite his hostility to Indonesia, Mgr Lopes accepted the services of a few Indonesian Church personnel to work in the areas of health, aid and education. The antipathy that the East Timorese felt towards the Indonesians wasn't confined to the military. They were suspicious of talking to

Indonesian civilians and Church personnel because they thought they would pass on information to the military.

Mgr Lopes was usually in his office, either at the Câmara Eclesiástica or at the house in Lecidere by 7.30 am, and there he received anyone who came to him. Every so often he tried to manage his schedule — certain days for dignitaries, certain days for ordinary people — but he could not turn people away. Sometimes the paperwork was not done, sometimes there were administrative hold-ups. Such was life during wartime. The walls of his house in Lecidere, patched with *palapa* thatching, had holes in them so big that chickens wandered in and out. Refugees shared the house. Nuns taught school out the back. Resistance fighters took refuge there. It was packed with people.

Under pressure from the military Mgr Lopes submitted a request to rebuild the cathedral in Dili. Church officials, aware that people in Timor were starving, were surprised at the request. When the plans arrived, Mgr Lopes took no interest in them. He set them aside saying, 'This is what the military wants. This will keep them happy for a while.'

After the invasion the East Timorese had to learn a new language. Outside every village the signs went up: '*Selamat datang*' and '*Selamat jalan*': 'Welcome' and 'Goodbye'. The people resisted on the most basic level. Old women and peasants made their choice: they refused to learn Bahasa Indonesia. The children learned it at school, but the older people were just waiting until the Indonesians went away. The resistance fighters had to use a code of scrambled Portuguese and Tetum that no one could understand.

By 1980 Mgr Lopes was on the record as favouring a

genuine plebiscite about self-determination. He corresponded directly with the Vatican but the Vatican, aware he was a nationalist, dealt with the East Timorese Church through its representative in Jakarta. In 1980 Cardinal Agostino Casaroli's advisors in the Vatican Secretary of State department privately regarded East Timor as an occupied country in which there had been no genuine act of self-determination. But did they make that position public? Did they press for Indonesia's removal? In June that year on American television, John Paul II talked about the 'drought-stricken victims of East Timor'. 'Drought' was a convenient euphemism.

Mgr Ettore di Filippo, the Vatican's permanent observer to the United Nations, had a passive brief regarding East Timor. He was to observe, listen and report back to the Holy See on UN testimonies and decisions, and private interviews. He did not intervene in UN discussions on behalf of East Timor, or take any initiative to advise on Vatican policy. Vatican policy, according to Mgr Filippo, was to leave action on local political matters to the episcopal conference of the country concerned, and not to intervene unless invited. While, in theory, the Pope was directly responsible for the East Timorese Catholic Church, in reality the Vatican accepted the Indonesian annexation of the territory. Mgr Filippo was aware that the Timorese were being starved and oppressed by the occupation forces to weaken their resistance. He knew of the guerrilla activities and he agreed that East Timor had a right to self-determination, but because of Indonesia's instransigence Mgr Filippo thought the only option was to concentrate on the preservation of East Timor's culture. If the Church in East Timor survived and developed it might have a civilising influence on the Muslim environment around it.

Six years after the invasion, the priests in East Timor were still stunned by the silence from the Vatican and the Indonesian Catholic Church, silence that allowed the Timorese to die abandoned. In 1981 the priests, under pressure from Indonesian authorities to use Bahasa Indonesia, received permission from the Vatican to use Tetum in the Mass. In 1981 in a personal letter Mgr Lopes requested a special audience with the Pope for the first time. John Paul II probably didn't realise what a blow his reply was: such an audience, he said, was neither timely nor necessary. When the priests from Timor tried to tell Mgr Pablo Puente, the Vatican pro nuncio, about the army's behaviour, Mgr Puente demanded more proof. The priests felt they would have to bring the bodies to him in Jakarta before he would believe them.

Privately, Mgr Lopes must have been bitterly disappointed by the Vatican's lack of real response to the situation in East Timor. While Catholics in Indonesia were a minority, some of them were extremely powerful in government, military, intelligence and business circles. Indonesia was largely Muslim but fairly tolerant of Catholicism and the Indonesian government funded Catholic schools and hospitals. The Vatican, for reasons of political expediency, appeased Indonesia instead of acting on behalf of the East Timorese; the institution to which Mgr Lopes had given his life was spurning his people in their time of need. Also, as Mgr Lopes said later, 'It was the great dream at the Vatican to expand the Catholic Church in Indonesia. The little ones are being sacrificed for the big ones.' In Timor in the early 1980s he kept his troubles to himself. He did not speak of the turmoil he must have felt about the Church's desertion of the Timorese. How he kept the faith alive in isolation under such terrible conditions was a testament to it.

After the siesta one afternoon in early September 1982 Mgr Lopes was sitting under the mango tree in the garden browsing through *Kompas*, an Indonesian daily newspaper, when a dishevelled man appeared at the gates and started towards him.

'I'm a member of Fretilin and I've come from the bush,' the skinny silhouette laconically said. He sat down beside the bishop.

'Where are you from?' asked the bishop.

'I'm from Laga, but I've walked from Lospalos. My name is Luís.' Luís and two other guerrillas had climbed mountains and scrambled down valleys. They were on a mission to supply Fretilin's central committee with intelligence about the exact position of the Bapas in Dili. They had traversed impossible terrain, cutting their way through bush. Luís had not eaten for three days.

Mgr Lopes asked his servant to organise something for Luís to eat straight away, 'until you can have a really good tuck-in at dinner time', he said.

Luís managed to munch and continue his story. 'We reached Laulara, and it was there, in a shoot-out with Hansips and Bapas, that the other men in my section were killed. I'd run out of ammunition, so it was impossible to put up any further resistance. I buried my friends on the outskirts of Laulara and I hid the Mausers. Eventually I made it to Dili, and to your door.'

Mgr Lopes gazed at him in silence for a moment.

'My friend, you have two alternatives.' He could be frank with Luís. 'Either you can stay here for good, and I will try and contact the military authorities on your behalf, or you can go back to the bush. You are completely free to make your own decision and you have all night to decide.'

The next morning Luís had made up his mind. 'But first, Ambispu, I need to contact my comrades in Dili to see if there's a clear path to the interior.'

'That's fine with me,' Mgr Lopes said. Before he left for the Câmara Eclesiástica, Mgr Lopes chose a quiet corner to say goodbye to Luís and to give him some money for the journey, in case he left for the bush immediately. He had to be frugal with his help; there were so many who needed it. He would much rather have spent the morning listening to Luís' stories than dealing with the mountain of paperwork in his office.

Mgr Lopes was having his lunch at home when Luís appeared again. Luís went to his room after he'd eaten, and the bishop went to talk with him there.

Luís said, 'I've been told that the Bapas have increased their surveillance, and all the exits from the city are unsafe.' He was utterly dejected.

'What are you going to do?'

'Would you please come to see the Bapas with me, Ambispu?' Luís asked. 'They'll kill me if I go alone.'

'I wouldn't dream of letting you go to the Bapas alone, even if you wanted to!' exclaimed Mgr Lopes, and perhaps his mouth made its characteristic and comic undefiable O shape. Luís of Laga must have been relieved as Mgr Lopes continued: 'Only over my dead body will anybody kill you.' But he was aware of his limitations and the unpredictability of interrogators when he added, 'Are you sure? Is going to the Bapas what you really want to do?'

'Yes, Ambispu. I've thought about it and that's what I've decided.'

Mgr Lopes left Luís and went to the telephone. The Korem sub-commander's number was no doubt engraved on his memory.

'Lieutenant-Colonel Francisco Xavier?'

'Monsignor Lopes?'

'Would you please come to my residence? We have an urgent problem to sort out.'

Fifteen minutes later Mgr Lopes was showing Lieutenant-Colonel Xavier into his visitor's room. He sent for Luís. Luís was surprisingly relaxed and at ease as he greeted the Korem sub-commander. Lieutenant-Colonel Xavier smiled and the two men shook hands. It was all going well. After a brief conversation Lieutenant-Colonel Xavier asked Mgr Lopes whether he could take Luís to Intel for questioning.

'Of course you may, commander,' Mgr Lopes said, 'on two conditions. Firstly, that he his not beaten and, secondly, that as soon as the questioning is over, he will be at liberty to return to my residence if he so wishes.' Luís was interrogated for two days, and even though Mgr Lopes knew the military would have loved to pulverise his bones, they obeyed the lieutenant-colonel's orders. Luís was allowed to return to the bishop's house, where he decided to stay.

Mgr Lopes represented his clients bravely and many people put their faith in him. He was pleased when the mighty hand of God could save a life using him as its humble servant, but he was starting to doubt the efficacy of his private protestations. Not all the commanders were as helpful as Lieutenant-Colonel Francisco Xavier. Some of them treated him with contempt and he was sure some wanted him dead. He knew some Timorese would be given a lot of money to kill him.

The military tried to intimidate Mgr Lopes. There were death threats and attempts on his life — hair-raising incidents in his car on the streets of Dili. It was part of the atmosphere of fear that all East Timorese endured. His outspokenness made him a target but his prominent position gave him some protection. In 1999 the Indonesian-backed militia members killed priests and nuns, but in the early 1980s they did not act against Church members with such impunity. The Catholic Church was the only organisation in East Timor with both its own infrastructure and independent links to the outside world. Indonesian authorities were becoming extremely frustrated and angry that the Church did not toe the line and accept East Timor's integration. With the Vatican's ambiguous position on East Timor, however, Jakarta must have surmised that assassination was not the only way of dealing with the problem of Dili's defiant bishop. The authorities were aware that an Indonesian bishop would be completely unacceptable to the people but a more co-operative Church leader would make the Indonesian military's task much easier.

Mgr Lopes had the protection of Xanana as well as God, and perhaps the threat of Fretilin reprisals made Jakarta adopt a more long-term strategy to oust Mgr Lopes. The resistance leader had written in a letter, 'If anyone kills you, we will know them.' Xanana, the fighter, surviving against all the odds, was also a poet. Mgr Lopes had gradually come to know that he was heading the resistance after the people started to come down from the mountains. The bishop knew Xanana well; Xanana had asked Mgr Lopes to send him philosophy books. Mgr Lopes hadn't been able to oblige, in case they were traced back to him and he couldn't help others. Still, he sent what he could, and the word reached the bush that the bishop was sympathetic to the struggle. On more than one occasion Mgr Lopes' help had been intercepted and he had had to explain his way out of the situation to the commanders. 'I'm a priest,' he said. 'If Indonesian soldiers were in need, I would give them food and money, too.' When Mgr Lopes visited Jakarta, the wives and children of Indonesian soldiers came to him asking for news of their husbands and fathers. The authorities often did not tell the wives what had happened to their husbands in Timor. The men were sent back to Java with terrible wounds. Mgr Lopes knew some soldiers respected human rights, but not enough of them.

He became more outspoken. When Andi Mohammed Yusuf, the Indonesian defence minister, visited Timor to review the troops Mgr Lopes pointed his finger at soldiers in the line responisble for atrocities: 'This one, this one, that one!' He spent five years complaining privately to the commanders and there was no change at all, really. He started to speak against the military in church. He spoke out clearly against the bad behaviour of the war. It was wrong for the Timorese to follow the Indonesian example of stealing and corruption. And it was wrong for the Indonesians to encourage people to hunt Fretilin members. But every day brought news that he couldn't keep inside himself.

The atrocities came dressed in such pretty words. The 7 December 1975 invasion was called Operasi Seroja (Operation Lotus). What was the metaphor? Were the paratroopers who landed on Dili bringing the fruit that would induce forgetfulness and dreamy languor? The 1978 offensive, designed to make Fretilin operatives in the bush surrender, was code named operation Skylight. They might as well have called that 'operation Hole in the Ground' or 'operation Bodies Cast into the Ravine', because that's where all its victims ended up. In 1981 Operasi Keamanan (Operation Security) began. Whose security?

Always the same story, hundreds and hundreds of times over. How Mgr Lopes hung onto his sanity while he tried to document each cigarette burn, each electric shock, each hanging, each slashing, each rape, each murder no one knows. He bought photographs of mutilated bodies from Indonesian army personnel. Some of the men in the army were sympathetic, others were just greedy, wanting the 20,000 rupiahs or whatever the shocking pictures cost. It was a disgusting trade, but he needed proof to show the world.

He remembered the names of those the military had tried to erase. Recording the names, compiling the lists — that was a dangerous business. Getting those lists out of Timor involved tremendous risks. Perhaps it was part of his debt as a human being, as a speaking mouth, to those who could no longer speak. The Mambai, one of the ethnic groups of East Timor, believed the dead returned to their mother, the earth, replenishing her with their decay. They joined the silent mouths — the rocks and the trees, the plants, birds, grass, insects, reptiles, fish, Mother Earth and Father Heaven, all animate and inanimate things except people. The speaking mouths — human beings — were the younger kin of the silent mouths. The speaking mouths had a debt to pay to the silent mouths for the livelihood they extracted from them. There were stories that Xanana could put his gun in the ground, stand on one leg and turn into a tree; that the guerrillas could lure Indonesian soldiers into a cave and disappear without trace. Where there were no longer villages, the stones and streams and gullies, the silent mouths, bore witness to the suffering.

It became unavoidably clear to Mgr Lopes that the procession in honour of Our Lady of Fátima, to take place on 13 October 1982, was the time and place to speak out. This was the anniversary of the Blessed Virgin Mary's last appearance to three peasant children while they tended their sheep in the olive groves outside the little village of Aljustrel, near Fátima in Portugal. It was here, at this holy place, where the leaves of the olive trees glistened silver and green against the bare earth and the Angel of Portugal exhorted Francisco and Jacinta Marto and Lucia Santos to: 'Take and drink the body and blood of Jesus Christ, horribly outraged by ungrateful men. Repair their crimes and console your God.' *Horribly outraged by ungrateful men. Repair their crimes.* Perhaps the angel's exhortation gave Mgr Lopes the sense of vindication he needed to write his homily.

Every year in Dili thousands of people joined the procession from the Motael church on the seafront to the monument of the Virgin of the Assumption in the park opposite the bishop's house in Lecidere. Their route took them from the suburb of Farol, past the port, the Câmara Eclesiástica, the government buildings and the rusting landing vessels used in the invasion, which had been left gaping in front of the Hotel Dili. The faithful from the surrounding villages didn't all fit in the park, they spilled over its knee-high wrought-iron fence onto the road and to the verge on the other side of the road, where they clustered under the thorny, wind-whipped bougainvillea bushes, the little eucalyptuses and the lanky coconut trees.

Perhaps the wind was blowing from the east that day, blowing Mgr Lopes' voice from where he stood on a podium in front of the statue of Mary to beyond the last person in the park across the town — the prisons, the barracks, the torture chambers, the yards and houses and shops — to the waiting hills and all the way to the border. He spoke about the massacre of 500 people who had surrendered after the siege at the Rock of Saint Anthony at Lacluta, the culmination of the fence-of-legs operation of 1981. The fence or circle had closed in around the mountain of Aitana. The people who had not been killed in the bombardment — by rocket fire, mortar fire or petrol bombs — were killed by the soldiers sent in after that. Mgr Lopes had heard terrible stories, reports it pained him to repeat. When the rains came, the blood wept into the sea with the water of the Laleia River, which had its source near Mount Aitana. Mgr Lopes talked about those murdered at Lacluta for the first time in public. He talked about the people forced to take part in the operations, dying from starvation, being abandoned by the roadsides. The statue of Mary looked heavenward from the shell on which she stood. The heads of cherubs clustered around the hem of her garment and her hands were over her heart. Although he did not name Indonesia, Mgr Lopes denounced the cruel crimes.

It was as if an atom bomb had gone off in Dili. The effects of the bomb were felt in Australia, the United States and England. The word was out.

That afternoon Mgr Lopes was resting at home when the phone rang. It was the Bapas inviting him to the Intel command at 1800 hours if possible. Mgr Lopes was not late, but the Intel commander was there already, surrounded by his officers who, despite the fact that they were all in plain clothes, would have presented a uniform sea of stern faces. The bishop greeted them all — he didn't want to offend anyone in particular.

The Intel commander smiled and said, 'Pastor, I know that you are doing the right thing when you defend human rights, but I must ask that you do not do so in the way you did this afternoon. Whenever you have a problem, please contact us privately.'

Mgr Lopes was ready. 'Commander, you seem to be in agreement with me because you have just said that I am on the right path, or words to that effect, because I defend human rights. Well, I can assure you that, God willing, I shall always stay on the path of good and truth.' The sea of faces remained unmoved. Mgr Lopes continued. 'As far as contacting the military authorities privately, I can tell you that I have already done so on several occasions — not just Kodim [Komando Distrik Militer or district military command] and Korem but also Brigadier-General Dading and even the defence minister, General Yusuf himself.' The names impressed. 'However, those contacts were to no avail. Taking into account the prophetic nature of my mission, I feel an urgent need to tell the whole world, as I did this afternoon, about the genocide being practised in Timor so that, when we die, at least the world knows we died standing.'

What could they say? Mgr Lopes always had a higher authority. 'The whole world' was a worrisome entity. Public opinion in the whole world was to be courted. Throughout the Timor campaign Indonesian authorities had been mindful of spinning the right stories for the whole world — that they were intervening in a civil war, that without the Indonesian presence there would be a bloodbath in East Timor. That afternoon Mgr Lopes' defiance started a chain of events that wouldn't come to fruition until some time later. The cards were being stacked against him.

• 12 •

Discredit

MGR PABLO PUENTE, the Vatican pro nuncio in Jakarta, was not an expressive man. When he visited Dili at the beginning of the dry season in 1981 Mgr Lopes and the vicar-general Father Ricardo tried to animate him. Surely, after being there nearly a year, Mgr Puente had some funny stories to tell about working in Jakarta? Apparently not. There was a knowing smile on Mgr Puente's long face and he spoke so slowly that even a short word seemed interminable. During Mgr Puente's nine-day visit Mgr Lopes and Father Ricardo tried to make the Vatican's man in Jakarta understand the situation in East Timor. They did what they could to show Mgr Puente what was happening, even if he chose not to believe what they told him.

Mgr Lopes and Father Ricardo knew that Mgr Puente thought that conditions in East Timor were better under the Indonesians than they had been under the Portuguese. Mgr Lopes was aware that his critics charged him with being a lusophile, a lover of Portugal, but he did not simply praise Portuguese colonialism. There were, he said, negative aspects to that colonialism, but he believed the Portuguese gave freedom to the people, which was more important than daily bread.

A couple of months before Mgr Puente's visit the Catholic Relief Service (CRS) and the International Committee of the Red Cross (ICRC) wound up their major operations, although some of their projects continued. Mgr Lopes was grateful for the work of the humanitarian organisations and the Indonesian church, which had alleviated the worst effects of famine. He agreed with Mgr Puente that conditions were better than they had been. However, the aid organisations had been prevented from alleviating the human rights situation. Mgr Puente did not question the Jakarta government's stance regarding justice, maintaining that the chances of getting any aid into East Timor were nil if politics and humanitarian concerns were conflated.

Mgr Lopes remained extremely concerned about the fence-of-legs exercises, which commenced each year in the dry season, and he tried to impress his concern on the pro nuncio. Mgr Puente visited Timor at a good time, the harvest was just in and there was food — corn, rice and pumpkin — in the markets. The shortages would come later, after the civilian population had been conscripted into the military exercises. Mgr Lopes tried to explain how unarmed civilians were forced to march in front of and behind the ABRI forces; how ABRI, despite its considerable resources, did not give the conscripts food or transport; how the villagers returned home too tired to farm. But Mgr Puente was unmoved. He regarded the presence of Indonesia as a fact of life.

At the new Dili airport, Mgr Puente and Mgr Lopes parted on good terms. The link with the Vatican was crucial for the Catholic Church of East Timor. The Vatican must understand what was happening; it might just take some time before they would come out publicly and say so. The Indonesian Bishop's Conference (MAWI) had been treading a fine line: they respected East Timor's autonomy but would not support its independence. Nevertheless, support, not interference, from the Indonesian Catholic Church was welcome. It is likely that Mgr Lopes chose not to dwell on his frustrations about Mgr Puente's acceptance of Indonesia's presence, or any private suspicions he might have held about Mgr Puente's assistant, Mgr Fontana, who was reportedly on very good terms with General Benny Murdani.

On the flight back to Denpasar and then on to Jakarta, Mgr Puente was no doubt satisfied he had seen the situation for himself. He would be able to report to the Vatican and to the Indonesian bishops. Perhaps he resolved to look up the file that Frank Carlin, head of CRS, had mentioned, the one the previous pro nuncio, Mgr Farano, had allegedly kept on the 'bishop' of Dili.

When a couple of months later President Suharto appealed to the Catholic hierarchy in Indonesia to bring the Catholic Church in East Timor in from the cold, so to speak, the secretary-general of MAWI, Archbishop Leo Soekoto, replied that it was the Pope, not the Indonesian Church, who should determine the status of the diocese of Dili. Nevertheless, following the meeting between the president and the clergy, MAWI informed the Holy See that it should acknowledge East Timor's integration into Indonesia and the Dili diocese's dependence on the Indonesian Church, and should adjust its policy accordingly.

Against the backdrop of these machinations, Mgr Lopes attended the MAWI conference in Jakarta in November 1981, where he received a letter from the Australian Catholic Episcopal Conference asking about the health and food situation in East Timor and if there was anything Australian Catholic sources could provide. While he was in Jakarta he replied to Bishop John Gerry, the chairperson of Australian Catholic Relief. His letter was personal. After the CRS and the ICRC had gone, there were no international relief agencies in Timor. Mgr Lopes described the situation wrought on the population by military operations throughout July, August and September. He mentioned the massacre of civilians at the Rock of Saint Anthony near Lacluta that had occurred in September. He warned that at best it would be a poor harvest and at worst it would be a famine. He asked for money for rice and corn.

Perhaps he didn't give a second thought to the letter after he sent it, apart from hoping for the food relief that might be forthcoming, because the bishops' audience with President Suharto, due to take place on 19 November, was more important. Mgr Lopes used his opportunity: he went straight to the point with the president. He told him about the disappearances of people who had come down from the mountains. He had a list of the people who had died. The list was priceless, not just because of the number of names on it and the needlessness and violence of the deaths, but because people had risked so much even to give information. Mgr Lopes gained his information from the priests and from the people. He checked and double-checked the stories, using all his authority in the community and all the confidence the people had in him to find out as much as he could.

The president suggested that the people on the list might be TBOs (people who followed the military with ammunition and supplies). Mgr Lopes countered that they had all been killed. If President Suharto could feel embarrassment, perhaps he felt it that day where, in front of Catholic and Protestant bishops and priests, as well as Muslims, that indefatigable troublemaker from Timor had shown that the presidential amnesty counted for nothing.

The following week, the Indonesian foreign minister Mr Mochtar issued a statement to say that Mgr Puente had advised him that the Vatican was convinced integration was the best way of ensuring East Timor's progress. Perhaps Mgr Lopes was not surprised at this further betrayal. Perhaps he believed that if he could visit John Paul II and explain to him in person what was going on in East Timor the Vatican would take a stronger stand. Despite the sense of abandonment Mgr Puente's pronouncement must have instilled in the East Timorese clergy, Mgr Lopes did not waver. If anything, he became more strongly and openly committed to the cause of the people he served.

The dignitaries started coming to East Timor. During his two-day visit in December the Australian ambassador to Indonesia was flown by helicopter to Lospalos, Baucau, Maliana and Liquiçá. He spoke Indonesian with the Indonesians. They told him Fretilin activities were 'no more than nuisance value' and in the report he duly filed to his superiors he unquestioningly stated that it was not possible to make an assessment of how onerous resettlement had been for those involved. The story he told — that people had better access to educational and health facilities than ever, that corn, cassava and vegetables were growing in the gardens and that there were enough chickens — was a comforting one. The other story, however, was starting to break.

Mgr Lopes did not foresee the reverberations caused by the letter he sent to Bishop Gerry. The news of the crippling military operations and impending famine in East Timor had a big impact in Australia and England. In January 1982 articles appeared on the front pages of the daily broadsheets in Sydney and Melbourne. Human rights and aid organisations in London kept the story running for months. Thousands and thousands of dollars was pledged from aid agencies in Australia, Germany and the Netherlands. At last the world was hearing. Not that Mgr Lopes knew the extent of the ripples made by the pebble he had thrown.

Jakarta stepped up its campaign to discredit Mgr Lopes, enlisting a well-known and effective accomplice, E. G. Whitlam, the former prime minister of Australia who had been favourable to the Indonesian annexation of East Timor in 1974. Mr Whitlam had been disturbed by the news reports of impending famine sparked by Mgr Lopes' letter. He contacted the Indonesian embassy in Canberra on behalf of a *Canberra Times* journalist wishing to visit East Timor and some weeks later Mr Poernomo, the embassy councillor for press and information, advised Mr Whitlam that if he travelled to

Indonesia a visit to East Timor could be arranged. Mr Whitlam decided to go and see for himself.

Flanked by senior Australian journalist Peter Hastings and Cedric Neukomm, the ICRC delegate in Indonesia, Gough Whitlam towered over Mgr Lopes. Whitlam was very knowledgeable about the region but he showed a devastating lack of insight into the issue of self-determination for East Timor. Perhaps Mgr Lopes regarded the former prime minister as a boastful student and felt compelled to put him right. Whitlam made him nervous, but he did his best to be affable. It didn't help that Hastings was recording the interview. Even though Whitlam maintained his visit was organised by the ICRC, the trip had been initiated and arranged by the Indonesian Centre for Strategic and International Studies, an organisation chaired by Ali Murtopo, minister for information and long-time 'friend' of East Timor.

It was March 1982, the end of the wet season. Mr Whitlam sweated profusely, took copious notes and ate at a speed that astounded even Mgr Lopes. Mgr Lopes openly condemned the Indonesians to Whitlam and Hastings. He told them about the imminent famine. Why not? These prominent men had access to all manner of help. It was obvious they didn't trust him. Had he heard Mr Whitlam make some thinly veiled derogatory reference to his term on Salazar's National Assembly? Mgr Lopes remained obstinately outspoken.

No one came to Dili unless they were briefed and it wasn't hard to guess who, in particular, had briefed these two. Gough Whitlam wouldn't hear of famine. He insisted that Cedric Neukomm had told Mgr Lopes in October, before his letter to Australian Catholic Relief in November, that 500 tonnes of Australian corn had been procured and that another 500 were under negotiation. And hadn't Pablo Puente told him the same thing at the Bishops' Conference in Jakarta in November?

'The Red Cross food that you were told about in October you have now heard, in February, would be coming from Australia?' Whitlam's voice was like a bludgeon.

'Yes,' the bishop answered.

Mr Whitlam went on. 'The thousand tonnes of corn that Australia will be sending to Dili, that will be sufficient to avoid any famine at all?'

'Unless there is poor distribution,' Mgr Lopes answered grimly. 'Of course, if the corn reaches us, it will be a good solution. I think it will be enough.'

Peter Hastings wanted verification. 'It will be enough?' he asked.

'Yes, yes,' Mgr Lopes said. 'Sometimes the problem is distribution.'

Whitlam said: 'That is, if I am asked in Australia, I could say the apostolic administrator said that a thousand tonnes of corn will be enough.'

It seemed the man chose to see no further than the curved arc of his nose.

Mgr Lopes told Whitlam and Hastings about the hundreds of people dying daily on Atauro, the detention centre for almost 4000 people who had committed the crime of allegedly being related to resistance members. Families from Lospalos and Baucau were brought to Atauro in an effort to destroy the support network for the resistance. Hastings and Whitlam were scheduled to go there the next day, Tuesday. They asked him whether he had visited Atauro recently and no doubt they looked smugly satisfied when he told them he hadn't been there. If condescension and interrogation are patience, Whitlam was patient, as the newspaper articles written by his companion later testified. He fired questions: Where was the famine? Where were the atrocities committed? How many people had been killed?

'I take it you were not in Lacluta when the alleged massacre took place?' Whitlam said.

'No,' answered Mgr Lopes.

'Where do you get your information?'

'From the priests.'

Did the journalist and the politician looked at each other, thinking they had won their point?

For the next two days the two Australians flew around Timor in ICRC helicopters with civilian pilots. They peered through cloud cover over the 'Fretilin-infested' mountains and on the ground they noticed new houses, roads, schools and medicine cupboards. Their focus was the future and Indonesia's plans for its newest province. They diligently took down notes about how long algebra had been taught at school and the aid equipment they saw: trucks, aircraft and four Massey-Ferguson tractors at the CRS compound in Dili. Mr Whitlam was impressed by the Portuguese street names, left intact with simply the Indonesian word for street 'Jalan' added to the front. He was impressed by the relaxed attitudes of doctors and nurses in the bush and by the detailed answers the Indonesians gave to his questions. When he was not permitted to visit six political detainees in Comarca prison, he made a note in his diary without pressing the point.

Whitlam and Hastings did their job quickly and well. By Thursday night they were back in Jakarta. On Friday morning Whitlam was received by acting foreign minister Pangabbean, the pro nuncio Pablo Puente and the secretary-general for foreign affairs Soedarmono. President Suharto returned early from Solo especially to see Whitlam before he returned to Australia. At the press conference at the Centre for Strategic and International Studies that day, Whitlam and Hastings claimed the authority to discredit Mgr Lopes. According to them, the bishop's letter was either false or grossly exaggerated. 'I cannot understand why he perpetrated this wicked act and sent this cruel letter,' asserted Whitlam. He said he saw no signs of famine or imminent famine and the International Red Cross's 1000-tonne buffer stock would be sufficient to cope with any local food shortages caused by drought. Perhaps he didn't realise, or simply forgot to mention, that he and Hastings visited Timor during a time of plenty and that the food shortages would be at their worst in the dry season, six months later, once the military operations resumed. Subsequently Whitlam maintained that if people wanted to comment on East Timor they should check with people who had been there.

At the press conference it transpired that Hastings had gleaned some information about the massacre at the Rock of Saint Anthony from Indonesian sources, who maintained that eighty people — Fretilin families and supporters, including several women — had been killed in small arms and rifle exchange with a company of Hansip forces. The 'exchange' wasn't mentioned in the newspaper and magazine articles they published in Australia. Atauro did get a mention and in Peter Hastings' version the deaths of many hundreds of people there were put down to gastroenteritis.

Whitlam went on to denigrate Mgr Lopes and half his clergy, saying that they simply lamented and resented the departure of the Portuguese, missing Portuguese language, systems and tradition. Mgr Lopes heard about the smear campaign but he didn't show it worried him. He stuck to his belief that material development meant nothing without justice and peace.

A week after Whitlam and Hastings met Mgr Lopes, Hastings reported that the life-saving 1000 tonnes of Australian corn were lying in sheds on a Brisbane wharf because, piqued about Australian press reports of Mgr Lopes' letter, the Indonesian government had decided not to accept the stock. That the corn was a gift from the Australian government to the International Red Cross wouldn't help it reach its destination if the Indonesian government didn't want it to. It was not the first time that Jakarta had obstructed attempts to send aid to East Timor. The Indonesian government's decision to reject the corn had already been made when Hastings and Whitlam interviewed Mgr Lopes in Dili.

The dry season of 1982 came. The March harvest had failed. Children in Dili were malnourished while the people of Lospalos and Viqueque faced severe shortages. The seasons were known by the degree of hunger they brought, in Bahasa Indonesia: *lapar biasa*, *lapar besar*, *lapar betul* (normal hunger, bigger hunger, severe hunger). When, in Viqueque, the people began to eat the *sagu* from palm trees, it was a sign for Mgr Lopes that famine was coming. When the ICRC claimed that there was enough food, Mgr Lopes knew it was because they didn't want to rock the boat with Jakarta and be thrown out of East Timor altogether.

The wet season came and went. According to Colonel Kalangie the *sekwilda* (provincial secretary), the previous year's fence-of-legs operation and the forced migration of families to Atauro had been a success for the occupation forces. Jakarta proclaimed that fewer than one hundred Fretilin guerrillas were left.

Transmigration was under way. Families from Bali were sent to the fertile area around Maliana and settled land that had belonged to Timorese. Their farming methods didn't work in Timor. Timorese and Indonesians borrowed money from Indonesian banks to develop the land, but the fertilisers were inappropriate and the crops failed. When the bank wanted the loans repaid the people had no money and no crop. People complained to Mgr Lopes that the migrants from Bali weren't really farmers, that they abandoned their land and got jobs as house builders and carpenters, and that the Timorese lost their jobs as a result. Mgr Lopes complained to the authorities. It wasn't a good situation for the Timorese or for the migrants. Transmigration eased off, but the Timorese weren't given their ancestral lands back.

When would it end?

The use of the contraceptive Depo Provera was reported in early 1983. Of course, Mgr Lopes had been against family planning, Indonesian style, from the beginning. He'd tried to mediate in families where the sterilisation of women, without their knowledge or consent, had resulted in terrible conflict. To Mgr Lopes it was an act of violence to seal a woman's fallopian tubes when she was having an operation for some other ailment. People in Timor needed big families. After all the loss of life, they needed them even more. In the countryside, people were suspicious of injections. When officials gave them boxes of contraceptive pills, the people gave them to the priest.

In the hospital the Carmelite nuns tried to watch who was being injected with what, but they couldn't be everywhere. A few years before, in Dili, Fátima Gusmão, a woman who had spent the early years of the occupation in the mountains, had been injected with God-knows-what at the top of each leg after her three-day-old baby died mysteriously in hospital. From abroad Fátima's mother had sent the bishop clothes for the baby, who had taken them to Fátima. They became the baby's burial clothes. The spots where Fátima had been injected had begun to itch and she got a fever. The lumps on her legs swelled from the size of a pea to the size of an orange. She couldn't walk and the pain made her mad. Fátima Gusmão screamed and shouted crazily for a year. Mgr Lopes gave her absolution. People thought that if she didn't die, the Indonesians would surely shoot her. At the hospital the Indonesian military doctor told her he could do nothing. Finally a Timorese nurse agreed to lance her. Without anaesthetic, he cut the lumps open. Blood and water came out. Fátima applied black paste, traditional medicine, to cure the wounds. After a few months she was walking, and later she became pregnant again. She paid a lot of money to leave Timor and gave birth in Jakarta before she went to Australia.

That was only the tiniest sliver of Fátima Gusmão's story, yet still the authorities tried to discredit Mgr

Lopes. However much he spoke out, he couldn't cover every wrong that needed to be righted. The whole story would take many lifetimes to tell.

He continued his pastoral work. Baptisms, confirmations. From one end of East Timor to the other. Maliana, Liquiçá, Bucoli, Tutuala. He exhorted the youth to stay strong and work hard. He was finally permitted to visit the prison island Atauro for five days, to administer the holy sacraments to the thousands of people interred there. He felt old. The medicine he took didn't seem to be helping his diabetes.

When he visited Maliana, he talked with his former pupil, Basílio Martins, about the old days. They were nostalgic — picnics at Corluli Bau Sai, riding through the yellow grass on the Maliana plain. Mgr Lopes asked Senhor Basílio about the situation around Maliana. Local ceasefires had been reported.

'How many fighters are up there on Mount Tapo?' the bishop asked. They were alone, it was all right to talk.

'About sixty,' Senhor Basílio estimated.

'Is it possible to increase the number of guerrillas here?'

'That would be good, Ambispu. You know who's up there?' He mentioned some names. 'You taught them when they were kids.'

'They're behaving well. I'm proud of them.'

One night in September 1982, while Mgr Lopes was on a pastoral visit to Lospalos, the *liurai* of Mehara near Tutuala came to him with a message from Xanana, asking him to receive the resistance leader in Lospalos. Xanana knew that the bishop would be receptive to a face-to-face meeting because the two leaders knew each other well. But Mgr Lopes couldn't stand the thought of Xanana being captured. The people of East Timor needed Xanana in the mountains as much as they needed the air they breathed. The east had always been a problem for the Indonesians and Lospalos was crawling with secret police and soldiers. Mgr Lopes sent word that it was impossible to receive Xanana. The *liurai* brought a message back from the resistance leader: 'Okay, Monsignor, I agree with you. I have another plan. I will meet you when you come back from Tutuala. I will co-ordinate everything.' Mgr Lopes left it to the will of God.

Mgr Lopes travelled through the bush with two priests, followed by a convoy of Indonesian military. The white trunks of the eucalyptus trees made squiggly lines against the earth and the new lime green foliage rustled in the breeze. Light penetrated their canopy and the understorey gave ample cover to those who might have preferred to remain hidden. Rough gullies traversed the road. It was ambush country: depending on whose side you were on, you could be scared here. The little trees growing on the verge of the road looked like soldiers in camouflage gear. On his return from Tutuala, as he was passing the house of the *liurai* Miguel dos Santos in Mehara, Mgr Lopes' vehicle stopped. Indonesian soldiers ran up to the jeep: 'Wait here, Monsignor,' they said. 'We are resolving a problem up ahead.'

Mgr Lopes went into the *liurai*'s house, past the Indonesian soldiers on the verandah, and who should the bishop find inside but Xanana himself.

'We simulated an attack about ten kilometres up the road, Monsignor.'

Two of Xanana's men stood guard while they talked.

Xanana gave the bishop an Indonesian military manual they had captured.

'Can you get this out, please, Ambispu? It's proof of what disgraceful conduct is condoned, encouraged here.' They were respectful of each other. They were a team.

'Yes, yes,' Mgr Lopes didn't hesitate. 'How's the situation?' he asked.

Xanana explained that the first national conference to reorganise the resistance had taken place on 3 March 1981. The bishop might have had word of the conference but the lines of communication between the resistance in the mountains and Mgr Lopes in Dili were not what could be called free. The bishop would have been under constant surveillance. Spies and counter-spies were abundant; half the population of East Timor were paid to spy on the other half. It would have been a dangerous mission to take news of the resistance's organisation to him. Even though Mgr Lopes was becoming more out-spoken and openly sympathetic to the resistance, Xanana would have had to be sure that the bishop was receptive to a meeting and cautious about the arrange-ments. After Alarico Fernandes surrendered Fretilin had lost their radio link, making it very hard to organise. Xanana estimated that the resistance had about 6800 people under arms throughout the territory. The regrouping aimed to unite all those fighting the occupa-tion as the Revolutionary Council of National Resistance.

'Would you take the documentation and send it to the Fretilin External Delegation?'

'Of course, of course.'

Mgr Lopes asked Xanana about the struggle. The bishop advised Xanana to put nationalism first. When he looked at the weapons Xanana and his men were carrying, his mouth might have turned down like a big old rounded hill as he tucked his chin into his neck. 'Do you receive these weapons from abroad?' he asked in a worried tone.

Xanana replied quickly, with a smile, 'No, these arms were seized from Indonesian troops.'

Mgr Lopes sighed with pride. 'You are very brave,' he said.

There was silence for a moment. The resistance leader was happy to have the bishop's support.

Mgr Lopes broke the silence. 'I'll continue to do everything I can to protect the people. Please transmit my greetings to your fighters. Tell them I said they should remain strong and stay in the bush to fight.'

'I will, Ambispu.'

'And I will make sure these documents reach their destination.'

Their time passed quickly. Neither could afford to talk for too long. No doubt Mgr Lopes returned to Dili hoping their meeting had not endangered those who helped to organise it. He wasn't afraid for himself, even though he knew Mgr Puente would be manoeuvring behind the scenes in Jakarta. By that time he would have felt he had very little to lose.

His exhaustion did not stop his eloquence in the filmed interview he gave from the steps of his house in Lecidere. The skin over his right eye drooped lower than the skin over his left, just as his father's had. There was joy in his face when he spoke of living in the hope of Catholicism, but there was pain and stoicism in his eyes as he nodded for emphasis, and turned his head in his proud way. 'We're separated from loved ones as you know … We care for people's souls and, where possible, their bodies.' Police observers were in the crowd. 'We do absolutely nothing against the government. In fact, we work with them.'

'The Indonesian government?' the journalist asked.

'The Indonesian government.' Mgr Lopes had the look of a man who knew his time was limited.

III

Journeys

• 13 •

Leaving Timor

THE ANNOUNCEMENT that Mgr Lopes was leaving East Timor was made suddenly. 'The diocese is to have another bishop,' Mgr Lopes told Father Ricardo. It had already been settled and organised: the new bishop had been elected and the documentation was ready to distribute. Shortly afterwards, the announcement was published in the diocesan news. The priests in East Timor did not know about the Vatican decision or that Mgr Puente had called Father Carlos Filipe Ximenes Belo to Jakarta to tell him that he was to be the new apostolic administrator. Belo had not been in Timor during the invasion. He was a thirty-five-year-old priest of the Salesian order who had recently returned from study abroad to work in the college at Fatumaca.

The priests were angry and they did not accept Belo. They thought he was too young and that he had had no experience. On the evening of 11 May 1983, the night

before Belo was due to be installed as apostolic administrator, the clergy visited the pro nuncio at the bishop's
residence at Lecidere to tell him their views and
announce that they would not attend Belo's installation
ceremony the next day. Mgr Lopes was there. With
dignity he said, 'I do the will of God and accept it in a
spirit of faith and humility.' When the priests asked Belo
for his response, he said, 'I am also obeying. The Holy
See asked me to take the position. I am doing what was
requested of me.'

Belo, promoted over Timorese priests who had ability
and apostolic preparation, had not been elected by the
clergy as Mgr Lopes had been. According to Mgr Puente
the Holy Spirit had ordained that Belo should be the
apostolic administrator of the diocese of Dili. The
priests had been excluded from the process and the
wounds on both sides took some time to heal. Jakarta
had succeeded in sowing discord in the Church.

Mgr Lopes' family, his brother Cristóvão's children
Rosa and Sebastião, found out that their Tio Bispo was
to leave Timor only a couple of days before his departure. They went to Lecidere to say goodbye but there
was too little time. They didn't know why he had to
leave. It was so sudden. Mgr Lopes wanted to stay in
Timor but Mgr Puente had advised him to leave. He was
preoccupied with Church business and packing. He was
surrounded by people. He wasn't well, but there was still
a lot to do before he left.

He appeared on the verandah of his house in Lecidere
wearing a white cassock with a large cross hanging in
front of the sash around his middle. He'd combed his
hair straight back, as he always did, and it disappeared

under his *zucchetto*. His round forehead stretched high, slightly shiny, scrubbed-looking. The tops of his ears stuck out, making his silhouette against the white wall look like a vase. With his hand by his sides he smiled. It wasn't a simple smile, even though his straightforwardness was written on his countenance. There was a residue of pain behind it. His eyes drooped down toward his handle-like ears. The furrows around his nose drooped down around his mouth to his chin. When he stopped smiling his mouth, too, made a downward swoop but, close up, his lips curled upward at either end. The lips that folded around his words, that sent them on their journey into the world, looked like some huge tropical flower or some smooth wood carving, totemic.

He said he was going abroad to raise awareness about Timor's situation. Of course he would rather stay with the people, but he could not. He didn't mention the pressure he was under. He told the young to stay united, stay strong, work for an independent East Timor.

About six months after his meeting with Xanana in the dry season of 1982, an envoy from the resistance leader had come to visit Mgr Lopes, bringing astonishing news. On 23 March Falintil command and an Indonesian delegation led by Colonel Purwanto had signed a ceasefire agreement. Xanana's envoy brought tapes of the talks, and even a photograph. There was Colonel Purwanto, wearing sunglasses, a cigarette in his mouth, smiling down at the piece of paper he held. Beside him sat Xanana, the corners of his eyes crinkling.

Purwanto had agreed to pass on to Suharto a letter with Fretilin's proposals. Fretilin asked for the unconditional withdrawal of Indonesian troops from East Timor, the admission of a United Nations peacekeeping force into the territory, free consultation with the people of East Timor and the maintenance of the armed resistance in the mountains so the people were free of any pressure. Falintil wanted Jakarta officially to inform the United Nations of the ceasefire. The Indonesians had offered to send in supplies for the Falintil guerrillas and to provide medical assistance for wounded guerrillas. Of course other offers made by ABRI had all been lies, but who could afford to give up hope?

The Falintil envoy asked Mgr Lopes to take the evidence of the talks out of Timor with him. The bishop agreed.

Mgr Lopes left Dili on 17 May 1983. The road to the airport was lined with people. It was unprecedented. Local transport was free and people mobilised to farewell their bishop of their own free will, unlike the time President Suharto came to visit when everybody was forced out. They wore yellow ribbons in their hair to mark the ceasefire. There were even two football matches between Fretilin and the Indonesians during the months the ceasefire lasted. The people cried to see Mgr Lopes go, their sadness adding to the grief the streets of Dili had already absorbed. Just when people thought things couldn't get any worse, they did. Houses had been turned into torture chambers, warehouses into incarceration centres, every corner, every tree, the gravel in the park, the electricity posts, held the story of an injustice. Perhaps better times were just around the corner. Perhaps Mgr Lopes would return to a free East Timor, but in any case he would be able to work for East Timor in the world outside.

He had had to leave his accordion in Dare but underneath the board at the bottom of his overnight bag he had the tape (removed from its spool so it was less likely to be detected) of the talks between Xanana and Purwanto that the resistance envoy had brought to him. Perhaps he had packed the slithery, seaweedy stuff himself, sliding it carefully under the board with his fingers so that he could take the news of the peace talks to the Fretilin External Delegation in Lisbon. The news of the ceasefire would reach the outside world even if the Indonesians did not honour their agreement to publicise it. Mgr Lopes hands had been fine and strong. Now his skin was blotched, his sores didn't heal. He wanted to rest.

Perhaps he was too tired to be nervous at the airport. What could they do to him now? Interrogate him? Deport him? Kill him? He had taken so many risks, at Tacitolu, at Santaiho, at Balide when the military tried to arrest him, at the commander's office in Dili ... The mission was much more important than the risk.

The priests had come to the airport to see him off. What awaited them now? The long days. The needs of the people. Mass. Prayers. Confession. Absolution. Hope. Father Cunha said, 'We hope to see you soon.'

Mgr Lopes wasn't optimistic. Despite his brave face, he couldn't lie. 'No,' he said, 'it's possible I'll die in exile.'

Maybe his feet were numb from diabetes as he climbed the stairs to the plane. He would have climbed voluntarily, lifting his feet himself, severing the connection with his land. These journeys gathered a momentum of their own. All he had done was board a plane. Then the engines and the engineering took care of the rest. Mgr Puente was on the same flight. No doubt the pro nuncio was masking his exultation until he arrived in Jakarta.

The plane zoomed down the runway; the palms and kapok trees whizzed by as the wheels lifted off the ground. As inertia pushed him back into his seat and the constant, impassive forms of the mountains receded, perhaps Mgr Lopes recalled the mythical journey undertaken by Ki Sa, ancestor of all the peoples of Timor, to find his younger brother Loer Sa, ancestor of all non-Timorese people.

The Mambai story went that Ki Sa and Loer Sa were the sons of Father Heaven. When he distributed their patrimony, Father Heaven gave Ki Sa the sacred rock and tree, tokens of the silent mouths. He gave Loer Sa the book and the pen, emblems of European identity. Heaven left other powerful symbols in Timor, but Loer Sa stole them and fled across the sea to Portugal. The people of the realm didn't recognise Ki Sa's authority and there was great chaos. Ki Sa went to find his younger brother, who was housebound and asleep in Portugal. Ki Sa explained the situation at home and reminded Loer Sa of his obligations to the place he had left. He asked for a token of status that would ensure his power was recognised and Loer Sa gave him gifts, including the flagpole, to take back to Timor. Loer Sa promised that his descendants would return at a later date with the flag.

After generations, descendants of Loer Sa arrived in Timor with the flag flying from the mast of their ship. Ki Sa's descendants were tired of ruling and handed over worldly responsibilities to the outsiders, but retained ritual authority over the cosmos, the silent mouths. Now Mgr Lopes was retracing Ki Sa's journey, leaving Timor to wake up the world.

Another Mambai belief was that forgetfulness posed a constant threat to world order. Those who travelled, who left the place they came from, risked forgetting their obligations to those who had stayed behind. Those who remained kept the collective memory intact, maintained the reciprocal ties that bind people and make the world cohesive. If, as according to the Mambai, true knowledge lay in the stomach, Mgr Lopes would have to have a committed stomach to keep the struggle alive so far away from home. But Mgr Lopes would never forget his obligations. He would never forget his brothers and sisters in Timor.

It was lonely on the ground after Dom Martinho had gone. Rosa and Sebastião wondered who would look after them and their families now. The priests were wary of the changes they felt were beyond their control. In 1983 East Timor was still a closed book as far as the world was concerned. Foreigners were not allowed to visit; the two humanitarian organisations that had gained access to the territory were strictly controlled. The population had been silenced. Who would have the courage to speak out for the people now Dom Martinho had been forced to leave? Who would unite them?

Mgr Lopes visited the Vatican on his way to Portugal, for his long-sought-after audience with Pope John Paul II. He wanted the Vatican to take a stronger stand on East Timor, and perhaps his words influenced John Paul II. Mgr Lopes was encouraged by the Pope's kindness and his awareness of the situation in East Timor. In the ensuing years the Pope asked Indonesian ambassadors to consider the ethnic, religious and cultural character of the East Timorese. Feeble words in the view of some, but Dom Martinho would not hear a word said against the Pope. He had met presidents and diplomats, but meeting the Pope was the pinnacle. He sent the photographs to his family in Timor. 'I'm all right,' he wrote to his friends. 'I talked with the Pope and I said everything I wanted to say.'

Mgr Lopes also met with Cardinal Casaroli, the Vatican secretary of state, whom he considered had been instrumental in preventing him from meeting the Pope until after he had resigned from office. Mgr Lopes told Cardinal Casaroli that the East Timor situation was a matter of politics. 'In matters of theology I believe the Vatican is infallible and I am obedient. But in matters of politics, you are only human and you are wrong about East Timor,' he said.

He arrived in Lisbon on 11 June, the Saturday of a holiday weekend. There was no one to meet him at the airport so he made his own way to the Pensão Flora, a place where Timorese refugees often stayed. From there he contacted the Portuguese Bishops' Conference and joined their retreat at Fátima, one of the largest gathering places in Christendom, where the stooped and sick came as pilgrims.

On the whole, the Portuguese bishops seem to have been as remote as the statues that watched the great square at Fátima from the top of the church buildings. The Portuguese episcopate did not regard Mgr Lopes as a bishop. 'Father' Lopes, some of them insisted, had been granted the title of 'Monsignor' as a courtesy by the Holy See. Some of them objected to the clothes he wore, clothes his station did not entitle him to wear. Mgr Lopes rarely spoke in self-defence. The people of East Timor had needed a bishop, and he had been their bishop.

The town of Fátima was full of souvenir virgins and Catholic comforts. Such abundance. When the East Timorese clergy had requested stocks of rosary beads, members of the Indonesian church had tersely reminded them that they were not their paymasters and that their social responsibilities were more important than pious devotions. In the olive groves near the village of Cova da Iria, where Our Lady appeared to three young shepherds in 1917, it was easy to forget the town of Fátima. Weathered, leather-faced men built stone walls. The poor country was built on, carved out. Whatever was indigenous to it had disappeared long ago. Eucalyptus trees grew in rows, unwanted plantation invaders. Still, the countryside wasn't as poor as Timor. It wasn't as invaded as Timor.

One day, while he was at Fátima, a phone call came through for Mgr Lopes. It was from Timor, apparently, an urgent message. The voice on the line was Abílio de Araújo's, president-in-exile of Fretilin. He wasn't in Timor. He was in Lisbon.

'I've been looking for you!' Mgr Lopes said.

Abílio arranged to go and pick up Mgr Lopes from Fátima. On the drive back to Lisbon they talked about the roads: bad, but not as bad as in Timor.

'Timor is poor because of Salazar,' Abílio said.

Maybe, for Mgr Lopes, Salazar was the least of Timor's problems now.

Whatever had transpired at the retreat, it hadn't resulted in permanent accommodation for Mgr Lopes. He planned to stay at Zitas Lar, a retirement home for priests and nuns, and had to pick up his bags from the residence of Dom José Ribeiro. By coincidence they saw a Timorese man on the street, whom they picked up.

At Zitas Lar, Abílio parked the car and waited for Mgr Lopes to sort out the arrangements. After half an hour he came out. 'There is no place for me,' he said. They tried another place. There was no room. It was six or seven in the evening. Mgr Lopes' predicament reminded Abílio of Joséph and Mary, searching for a place at the inn. In a magnanimous gesture, Abílio made a suggestion: 'If you were pro-Indonesian, pro-oppression, you would continue to live in your bishop's palace in Dili. As we are both here, I'll pay for your accommodation in a hotel.' Calling the bishop's residence in Dili a 'palace' showed how long Abílio had been away from Timor.

The Residencial São Pedro on the Rua Pascoal de Melo became Mgr Lopes' new home. It had a tiled façade and an impressive foyer. Through the glass security door were pink-tinged shiny marble steps with a gold handrail and dark wood panelled the wall on one side. It was almost church-like. The foyer smelt of cleaning fluids.

Seventy metres or so from the São Pedro was the Largo de Dona Estefania, a roundabout at the junction of a few cobbled roads. In a pond in the centre of the roundabout a statue of Neptune sat on a shell supported by two happy fish. The god had a wide torso, a benign, conceited expression and long locks. Water spurted at him from all around. His trident pointed downwards and was tinged green with moss. Around the pond a garden of low rose bushes was in bloom. There was a straggly wire fence around the whole affair, reminiscent of parks in Dili. It was a central part of Lisbon. There were cafes and shoe shops for the better off. Conservative-looking, elderly Portuguese in dark skirts and trousers strolled along the street.

In the opposite direction from Largo de Dona Estefania, Rua Pascoal de Melo passed Jardim Constantino, a small scruffy park with wooden seats. On the corner of Rua Pascoal de Melo and Avenida Almirante Reis, in a grey building with arched windows and thick, castle-like walls, was a restaurant called The Portuguese. Traditional, old-fashioned and clean, it offered its chubby clients wide tables with white linen tablecloths to eat steak with eggs on top for Sunday lunch. Substantial Portuguese-ness, big meat meals.

The news of the ceasefire in Timor was out. Mgr Lopes had reported the developments to Fretilin's delegates in Lisbon on his arrival, but Fretilin only divulged that they had the tapes and the photographs weeks after an Agence France Presse report from Jakarta broke the news on 10 June. Simultaneously, Mgr Lopes announced that Jakarta had failed to honour the agreement to publicise the ceasefire internationally. As far as Jakarta was concerned, there was no question of bringing the United Nations into what Indonesian authorities termed an internal affair. Shortly afterwards Jakarta announced that the talks had been solely concerned with the question of an amnesty. The negotiations had been a ploy to extricate ABRI from the military situation on the ground and to undermine international lobbying on East Timor in the months leading up to the 38th session at the UN.

Another motivation on Jakarta's part for the talks may have been the change of government in Australia. The Labor Party, which had had a policy of supporting East Timor's right to self-determination, replaced the more conservative Coalition government in early March. Bill

Hayden, the Australian foreign minister, visited Indonesia in April and perhaps was then informed of the developments. When Bob Hawke referred to the 'changed situation' on his visit to Jakarta in June the news of the ceasefire had not been made public, so what was the 'changed situation' that enabled his government to abandon ALP policy? Indonesia did not want Australia to support the UN resolution for East Timor.

Year by year the votes in favour of the UN resolution condemning the invasion, calling for the removal of Indonesian troops and an act of self-determination in East Timor had been falling. Despite a 1982 resolution requesting that the secretary-general of the UN should initiate consultations with all parties directly concerned, Jakarta's objective was to remove East Timor from the United Nations' agenda altogether. For one year the strategy succeeded because in 1983, due to unspecified 'recent developments', debate on East Timor was postponed until 1984.

In July the Indonesians withdrew permission for the International Red Cross to continue relief work on Atauro. In August 1983 the ceasefire in East Timor ended and Operasi Persatuan (Operation Reunion) commenced. It involved increased personnel, helicopters, tanks, Skyhawks and bombers. This time there was no fooling around. According to Benny Murdani: 'We are going to hit them without mercy.'

Mgr Lopes declined pastoral work in Lisbon because he wanted to devote himself exclusively to the East Timorese people. He was sixty-five years old. Caritas, the Catholic charity, helped him at first, until he started to receive his pension of about 54,000 escudos a month (the equivalent of US$400) — less than half the pension a Portuguese primary school teacher was paid on retirement — from the Holy See, and 70,000 to 80,000 escudos (US$518–US$592 approximately) from the Portuguese state, as a result of his time on the National Assembly.

After a few months at the São Pedro, Mgr Lopes told Abílio he had bought an apartment, a left-hand basement at Lote 109, Rua da Eira, in Alto de Alges. He also bought a black Renault 5. Did Abílio ever pay the bill at the São Pedro? Some say that he didn't, and that it caused quite a bit of embarrassment. The Timorese community helped Mgr Lopes move. He had a few personal belongings and his altar stone, chalice and equipment for Mass. He had permission to say Mass at home.

•14•

Travelling

IN AUGUST 1983 the war in Timor well and truly started again. When a group of Falintil fighters were captured and killed, there was an uprising in the village of Kraras, a resettlement area near Viqueque. In reprisal, the military killed hundreds of people and burned the village down. The survivors were left without food or clothes and when they sought refuge in the mountains at Bibileu they were bombed. Hundreds more were captured and massacred at the river Be Tuku. In October Mgr Carlos Ximenes Belo, the new apostolic administrator of Dili, denounced the killings and condemned the mass arrests. Also in August about five hundred Timorese soldiers defected to Fretilin from the Indonesian army, taking their weapons with them. In mid August Fretilin attacked the military airport in Dili and a door-to-door search in the capital ensued. It was back to the tension of 1977.

Meanwhile, throwing himself into the campaign to

raise awareness about East Timor, Mgr Lopes hardly sat
down during his first months of exile. His travels started
in Europe: London, Dublin, Paris and Holland in September. He met government representatives and lobbyists,
spoke with parliamentarians and gave press conferences.
He didn't have to look about to see whether the secret
police were watching, whether he was incriminating
anyone. He answered questions directly. He gave the
specifics and the generalities. Why did Indonesia want to
annex East Timor? He saw it as a matter of egoism, they
wanted to prove how strong and superior they were. They
had no humility at all and with such terrible arrogance
they were blind to everything. They simply refused to see
that imperialism was finished! The movement of history
was towards independence, but Indonesia didn't seem to
be learning from the lessons of history.

In his view the new offensive proved that the annexation had failed completely. There were 20,000 Indonesian
troops in East Timor. The Indonesian government continued to make the terrible mistake of refusing to see
that the East Timorese did not want to be integrated. If
they did want integration, Mgr Lopes maintained, he
would support them. If his people wanted to be independent, he would do everything possible to help them.

The Western governments, he presumed, were
remaining silent because of their trade links and huge
investments in Indonesia. Their materialism overrode
any idealism, morality or concern they might have about
human rights, although they paid lip service to such
notions. All they cared about were profits. In Mgr Lopes'
eyes the people in the West were losing their sense of
sin. Nothing seemed wrong to them any more; every-

thing was allowed. Because they had lost their sense of sin, they had lost their sense of God. People needed God because they were sinners. It was a terrible thing for people to regard themselves as superhuman, to think they didn't need God any more.

The Indonesian soldiers in East Timor, according to Mgr Lopes, were forced to do what they did. They were carrying out orders. The government of Indonesia was responsible for killing hundreds of thousands of people in East Timor. It was the sin of the government.

When Mgr Lopes visited Australia in late September and October, he found the Timorese community divided. Many had gone to Australia during the civil war and some UDT supporters tried to discredit him. Other Timorese in Australia didn't hear about his visit until it was too late. Some wondered why he was bringing up bad memories. They thought he was a communist, allied with Fretilin. But he said, 'I do not know if [Fretilin's] ideology is marxist or not. What I do know is that the Timorese people want to be free and independent and to govern themselves like other small Pacific islands.' When people asked him why Fretilin didn't change their name he answered, 'Why don't you change yours?' For Mgr Lopes, Fretilin was the symbol of national resistance.

Right-wing church commentators in Australia stuck the boot in, reminiscent of those fine accomplices of the New Order, Gough Whitlam and Peter Hastings. Mgr Lopes said he couldn't worry about such people, that he had to say what he knew to be true and that the people relied on him to do this. The Catholic hierarchy was divided. Some didn't receive him. He wanted to work with the local Church and was delighted when one bishop's greetings were passed on to him. He met with representatives from charities, the Church, the Australian Labor Party and trade union leaders. He expressed his belief that the Church was the servant of the people and told his story simply.

'The Church must follow the faith of its people. If the people want integration, the Church will accept that. But I insist they must have the right to decide for themselves.' He repeated what he had been saying for years: 'The only legitimate way to know what the people really want is to hold a referendum free from all pressures, internal or external.'

Someone mentioned Australians being 'realistic' about Indonesia's takeover. Mgr Lopes had a few words to say about that: 'You talk of "realism", but the reality is that the Timorese people do not want to be part of Indonesia. They have had a different history for 400 years, under a different colonial power, with a different culture, religion and values. They will never accept integration. To recognise this is realism.'

Whenever, wherever he travelled, he took his chalice and altar stone and said Mass daily. If he hadn't had a chance all day, midnight was not too late. He often slipped away to his room to pray. At St John's church in East Melbourne, in a clear voice full of suffering, he asked the Timorese congregation to remember their brothers and sisters in Timor, the land that was their mother. He told them not to let fear, shame or concern for their relatives stop them from speaking out about the terrible things that had happened. Their people were running like deer in the mountains, sleeping in mud. It could not get worse.

After the service Mgr Lopes was taking off his old-fashioned vestments in the sacristy when two girls greeted him. They hugged him, crying. He soothed them. 'It's all right. You're still alive. It's all over now.' If it hadn't been for him, they said, they would be dead. When the military had taken them he had faced the soldiers and taken them back. There were many similar stories of how he had saved people among the Timorese in Melbourne.

He was worried about the new offensive, though of course it was really nothing new. The resistance would withstand it, but it would be the civilian population who would suffer. He found it hard to talk about the atrocities. His voice trailed off when people interviewed him. He digressed, trying to understand how human beings could do such things to each other.

One evening, with a space in his schedule because of a cancellation at one of the Timorese soccer clubs, he had dinner with the Pires family. Alfredo Pires had been an administrator in Timor during the Portuguese time.

'What can I do?' said Mgr Lopes about the soccer club not receiving him. 'If the people think like that, what can I do? They're inflexible. You kill a person because they're a communist. Doesn't a communist have a right to life?'

Mgr Lopes said grace in Latin and the Pires family all tucked into the delicious *bacalhau* (cod) cooked in the Portuguese style. Mgr Lopes hadn't eaten Portuguese food for a while and everyone knew how he loved his food, particularly Portuguese food. Of course he wanted some more. But Tia (Aunt) Albina had made the unprecedented mistake of cutting the fish in half and mixing only half of its flesh with potatoes and cream and cooking it. So there was no more. The Pires family remembered the mistake for years.

Alfredo Pires and his daughter Emília took Mgr Lopes to the airport. There weren't many people to see him off. He visited Canberra, Sydney, Darwin and Perth while he was in Australia. In Darwin, with Agio Pereira, he went to a fish-feeding display. There were tears in his eyes when he said, 'This is what civilisation is all about. Feeding the fish in peace. People aren't taking them straight to the fire to cook.' He talked about peace for the rest of the afternoon, and at night they drank whisky and Coke. 'Your Portuguese is good!' he told Agio, astounded. Agio used to hide in the cemetery during Father Lopes' Portuguese lessons at Bispo Medeiros to avoid being hit with a ruler when he couldn't remember the vocabulary. Mgr Lopes kept his cassock on and sweated through the streets of Darwin. He saw Australian Aborigines for the first time.

The church conference in Darwin was filled with conservatives. Maybe Mgr Lopes was beginning to look tired: the skin of his eyelids drooping, his face puffy with perhaps the shadow of a beard. Perhaps his neck bulged over his stiff collar and the light reflected from his glasses with their heavy black rim on top, silver underneath as he explained: 'We are not asking you to go and fight for us. We are asking you to give us guns.' It caused a stir among the talking heads. He was 'comrade bishop' to some of the activists after that.

He had failed to receive the support he needed in Australia. He was short of money. Because of an oversight in the organisation of his trip, when his plane landed in Fiji it landed in Nadi, not Suva. Mgr Lopes had no way of getting to Suva. There was no one to meet him. He stayed in the airport for two days without any food until his onward flight. His other ports of call in the Pacific — the Solomons, Western Samoa, Vanuatu and New Guinea — weren't as bleak. He travelled on to North America, where he thought all the people looked the same. In the course of his broader United Nations address that year Father Walter Lini, the prime minister of Vanuatu, attacked 'the moral bankruptcy of those who speak so eloquently on other matters but who remain silent on the question of East Timor'.

The following February Mgr Lopes spoke before the United Nations Commission on Human Rights in Geneva. He had received a heartbreaking letter from Mgr Belo. 'It is a misery, Monsignor,' Belo wrote. He described mass military trials, the people being corralled and suffering from illness, hunger, loss of liberty and persecution, the conscription of the civilian population, going off with swords and knives and leaving their gardens untended. He described 'popular judgments' where those implicated with the fighters in the bush were murdered by their own families with knives, swords and sticks in front of the assembled people.

'They thought to finish things off by the end of December 1983, but we are already in February 1984 and there is no end in sight,' Belo wrote. He asked for people outside 'to pray for us, and appeal to the free world to open its eyes to the barbarities of which the Indonesians are capable'.

East Timor was now an official transmigration zone. In the following years, when Timorese were finally permitted to leave the resettlement villages and go home, their land was occupied. In 1985, in addition to its plans to settle almost 7000 people from the Indonesian archipelago in East Timor, the Indonesian government announced a five-year plan of birth control for 95,000 East Timorese women. Mgr Lopes wrote to President Reagan protesting about the birth control program. There is no record of Reagan's reply.

There was only so much travelling one man could do. Mgr Lopes started to become forgetful. On a trip to North America he arrived at an airport with no one to meet him. He was due to talk at the United States Senate the next day, but instead he got on a plane and went back to Portugal. He almost cried when somewhere in Germany he admitted to José Ramos-Horta that 'after serving the people and the Church for so many years, I was forced to resign'. He still never wanted anyone to think badly of the Pope.

He once spent a whole day in New York watching the boxing on television with José Ramos-Horta — a good break from the United Nations. He watched it quietly, not crying out with enthusiasm. His enjoyment was as elemental, as involuntary as breathing. Boxing wasn't as fine or as skilled as the Timorese sport *pontapé* but no doubt he was still mesmerised by the speed, and grace, of the fighters as they moved around the ring. Perhaps he felt an unproblematic satisfaction in watching an assault in the form of a series of well-placed punches. The sweat, swollen eyes, bruised bodies and fatigue of the fighters were as much a part of life as the dignity and restraint required of the priest in his luminous white vestments embellished with purple or gold, administering mystical rituals.

Since 1976 US administrations had recognised Indonesia's presence in East Timor without giving Indonesian sovereignty legal recognition. Before President Reagan's 1986 visit to Indonesia Mgr Lopes met with staff of the Committee on Foreign Affairs of the US House of Representatives to raise the issue of the Indonesian occupation of East Timor and the Timorese people's right to determine their own future. When a committee aide asked Mgr Lopes what the State Department's position on the question was, he replied that they recognised Indonesian control of East Timor.

'Then you're out of luck,' the aide said.

Mgr Lopes, in his black slippers and his black clerical suit, moved across the room as fast as a fighter in the boxing ring. *'Out of luck?'* he shouted angrily. 'You send the arms that kill my people and then you tell me I'm *out of luck?'*

Dom Martinho's message was clear and not quickly forgotten in the US Congress.

When Jenny Herera, a supporter in Tasmania, wrote to Mgr Lopes and mentioned that her Tasmanian solidarity group proposed to nominate him for the Nobel Peace Prize he had no objections. With or without the Nobel Prize, he said, he would continue to work for East Timor's freedom and independence.

Alberto Soares visited him from time to time in Lisbon and they talked about the old days, about the day Senhor Alberto broke Dom Martinho's arm. He'd recovered so quickly then; now his diabetes affected him more and more. There were more churches than people in Lisbon. In Timor he had never been alone. Now they were just two old men, Senhor Alberto and Dom Martinho, talking about the struggle they had come to know so well.

Not all his friends in Lisbon agreed with his defence of the fighters in the bush. Father Jorge Barros Duarte was a little older than Dom Martinho. Like Mgr Lopes, he had been a representative for Timor on the Portuguese National Assembly. Father Jorge was a scholar, a linguist, and a fine musician and composer. Mgr Lopes had a lot of respect for him, but he didn't understand the struggle. Mgr Lopes knew that, behind his back, Father Jorge called him a communist because of his links with the resistance.

'You have to open your eyes,' Father Jorge said to Mgr Lopes. 'You're being used by Fretilin.'

'I know what I'm doing,' Mgr Lopes responded.

They saw each other less and less.

Late in 1986, looking childlike and very tired at a conference table in Japan, Mgr Lopes refused to concede that the situation for East Timor was hopeless. He spoke optimistically. 'When I was in East Timor ... no news could go out and no news could come in. But now it is impossible to hide what is happening in East Timor. I and the Fretilin members are going everywhere in the world. I am trying to make all the governments of the world, and the people of the world, sensitive to our right to fight for justice.' Despite the slow process of international relations, little by little, year by year, others — the European Community, the United States, Japan — were taking steps.

'As long as we are alive,' he said, 'we have hope. God is in heaven looking down on us. So I trust God to change the minds of the government of Indonesia and the government of the United States.' Fretilin were ready to sit down and talk, but not without the United Nations. It was a question of Indonesia's losing face. 'One small island with only half a million people, and they are 155 million. So they are feeling ashamed because they are losing face. And for the Asian countries, for the underde-veloped countries, that has a very great influence on the psychological thinking. We are very small; they are very big.' The solution was simple, according to Mgr Lopes, if only Indonesia would accept the United Nations resolu-tions. Instead they were trying to buy off UN members. 'We have no money,' Mgr Lopes said, 'our force is only reason, justice and God.'

Earlier that year Fretilin and UDT had issued a joint statement. They had decided to work together in the defence of the interests of all Timorese people and for democracy in East Timor. Long memories died hard, but it was a step forward. In line with the new convergence Xanana Gusmão resigned from Fretilin in 1987. The fol-lowing year José Ramos-Horta and Xanana restyled the Revolutionary Council of National Resistance to become the National Council of Maubere Resistance (CNRM).

The years passed. Timorese refugees arrived in Lisbon. Mgr Lopes helped them how he could, in practi-cal ways. When Laura Barreto arrived, he gave her a stove. He travelled, baptised babies, drove around in the Renault 5. Anselmo Aparício, who as an eighteen-year-old seminarian had visited Atauro with Mgr Lopes in 1983, went out to lunch with him a few times. Anselmo didn't want to ask the bishop for help with his education or career. He didn't want to put pressure on him.

Mgr Lopes went on holiday to the Holy Land, naive and full of wonderment. He had dinner with Portuguese digni-

taries and enjoyed the good life. With characteristic inde-
fatigability he rarely turned down an invitation to attend
meetings or to talk about East Timor. With characteristic
simplicity he said what he believed was true. The Church
spurned him. Political opportunists used him. He was
caught up in the cause. It was exhausting him.

In 1989 the Indonesian authorities started their
Smiling Policy in East Timor. It was a quest for the
hearts and minds of the East Timorese. No Timorese
smiled for the tourists, however, who were allowed into
East Timor for the first time in fourteen years. John
Paul II himself was one of the first visitors, in October
1989. He spoke at Tacitolu. The youth unfurled their
banners: 'Independence or death!' An old battle cry. An
old story with the same results: detentions, torture, disappearances, death. Silence.

The family of Pedro Correia stopped coming to look
after the apartment in Alges in 1989 when Lídia Tilman
and her family, recently arrived from Timor, took over.
Pedro used to drive for Mgr Lopes when his cataracts
grew bad. He much preferred to eat out than to eat at
home. He was lonely in Lisbon. In Timor, people always
knew where to find him. In Lisbon people were busy. No
one had time.

When the resistance in Timor nominated Mgr Lopes
as their representative, he declined. He knew exactly
what the people in Timor needed, but he felt that some
factions in Portugal were using Timor for their own self-
interest, wanting the leadership role for themselves. He
was disappointed with the political structure in Lisbon
and he wasn't in touch with local politics. His outspokenness made his position problematic. Should he have

been more prudent? Should he have had a better defined strategy?

After a Portuguese newspaper published some of Xanana's comments, Mgr Lopes sent a message to Xanana to say 'We cannot lose Portugal'. Abílio was the man he asked to transmit the message, but who could trust Abílio? A couple of years later Abílio changed his position; the self-proclaimed leader of Fretilin in Portugal began to support integration. He had his price, no doubt. However, Abílio's tactics contributed to Dom Martinho's isolation. In September 1990 Mgr Lopes met Bishop Belo. They cleared up some misunderstandings, but after the meeting he sank into depression.

He became increasingly detached. His diabetes worsened. His sight was failing. He declined lunch invitations. 'I'm old. I'm tired,' he said when people asked him out. He didn't answer the door when people came to visit. He, who so loved dining, who had had so much energy to discuss Timor, had withdrawn from public life. He started to distance himself from Fretilin in Portugal. There were no angry words between them that Abílio recalled. Their relationship had simply grown cold.

Dom Martinho believed that the Timorese people were fearless and in his last interview he proclaimed that, one day, *oxalá*, their day would come. His talk was littered with the word *oxalá*, a whispered wish, a soothing, familiar word. 'God please bring as soon as possible to the East Timorese people what they deserve, *oxalá*, which is peace and justice.' His public statement was almost a prayer. *Oxalá*, 'God willing', from the Arabic. His hope was in God, not humanity.

•15•

Alto de Alges

THE MAN WHO WAS helped into his basement flat after he slipped in the stairwell at 109 Rua da Eira on 5 December 1990 was tired and lonely and sick. There was no food in his flat. He didn't cook; he preferred to eat out but, even so, the table was set for a meal. There was no one to set and clear away the table. He just left it set. The contract with the woman who used to come and clean his house had ended and he hadn't got around to renewing it.

All he had in the house was milk and biscuits. It wasn't like being at school with the priests — he could have milk whenever he wanted it now. Perhaps he thought about food while he was alone in that basement flat eating milk and biscuits. Perhaps he looked forward to a good meal: fish, chicken, any meat, any healthy food — that's what he really liked. And some wine, too. All those meals, round tables full of people, and Dom Martinho finishing off the plate as it was passed around.

Food was his pleasure. Perhaps he loved to eat because starvation lurked behind every meal. Perhaps he ate because if he fed his stomach, his memory would stay strong and he wouldn't forget his obligations to those who had stayed at home in Timor, to those who were running like deer in the mountains. Perhaps he ate to combat the bodily degradation he had witnessed and heard about. Why not eat? Because human life was inconsequential, because the human body was frail and could not withstand torture. Perhaps he ate because he didn't permit himself other forms of physical pleasure, because he was isolated from human intimacy but was a passionate man. Perhaps his appetite was voracious because the struggle continues. The body fights; the body can bear this overloading. And in this world where there is so much pain and pleasure is irresponsible, those chickens and cows might as well have died to nourish the fight.

Some said he was fat because of Fretilin. The criticism didn't worry Dom Martinho. He wasn't close to Fretilin now, not in Lisbon. Still, for Dom Martinho, Fretilin represented the people of East Timor, and they were fighting for the people of East Timor. The Indonesians would have to kill every last Timorese if they wanted to wipe out Fretilin.

Either Abílio called Dom Martinho to ask him to participate in the fifteenth anniversary of the invasion of Dili or he didn't. Perhaps the bland taste of soggy, crumbled biscuits was still in Dom Martinho's mouth if he answered Abílio's telephone call. Some said Abílio didn't call. Whether Abílio asked him to the ceremony or not, Dom Martinho couldn't go.

Politics were complicated in Lisbon. Dom Martinho had known what the people in Timor wanted. That was simple. Every day he heard what they wanted because they came to him and told him everything. The resistance in Timor had asked him to be their representative in Portugal but he had declined, leaving the job to others. Now there were people saying that those to whom he had left the job were opportunists, using Timor for their own self-interest. Despite the intricacies of politics in Portugal, he had to speak the truth.

He had been away from Timor for seven-and-a-half years. That was as long as he managed to stay in Timor after the Indonesian invasion. Seven-and-a-half long years and no sign of a change. In Lisbon the Timorese were divided: factions and fights. Perhaps he wasn't diplomatic or prudent enough. But he had spoken out when the people of Timor had needed him. What could he do now, when the world would not listen?

There had been such a long history of silences in Timor. The people had been silent because they couldn't speak Portuguese. Later, during World War II, people had struggled to survive. No one could speak about the Japanese occupation. After the war, the Portuguese returned and, later PIDE, the secret police, arrived. To speak against Portugal was to commit treason.

But Dom Martinho believed in the heavenly and prophetic mission of the Church to do its work, here and now, on Earth. Justice in this lifetime is what he believed in.

Silence in Timor, now silence in Lisbon. The little flat in Alto de Alges was crowded with furniture: sofa, TV, bookcase and a vase of fabric roses, reminiscent of the arrangements of artificial flowers in the reception rooms of houses in Dili, covered in plastic against the dust. One of the drop sides of the round rosewood-veneer table was lowered so the other sofa could fit in. The walls were damp.

The television set was beside the table where he ate and said Mass daily. On top of the television was a photograph of Dom Martinho meeting the Pope. In the photo the Pope was dressed in white. His white-clad figure dominated the picture. His white hands, ring glistening, reached out to encircle Dom Martinho. Dom Martinho's expression in the picture was one of dignity, humility, respect, joy. There was also stern necessity in the cast of his carved lips, in the flare of his nostrils. John Paul II should have understood. He was from Poland! Surely the people of East Timor, after all their suffering, had the right to peace and freedom, just as the people of Eastern Europe had the right to free themselves?

It was two weeks before the telephone rang again, on the evening of Friday 21 December 1990. 'Can you come and have dinner with us?' asked his niece, Lídia Tilman. 'Some friends have just arrived from Timor.'

'I'm sorry, I can't come. I'm sick,' he said. Lídia was worried. Later that night she, her son and her brother came over to Alto de Alges. They found Dom Martinho sitting on the lounge. Lídia had brought some chicken soup with her.

'Who's been looking after you?' Lídia asked.

'No one,' replied Dom Martinho.

Lídia was aghast. Dom Martinho, whose appetite was as large and famous as his outspokenness, had been living on nothing but cold milk and biscuits.

'Let me stay here for the night, so someone's with you,' Lídia said.

'There's no need,' he answered.

The next day Lídia's older son drove Dom Martinho in the black Renault 5 to São Francisco Xavier Hospital for a check up. At the hospital they found a small bruise on his back, gave him some medicine and sent him home. He took Panadol and ate the chicken soup Lídia had left for him.

When Lídia rang Dom Martinho on Christmas Eve he couldn't stand up. Lídia wouldn't allow him to be alone any longer. Without asking her husband's permission she insisted the bishop come and live with her and her family. Dom Martinho didn't want to trouble or to be a burden to them. Nonetheless, Lídia sent her son straight over to pick him up.

With his important belongings in an overnight bag, Dom Martinho climbed the stairs out of his basement flat, moving slowly across the grey-and-white chequer-board floor, past the green four-tile wall pattern. The ceiling, with its remote light fitting, was bright blue, brighter than the sky could ever be.

They passed the shanties on the corner. In heaps of corrugated iron, wood, cardboard, mattresses and scrap lived the people from the former Portuguese colonies who had come to seek a better life in the old metropolis. Their proximity kept things in perspective, the way things had been in perspective in Timor. How could anyone develop unnecessary desires when there was such need everywhere? The road curved right and they travelled the long, slow hill down to Alges. Alges was bustling. Christmas decorations brightened the busy streets and people were preparing for the festivities ahead. Yes, people in Portugal still hung Christmas decorations.

At Alges the River Tagus opened out. The sandbar curved across the river, God's calligraphic brushstroke, pointing to a space where sea receded into sky, space that offered new worlds, old worlds, the way west, the way east, the sea route back to Timor. Out there Dom Martinho's pain might disappear. He might feel vital again. He would be closer to home. He would have the energy to continue.

They climbed again from Alges to Carnaxide. Carnaxide was now a suburb of Lisbon but it had been a village amid the olive groves once. Pastel-coloured flats rose from the sparsely foliaged hills. From Carnaxide they could see Linda a Velha, more box-like buildings going up. Lisbon was growing. Cranes tickled insensible heaven.

•16•

Christmas 1990

THE CHRISTMAS that Dom Martinho came to stay Lídia was working as a cleaner. She lived with her unemployed husband and their sprawling family in *pensão*-style accommodation. Their apartment was two rooms and a kitchen. Lídia and Armindo Tilman had seven children, a number of whom were living with them, as well as three war children (fighters' orphans), and other friends were staying. Lídia lost count of how many people shared their flat that Christmas. Rogério Lobato, a nephew of Lídia's, was one of them. A bed for Dom Martinho was made up on a lower bunk of the three-metre-by-three-metre room where their daughters slept. He stayed in bed and ate heartily.

Here in crowded conditions in Lídia's flat were children, adolescents and adults, with their shyness, their spontaneous noise, humour and frustrations. The Tilman family had arrived in Lisbon from Timor in

1989. Life during wartime wasn't long ago. It was a difficult Christmas for Lídia and the household but it was a good change for Dom Martinho.

His body was failing. It refused to function, but he didn't want to trouble other people with his own suffering. His capacity for suffering was great. 'A Christmas present from the baby Jesus,' he told Rogério.

If Dom Martinho didn't sleep well on Christmas Eve, he didn't complain. As he said, his pain was a Christmas gift from Jesus; it united him with Christ and with all of suffering humanity. He wasn't up to much that Christmas Day. The parish priest from Carnaxide came in the afternoon to give him Holy Communion and they talked for a long time. Who knows what priests talk about? They had listened to so many people: heard their foibles, cruelties, doubts and hopes. The confidentiality of the confessional sealed their lips. It is said that doctors don't go to the doctor; they believe they know what the doctor will say, so they self-diagnose. A priest cannot take his own confession. Like other Catholics, he must go to confession. What regrets did Dom Martinho have? It is said that you don't regret the things you have done, just those you haven't done. Perhaps Father Manuel Chicharo offered solace to Dom Martinho's soul. Perhaps that was his Christmas present.

Rogério Lobato and Dom Martinho reminisced about the civil war — Rogério's feats of endurance, the funny parts. 'Remember the time,' said Dom Martinho, 'you lent me the car and provided the bodyguards so I could visit the missions? And then the police stopped me and asked me whether I was carrying weapons! "How could I be carrying weapons?" I said. "I'm a priest!"' Dom Martinho hadn't thought much of weapons in 1975. He still didn't think much of their misuse, but he saw their necessity now. They laughed. They talked about the struggle. They talked so they could feel invincible.

No matter how strong his memories were, Dom Martinho's body was weakening. He ate a lot. Lídia rang home from work at 10 am, noon and 4 pm with instructions for her sons, who were cooking for him. He ate, but he couldn't excrete anything. At first he could urinate, and then not even that. He still consumed the soup Lídia prepared: vegetable, fish or chicken, plenty of it. Abiding appetite. He would have preferred meat and sausages, but they weren't good for him. He tried to go to the toilet thirty times one night. He hid his pain from Rogério — it wasn't pain, he maintained, just discomfort, nothing compared to what others had suffered.

On the Friday after Christmas Dom Martinho was rushed to São Francisco Xavier hospital with a severe intestinal occlusion. São Francisco Xavier was a modern hospital, but the five-hour wait in casualty aggravated his suffering. There were fluorescent lights and the smell of pine needles from the park across the road. After his treatment, Lídia's family took him home to Carnaxide but he didn't improve.

Lídia continued to cook soup. Sometimes Dom Martinho ate yoghurt or stewed fruit. He liked having people around, but what could they do to alleviate his suffering, his special gift from Jesus? Perhaps the younger ones were shy of the sick old man. Maybe they found it terrible to watch him, the fighter, beaten by his own body.

By Sunday Dom Martinho was worse. Father Manuel came from the church at Carnaxide to give him

Extreme Unction. His body, despite food and medical attention, continued to deteriorate. Rogério convinced Lídia that Dom Martinho needed to go to hospital late on the last day of 1990. They packed his overnight bag. They called the local priest from Carnaxide, and Dom Martinho received Holy Communion. At 2 am on 31 December he was taken in an ambulance to São Francisco Xavier hospital.

He was beyond fighting now. Perhaps this would be their indefatigable bishop's final journey.

As it turned out, Dom Martinho spent only one night in São Francisco Xavier. On New Year's Day 1991 he was taken down the hill to Egas Moniz hospital. Egas Moniz wasn't modern and clean like São Francisco Xavier. Egas Moniz, the person, was a renowned lobotomist. When Dom Martinho had edited *Seara* he had printed a joke about a man who went to the bank and asked the teller to remove his appendix. When the teller said, 'I'm sorry, sir. This is a bank, not a hospital,' the man said, 'I'm sorry, sir, there is a sign here that says "All operations performed."' It wasn't a new brain Dom Martinho needed.

No one consulted Lídia about Dom Martinho's transfer; when she rang São Francisco Xavier they simply told her that he had been moved, she didn't find out why. The bougainvillea and oleanders in the grounds of Egas Moniz were not in flower when Dom Martinho arrived there. There was no sign of life in the branches of the poplars, and the stiff green shoots of the cliveas pointed up defiantly, waiting for spring.

Dom Martinho didn't go outside. He didn't see the palm trees around building A. They would have reminded him of Timor. There were gigantic statues outside building A — a bearded man with a piece of paper and a snake wrapped around a staff, a woman holding a bowl and a leafy branch, a nun with a microscope, her arm around a figure who looked like Apollo. Perhaps he was intended to look like Apollo, with an aquiline profile and a bear chest, when he left Egas Moniz.

He shared his ward with four or five others, heart patients and diabetics. He had the bed near the window and in the two months he spent there he improved. Some nights, it was true, in the small hours he fell out of bed and his calling the nurse must have disturbed the other patients. During the day he talked with them. The nurses were nice, and Dr Corrêa was a fine man. They talked and joked. He liked his conversations with Dr Corrêa.

In the evenings at Egas Moniz he sang the Mass. That was the only music he had. Food and music. Apart from devotion to God, food and music were what brought joy to each new day. He had the Mass but no Donizetti, no Spanish songs. He could hum them to himself, of course, but what if he wanted to hear them? What if he wanted to hear the thirty-four-piece orchestra in Macau? or the boys' choirs in Dili surge and fade as he conducted? or some sacred harmonies?

•17•

Hospital

ON 10 JANUARY 1991 Lídia gave up her job to care for Dom Martinho. It was the same day that Rosa wrote from Timor to let him know that her papers would soon be ready and that she would be able to come and look after him. The winter solstice was over. The days were getting longer but the oil heaters at Egas Moniz still didn't warm the room properly. Dom Martinho's feet were always cold. Rosa's postcard didn't arrive in Lisbon until late February, and by then it was too late.

Lídia and Irmã Marina visited him every day. Other people came, too, between three and four in the afternoon. Lídia cooked soup — vegetable and chicken — but she didn't bring sausages and red meat, which disappointed Dom Martinho. No *piri piri* (chilli sauce), no salt, only yoghurt or stewed fruit. He wouldn't eat the hospital food. Who would? He'd never get well if he ate that food. He was glad to see Irmã Marina and Lídia when they arrived. His face lit up with his big broad smile despite the pain in his stomach and his chest. It hurt Lídia, she didn't like it, but he preferred it when Irmã Marina fed him. She was a nun who had worked all over Timor — Ossu, Suai, Ermera, Ainaro, Soibada. She and Dom Martinho had never worked in the same place at the same time, but he had known her in the way priests know nuns, respectfully and at a distance, with a knowledge that their lives had the same framework, the same priorities.

Dom Martinho started to improve. He left his bed, moved around in a wheelchair and watched television. Perhaps he saw on the news that Australia and Indonesia were continuing their plan to divide the oil in the Timor Sea. He had had such hopes for the money from that oil. Now, like everything else, it was being stolen.

Planes flew over Egas Moniz from the south. Transport. Communications. Such great advances in his lifetime. Mgr Belo had always wanted to travel. That's what he'd said when he'd become the apostolic administrator of Dili. Perhaps they could swap. Dom Martinho could just go home and stay put, and Belo could take on the travelling, talking role.

Traffic moved across the Tagus on the new bridge, like a never-ending rosary. Now even the Tagus was receding, silting up, leaving the tower at Belém high and dry, refusing to provide enough water for big ships. Would the rivers of Timor ever give up like that?

Towards the end of February Dom Martinho's condition deteriorated. On Sunday 24 February he was given the last rites again. The ritual must have given his soul just one last burst of fight. His health improved and the next day Dr Corrêa suggested it might be time for him to leave Egas Moniz. Irmã Marina and Lídia had been looking for lodgings for him, somewhere clean where he would be looked after. They didn't like to tell him too much about the places they had seen. They forced themselves to stay optimistic. Lídia was ready to move into the flat in Alto de Alges to care for him. But Dom Martinho felt like a burden. No place for him. It was just like when he'd arrived in 1983, only worse. If only Rosa would come. 'Look after Rosa,' he said to Irmã Marina as she dipped the spoon into the chicken soup Lídia had cooked. Rosa would be on her way from Timor.

The shutters were lowered against the low winter sun. Irmã Marina fed him the soup Lídia had cooked, spoonful by spoonful. He had eaten most of it. When Irmã Marina turned her back to put the bowl down, Dom Martinho died.

Where does a life end? In the ward at Egas Moniz, a few centimetres from Dom Martinho's pained face as his last breath dissolved into the air? In a corner of the cemetery at Carnaxide after his coffin, covered with a Timorese cloth, a *tais*, was lowered onto Timorese soil and then buried under local dirt, which, in turn disappeared under white marble and plastic flowers? In Lahane, Dili, where Rosa, waiting for her papers to come through, received the news from Bishop Belo that her Tio Bispo would no longer need her in Lisbon?

For the living there were more of the ceaseless activities life demands. For the doctors there was the autopsy, which revealed Dom Martinho had chronic diabetes, liver, prostate, intestinal and arterial problems and a poor state of nutrition. The cause of death was a heart attack. For Irmã Marina and for Lídia, who arrived at the ward not long after Dom Martinho had closed his eyes for the last time, there was the rosary to be said, the collection of his clothes and the preparation of his body for the mortuary. For Dom Albino Cleto and for the many who knew him there was the requiem Mass and the burial at Carnaxide.

For Dom Martinho's spirit there was the slow flow of the Tagus west, the beginning of the long journey home.

And when does a life end? When can a soul rest?

Notes

IN THE PROCESS of compiling this biography I have read books and newspapers, interviewed people and retraced Dom Martinho's footsteps. Some sections are drawn from many sources. I'm very grateful to the people who shared their insights on Dom Martinho with me, many of whom I have not named here because I fear for their safety.

Introduction

1. Jose Ramos-Horta, *Towards a Peaceful Solution in East Timor*, East Timor Relief Association (ETRA), Sydney, 1996, p. 12.
2. Benedict Anderson, 'Gravel in Jakarta's Shoes', in Benedict Anderson, *The Spectre of Comparisons: nationalism, Southeast Asia, and the world*, Verso, London and New York, 1998, p. 133.
3. Horta, p. 12.
4. Anderson, p. 135.
5. Horta, p. 25.
6. Horta, p. 33.
7. Gerry J. Simpson, 'The Timor Gap Treaty Case at the World Court' in ETRA (ed.), *It's Time to Lead the Way: writings from a*

conference on East Timor and its people, ETRA, Melbourne, 1996, pp. 90–8.

8. Paulo Guterres, 'The Timor Gap Treaty' in *It's Time to Lead the Way*, p. 85.

9. For more information on Kamal's murder and Helen Todd's legal action, see the film directed by Anne Goldson, *Punitive Damage*, Occasional Productions, 1999.

10. Anderson, p. 137, attributes this phrase to Ali Alatas, Indonesian foreign minister, in the aftermath of the Dili massacre.

11. Catholic Institute of International Relations (CIIR), *East Timor: the continuing betrayal*, Comment series, CIIR, London, 1996, p. 12.

12. CIIR, p. 30.

13. *ibid.*

14. The outline of the CNRM peace plan is taken from Horta, pp. 18–20.

15. CIIR, p. 33.

16. Helen Hill, 'A Timor Settlement: can it be achieved before 2000?', *Arena Magazine*, June–July 1999, p. 26.

17. Hill, p. 25.

18. ETRA, 'East Timor: the final vote', May 1999 supplement to *Matebian News*, January–April 1999, p. 4.

19. *ibid.*

20. James Goodman, 'Examining East Timor issues', *UTS News*, no. 18, 27 September – 10 October 1999, p. 4.

21. ETRA, 'East Timor: the final vote', p. 4.

22. *ibid.*

23. Transcripts of the UN Agreement between the Republic of Indonesia and the Portuguese Republic on the question of East Timor, signed in New York, 5 May 1999, are available on the ETRA website. In October 1999 the website was in the process of moving from its current address (www.pactok.net.au/docs/et) to a new address (http://www.etra.zip.com.au).

24. John Lyons, 'The Secret Timor Dossier', *Bulletin*, 12 October 1999, p. 26.

25. Hill, p. 24.
26. Senate Foreign Affairs, Defence and Trade References Committee, *East Timor: interim report*, Commonwealth of Australia, Canberra, 1999, p. 10.
27. Senate, p. 11.
28. Senate, p. 12.
29. Lyons, p. 28.
30. Senate, p. 12.
31. Senate, pp. 12–13.
32. Senate, p. 19.

1 Fall

The account of Dom Martinho falling in his stairwell is drawn from Manuel Vilas-Boas, 'Bispo de Timor-Leste morreu à fome' [Bishop of East Timor died of hunger], *O Jornal*, 8 March 1991.

Page 6   AIA FORFORA BIRD AND THE GRANARY RITUAL: Margaret King, *Eden to Paradise*, Hodder & Stoughton, London, 1963, p. 153.

2 Beginnings

The bare bones of Martinho da Costa Lopes' life in this and subsequent chapters (including his parents' names, schooling and professional life from Soibada onward) are drawn from Martinho da Costa Lopes, unpublished curriculum vitae, Lisbon, 1985, referred to subsequently as Martinho da Costa Lopes, CV.

    GENERAL HISTORICAL BACKGROUND (SALAZAR'S ASCENT, PORTUGUESE LEGISLATION): James Dunn, *Timor: a people betrayed*, 2nd edn, ABC Books, Sydney, 1996, ch. 2; Gudmund Jannisa, *The Crocodile's Tears: East Timor in the making*, Lund Dissertations in Sociology 14, Department of Sociology Lund University, Lund, 1997, ch. 8; Jill Jolliffe, *East Timor: nationalism and colonialism*, University of Queensland Press, St Lucia, 1978, ch. 1.

7–8   PHOTOGRAPH OF MARTINHO DA COSTA LOPES AT LIQUIÇÁ: This photograph belonged to Father Jacob Ximenes and I saw it when I visited him in his room at the São Sebastião church in Lisbon in October 1992. Unfortunately, I did not take a copy of the photo, and Jacob Ximenes died before I visited Lisbon again to research Dom Martinho in 1997. There are other photographs of Dili and Maliana that I regret I did not borrow to copy when I was in Timor in 1997. After the rampage of 1999 the photographs, as well as the buildings and towns they depicted, have probably been destroyed.

8–13 GREAT REVOLT OF 1912: Dunn, pp. 16–17; Jannisa, pp. 137–43; Jolliffe pp. 34–9.

13–16 BINAMO AND MARTINHO DA COSTA LOPES' BIRTH: anecdote.

15 'THE SWEET MONOTONOUS CHANT OF WATER': Martinho da Costa Lopes, 'Os que eu amo' [Those I love], *Seara*, July–August 1953, tr. Jocelyn Vieira. The original reads: 'Eu amo a doce melopeia da agua,/Ja derivando mansa,/Ja fugindo a cantar, como que a medo,/Entre algas cor de esp'ranca.'

15 CUSTOM OF REMOVING NEWBORN BABY'S PLACENTA: King, p. 163.

16–20 TENDING THE SHEEP, FINISHING ELEMENTARY SCHOOL AND RUNNING AWAY FROM LIQUIÇÁ TO DILI: anecdote. I do not know how old Martinho da Costa Lopes was when his family moved from Laliea to Liquiçá, or how old he was when he travelled from Liquiçá to Dili. He finished elementary school in record time — before he lost his baby teeth.

20–1 SCHOOL IN DILI: author intrview with Alberto Soares, Lisbon, October 1992.

22–3 MAMBAI CREATION MYTH: Elizabeth Traube, *Cosmology and Social Life: ritual exchange among the Mambai of East Timor*, University of Chicago Press, Chicago and London, 1986, pp. 37–41.

23–6 SOIBADA: anecdote; author interviews with Helena Brites, Sydney, July 1997; José Ramos-Horta, Lisbon, October 1992.

24 FOREST FOOD: Abel Guterres in Michele Turner, *Telling East Timor: personal testimonies 1942–1992*, University of New South Wales Press, Sydney, 1992, p. 64.

3 Macau

27–31 LEAVING DILI AND SEMINARY LIFE IN MACAU: author interviews with Father Francisco Fernandes, Macau, August 1997; Father Lancelot Rodrigues, Macau, August 1997; Father M. Texeira, Macau, August 1997; Father Jacob Ximenes, Lisbon, October 1992; seminary records.

31 SPIES IN TIMOR: Robert Lee, 'The Pacific War in Timor', paper presented at *East Timor: towards self determination* conference, Sydney, July 1999.

31–3 WORLD WAR II IN TIMOR: Dunn, ch. 2.

32 DOM JAIME GOULART: anecdote; Francisco Fernandes.

32 'IN THE CELESTIAL EDEN': Martinho da Costa Lopes, 'As pétalas da vida' [The petals of life], *Seara*, January–February 1952, tr. Jocelyn Vieira. The original reads: 'Que no éden celestial, na tua c'roa/Pérola mais brilhantes se encastoa.'

32–3 RETURNING TO DILI: Jacob Ximenes.

33 ANTÓNIO'S GREETING: author interview with Alfredo Pires, Melbourne, October 1997.

4 Rebuilding

34–5 PILGRIMAGE TO PORTUGAL: author interviews with Simão Barreto, Macau, August 1997; Jacob Ximenes.

35–9 LIFE AT MISSION AT BOBONARO: Simão Barreto; Francisco Fernandes; author interview with Basílio Martins, Lisbon, September 1997.

39–43 INDONESIAN INDEPENDENCE: Jannisa, pp. 169–85.

43–6 ARCHITECTURE OF COLÉGIO INFANTE SAGRES; VISIT OF THE PILGRIM VIRGIN: Martinho da Costa Lopes, 'Ecos da missao de Bobonaro' [Echoes of the mission of Bobonaro], *Seara*, September–October 1951, no. 5, tr. Joan Oliveira and Jocelyn Vieira.

46–8 CORLULI BAU SAI: Simão Barreto; Basílio Martins.

47 LULIK OBJECTS AND CEREMONIES: author interview with Rogério Lobato, Lisbon, October 1992; King, pp. 154–5.

48–50 LIFE AT DARE: Francisco Fernandes.

50   ORGANIC LAW OF OVERSEAS TERRITORIES: Dunn, p. 25.

50–1   CONSCRIPTED LABOUR: Jannisa, p. 153.

51   CÂMARA ECLESIÁSTICA: when I visited the Câmara Ecle-
        siástica in 1997 there were letter boxes for the parishes
        arranged in alphabetical order as described. I can't be
        sure they were like that in 1954, but it looked like an old
        cabinet.

51–2   MARTINHO DA COSTA LOPES' WRITING ABOUT LABOUR CON-
        DITIONS, DILI HARBOUR: Alfredo Pires.

52–4   LIFE AT BAUCAU: author interview with Elvira Guterres,
        Melbourne, October 1997.

5 Faith and empire

56   PORTUGAL'S ADMISSION TO UN: Jolliffe, p. 48.

56   PHOTOGRAPH AND DESCRIPTION OF MARTINHO DA COSTA
        LOPES: Republica Portuguesa, *Anais da Assembleia Nacional
        e da Câmara Corporativa (VII Legislatura)*, 1st sessao legisla-
        tiva, 1957–58, Assembleia Nacional, Lisbon, 1960, p. 12.

56–7   LEGISLATIVE COUNCIL IN TIMOR: Dunn, p. 34.

57   POPULATION; AGRICULTURAL METHODS AND CROPS:
        Finngeir Horth, *Timor Past and Present*, South-East Asia
        Monograph no. 17, James Cook University, Townsville,
        1985, pp. 1–14.

58   LEGALITY OF CONSCRIPTED LABOUR: Jannisa, p. 148.

58–67   MARTINHO DA COSTA LOPES' PARLIAMENTARY SPEECHES: Por-
        tugal in the Far East: Republica Portuguesa, *Diário das
        Sessões*, Sessao no. 8, 14 December 1957, Secretaria da
        Assembleia Nacional, Lisbon, 1957, pp. 218–19; faith and
        empire: no. 39, 17 April 1958, pp. 831–3; lament for Pope
        Pius: no. 48, 9 October 1958, p. 1023; development plan:
        no. 59, 29 October 1958, pp. 1244–7; Governor Barata:
        no. 115, 3 June 1959, pp. 862–3; constitutional reform:
        no. 123, 17 June 1959, pp. 1003–5; pension entitlements:
        no. 148, 27 January 1960, pp. 319–20; general accounts:
        no. 176, 29 April 1960, pp. 862–4; Henry the Navigator:
        no. 177, 30 April 1960, pp. 870–2; insidious slander: no.

180, 2 December 1960, pp. 108–9; tears and sorrows of Angola: no. 206, 6 April 1961, pp. 531–2, tr. Joan Oliveira and Geoffrey Hull.

59–66   LIFE IN LISBON: records of the Assembleia Nacional, anecdote.

63–4   1959 REVOLT IN TIMOR: Jannisa, pp. 154–5; Jolliffe, pp. 48–9; Francisco Fernandes.

64   AEROPLANE FLIGHT FROM TIMOR TO PORTUGAL; GOV. BARATA'S HUMANE AND CHRISTIAN ROLE: Martinho da Costa Lopes, personal communication to Governor Barata, Lisbon, 12 November 1959, tr. Joan Oliveira.

66   IRRITATING DELAYS: Martinho da Costa Lopes, personal communication to Governor Barata, Lisbon, 29 May 1960, tr. Joan Oliveira.

67   EVENTS IN ANGOLA: Jannisa, p. 155.

6 Could the centre hold?

68   WARS IN AFRICA: Eduardo Mondlane, *The Struggle for Mozambique*, Zed Books, London, 1983 (originally published by Penguin, 1969).

72–4ff   LIFE AT OSSU; ADMINISTRATOR AT VIQUEQUE: Francisco Fernandes. I've invented the conversation between Father Lopes and the people of Viqueque based on information Father Francisco told me.

75–7   FAMILY STORIES: anecdote.

7 Awakening

GENERAL HISTORICAL BACKGROUND: Dunn, chs 4 and 5; Jannisa, ch. 10; Jolliffe, ch. 2.

84–5   GOV. ALDEIA: Francisco Fernandes.

85–6   MARTINHO DA COSTA LOPES' *SEARA* ARTICLES: heroism: 'A heróica resistência de um punhado de bravos', 9 September 1972; revolution in schools: 'O ano da revolucaõ escolar', 2 December 1972; Bishop Ribeiro's anniversary: 'Dois aniversários do nosso bispo', 10 February 1973, tr. Joan Oliveira.

86   CLOSURE OF *SEARA*: *Seara*, 24 March 1973; José Ramos-Horta.

90–1   PORTUGUESE FLAG: Constâncio Pinto and Matthew Jardine, *East Timor's Unfinished Struggle: inside the East Timorese resistance*, South End Press, Boston, 1997, p. 32.

92–3   PARTY CAMPAIGNING AND XAVIER DO AMARAL'S SPEECH: Francisco Fernandes.

94–5   BISHOP RIBEIRO'S PASTORAL LETTER: Jolliffe, ch. 2.

95–6   'UDT PARENTS ...': José Alexandre (Xanana) Gusmão, extract from *Timor-Leste*, an autobiography, *Arena Magazine*, December 1995 – January 1996, p. 43.

8 Civil war

GENERAL HISTORICAL BACKGROUND (INCLUDING CIVIL WAR, RECONSTRUCTION OF DILI, ROME TALKS, ASSAULT ON BALIBÓ): Dunn, chs 8, 9; Jannisa, ch. 10; Jolliffe, chs 3–8.

106   MARTINHO DA COSTA LOPES' CONVERSATION WITH ROGÉRIO LOBATO: Rogério Lobato.

108   MARTINHO DA COSTA LOPES' BLAMING PORTUGUESE: Martinho da Costa Lopes quoted in Michael Richardson, 'Under the double-talk, Timor suffers', *Age*, 15 January 1976.

109–10 SEPTEMBER RAIDS ON BOBONARO GARRISON: 'Alexandrino' in Turner, pp. 87–9.

111   'IF YOU LISTEN TO BENNY YOU'LL BE IN A WAR EVERY DAY': attributed to Suharto, Dunn, p. 204.

113   MARTINHO DA COSTA LOPES' CONVERSATION WITH XANANA: author communication with Xanana Gusmão, July 1999.

113   XANANA'S UDT PRISON EXPERIENCES: Xanana Gusmão, *Arena*, p. 43.

9 Invasion

My sources for this chapter are: David Jenkins, 'Day of fear and fury', *Sydney Morning Herald*, 2 December 1995; Martinho da Costa Lopes, 'Interview with former bishop of East Timor', *Tapol Bulletin*, September 1983; anecdote.

116   'DIPLOMACY IS FINISHED …': Adam Malik quoted in 'Malik warns', *Canberra Times*, 3 December 1975.

122–3   ALARICO FERNANDES' RADIO SOS: Jolliffe, p. 3.

125   SHOOTINGS ON DILI WHARF: Jolliffe, pp. 3–8; 'Mr Siong' in Turner, pp. 103–4.

125–6   PEOPLE LEAVING DILI; SHIPS BEING LOADED WITH LOOT: Xanana Gusmão, *Arena*, p. 44.

126–8   SITUATION FOR THE PRIESTS: anecdote.

10 Integration

Once again, I've used Dunn, Jannisa and Jolliffe for general background, as well as Martinho da Costa Lopes in Turner pp. 164–8.

129–30 STATUS OF THE DIOCESE OF DILI: Pat Walsh, unpublished notes on the East Timor issue based on an international visit, 7 June 1980–18 August 1980, Action for World Development, Melbourne, 1980.

131; &   YOUNG WOMEN TRYING TO BE UNATTRACTIVE; RUBY AND
136–9   OLINDA AT THE BISHOP'S HOUSE: 'Ruby' and 'Olinda' in Turner pp. 146–9. I've invented the conversation between Ruby and Olinda and Mgr Lopes regarding the 'peace map', but other details of the story are as they are given in Turner. I've also made up Olinda's thoughts.

131   TIMORESE PAYING FOR THE BULLETS THAT KILLED THEM: 'Edhina' in Turner, p. 111.

132–4   INDONESIAN SOLDIERS GIVING ARMS TO FRETILIN; *BABINSAS*, KORAMIL AND OTHER TERMINOLOGY; CHOICE OF FATHER LOPES AS APOSTOLIC ADMINISTRATOR: Martinho da Costa Lopes, 'Interview', *Tapol Bulletin*, pp. 3–8.

139–42 MARIA GORETE: Maria Gorete Joaquim in Turner, pp. 168–71. I've invented the conversation between Mgr Lopes and Maria Gorete based on information in Turner. 'I have to humiliate myself many times …' attributed to Maria Gorete by 'Lourenço', Turner, p. 170; 'My body is no longer mine …' attributed to Maria Gorete by Ines Almeida, 'The role of women in the struggle', in East Timor Relief Association (ETRA), *It's Time to Lead the*

Way: writings from a conference on East Timor and its people, ETRA, Melbourne, 1996, p. 101.

143   Split in Fretilin leadership: Hamish McDonald, Suharto's Indonesia, Fontana, Blackburn Vic., 1980, p. 213.

144   Luís da Costa: author interviews with Luís da Costa, Lisbon, October 1992 and September 1997.

144–5   Xanana regrouping resistance: author communication Xanana Gusmão, July 1999; Xanana Gusmão, Arena, p. 44.

145–6   Martinho da Costa Lopes' collapse in Jakarta: anecdote and information about diabetes.

146–8   ICRC and CRS aid programs: Australian Council for Overseas Aid (ACFOA), 'The politics of aid to East Timor', ACFOA Development Dossier, 2nd edn, ACFOA, Melbourne, July 1980.

148–50   Lourenço: Martinho da Costa Lopes, CV.

150–1   Fretilin attack on Dare: Walsh, notes on East Timor issue; Amnesty International, East Timor Violations of Human Rights: extrajudicial executions, 'disappearances', torture and political imprisonment, 1975–1984, Amnesty International Publications, London, 1985.

152   Fretilin links with civilian population: Martinho da Costa Lopes, 'Interview', Tapol Bulletin, p. 6.

153   Pablo Puente's acceptance of annexation: Walsh, notes on East Timor issue.

153–7   Meeting at Baucau: Martinho da Costa Lopes, CV.

154   Dading Kalbuadi's allegations of Timorese cannibalism: Martinho da Costa Lopes in Turner, p. 167.

154   Dading Kalbuadi's comments on the weather 7 December 1975: cited in David Jenkins, 'Day of fear and fury', p. 6A.

11 Speaking out

158–9   Sermon in chapel at Lecidere: I have drawn the general scene from my visits to Bishop Belo's early morning Mass at Lecidere, Dili, in September 1997. The words of Mgr

Lopes sermon are drawn from Belo's sermon, which features in a film by Max Stahl, *Carlos Ximenes Belo: sometimes I speak out*, Yorkshire Television, 1997.

159   II Corinthians 4, 6–11 was a reading in *Seara*, 10 March 1973, the second last issue before the journal was closed down by the secret police.

160   ANIMIST NAME: Jacob Ximenes.

160   BAPTISM AND FREEDOM OF MOVEMENT: Rogério Lobato.

161–4   CHURCH ORGANISATON; VATICAN POSITION: unpublished notes on list of personnel in the diocese of Dili; notes on Martinho da Costa Lopes taken from interview material in the ACFOA office, Melbourne; Walsh, unpublished notes on the East Timor issue.

164–5   VATICAN AND INDONESIA: Arnold S. Kohen, *From the Place of the Dead: Bishop Belo and the struggle for East Timor*, Lion Publishing, Oxford, 1999, p. 141.

164–5   'THE LITTLE ONES …': Martinho da Costa Lopes cited in Kohen, p. 142.

165–8   LUÍS DE LAGA: Martinho da Costa Lopes, CV.

168–69   DEATH THREATS; MARTINHO DA COSTA LOPES' POINTING OUT PERPETRATORS OF ATROCITIES: Kohen, p. 139.

169   XANANA ASKING MARTINHO DA COSTA LOPES FOR PHILOSOPHY BOOKS: 'Lourenço' in Turner, p. 112.

170–1   SPEAKING MOUTHS AND SILENT MOUTHS: Traube.

171–4   13 OCTOBER 1981 MASS: Martinho da Costa Lopes, CV.

12 Discredit

175–7   PABLO PUENTE'S VISIT TO DILI: anecdote; Walsh, Unpublished notes on the East Timor issue.

177   PRESIDENT SUHARTO'S APPEAL TO INDONESIAN CATHOLIC HIERARCHY: Pat Walsh, 'Church may hold the key to Timor's future', *National Outlook*, January 1982, pp. 12–14.

178   IMPENDING FAMINE IN EAST TIMOR: 'Famine looms in East Timor', *Sydney Morning Herald*, 11 January 1982; 'Backing for Timor plea', *Northern Territory News*, 11 January 1982;

'Territory move on Timor aid', *Northern Territory News*, 12 January 1982; 'Big response to Timor fund', *Northern Territory News*, 8 February 1982; 'Red Cross to check E Timor', *Sydney Morning Herald*, 3 March 1982.

179–80 Australian ambassador's visit to East Timor: Rawdon Dalrymple quoted by E. G. Whitlam in Senate Standing Committee on Foreign Affairs and Defence (Reference: East Timor), *Hansard Report*, 14 May 1982, Canberra, Commonwealth of Australia, pp. 40–1.

180–5 Hastings and Whitlam's visit to East Timor: Bill Gray, 'Whitlam slips into Timor', *Herald* (Melbourne), 3 March 1982; Ian Davis, 'Aid body attacks Whitlam's Timor visit', *Age*, 4 March 1982; Jim Dunn, 'In perspective', *Northern Territory News*, 18 March 1982; 'Whitlam visit "hasty"', *Northern Territory News*, 5 April 1982; Pat Walsh, 'Timor people support the Church in its opposition to Indonesian takeover', *National Outlook*, November 1982, pp. 10–12.

181–3 Conversation between Martinho da Costa Lopes, Gough Whitlam and Peter Hastings: Senate Standing Committee on Foreign Affairs and Defence (Reference: East Timor), *Hansard Report*, 14 May 1982, Canberra, Commonwealth of Australia, pp. 57–8. Whitlam's quote 'check with people who have been there' appears on p. 69 of this report.

184–5 Whitlam's version of his visit to Timor: Gough Whitlam, 'The truth about Timor', *Bulletin*, 30 March 1982, pp. 78–81. A complementary article is 'Timor report false, says Whitlam', *Age*, 6 March 1982.

184–5 Hastings on the visit to Timor: Peter Hastings, 'Food a worry but no famine in E Timor', *Age*, 6 March 1982 (Hastings' term 'Fretilin-infested' appears in this article); 'Priest's tale of woe could cost Timor aid', *Age*, 8 March 1982; 'Indon [sic] officials warm to the Whitlam style', *Age*, 8 March 1982.

185–6 FAMINE AND THE SITUATION ON THE GROUND IN TIMOR: Senate Standing Committee on Foreign Affairs and Defence (Reference: East Timor), *Hansard Report*, 12 August 1982, Canberra, Commonwealth of Australia, pp. 1142–1235; Peter Griffiths, 'Fretilin guerrillas virtually beaten', *Northern Territory News*, 21 May 1982; Rod Nordland, 'Famine signs clear in East Timor', *Northern Territory News*, 11 June 1982; Kenneth Whiting, 'Timor's famine abates ... but hunger remains', *Northern Territory News*, 13 July 1982.

187 FÁTIMA GUSMÃO'S STORY: Fátima Gusmão in Turner, pp. 141–2.

188 CONVERSATION BETWEEN MARTINHO DA COSTA LOPES AND BASÍLIO MARTINS: Basílio Martins.

188–91 MEETING BETWEEN MARTINHO DA COSTA LOPES AND XANANA: 'Interview with Monsignor M. da Costa Lopes', *AMPO Japan-Asia Quarterly Review*, vol. 19, no. 1, pp. 44-8; author communication with Xanana Gusmão, July 1999

191–2 INTERVIEW AT LECIDERE: Stahl, *Carlos Ximenes Belo*.

13 Leaving Timor

195–6 SELECTION OF BELO AND THE PRIESTS' ATTITUDES: anecdote; Kohen, pp. 145–6.

196–7 MARTINHO DA COSTA LOPES' DEPARTURE AND HIS ADVICE TO YOUTH: anecdote; author interview with Jacinto dos Santos, Melbourne, October 1997.

197–8 MEETINGS BETWEEN FALINTIL AND ABRI; CEASEFIRE: Dunn, p. 301; author interview with Jill Jolliffe, Lisbon, October 1992; author communication with Xanana Gusmão, July 1999.

200–1 KI SA AND LOER SA: Traube, pp. 55–6.

201–2 MARTINHO DA COSTA LOPES' VISIT TO VATICAN: anecdote; Kohen, pp. 140–2.

202–4 MARTINHO DA COSTA LOPES' ARRIVAL IN PORTUGAL: author interview with Abílio de Araújo, Lisbon, October 1992.

205–6   ANNOUNCEMENTS OF FRETILIN–ABRI CEASEFIRE; AUS-
TRALIAN LABOR PARTY AND EAST TIMOR: *Tapol Bulletin*, no.
58, July 1983, pp. 6–7.

206   UN RESOLUTIONS: Jannisa, pp. 243–4.

14 Travelling

209ff   MARTINHO DA COSTA LOPES' VIEWS AND STATEMENTS: Martinho da Costa Lopes, 'Interview', *Tapol Bulletin*, *AMPO
Japan-Asia Quarterly Review*; CISET, *Newsletters*.

210–14   VISIT TO AUSTRALIA AND PACIFIC, 1983: Martinho da
Costa Lopes in Turner, pp. 164–8; Chistians in Solidarity
with East Timor (CISET), *Newsletter*, vol. 1, nos 1–3, September–November 1983; author interviews with Emília
and Alfredo Pires, and Pat Walsh, Melbourne, October
1997; Agio Pereira, Ceu Brites and Ines Almeida, Sydney,
October 1997.

214   BELO'S LETTER: Jannisa, pp. 244–6.

215   'AFTER SERVING THE CHURCH …': Martinho da Costa
Lopes quoted by José Ramos-Horta in interview with
author, London, October 1993; also quoted by Horta in
Stahl, *Carlos Ximenes Belo*.

216   'OUT OF LUCK': Martinho da Costa Lopes in Kohen, p.
155–6.

216   NOBEL PEACE PRIZE NOMINATION: personal communication from Martinho da Costa Lopes to Jenny Herera,
Lisbon, 25 May 1986.

216–20   LIFE IN LISBON: author interviews with people in Lisbon
conducted in October 1992: Anselmo Aparício, Laura
Barreto, Gregorio Henriques, Jill Jolliffe, Luisa Pereira,
Alberto Soares.

220   MEETING WITH BELO: Abílio de Araújo quoted in 'Timo-
renses apoiaram sempre D. Martinho' [Timorese always
supported D. Martinho], *Diário de Noticias*, 12 March
1991, tr. Joan Oliveira.

220   *OXALÁ*: Martinho da Costa Lopes in an interview with
Maneul Vilas-Boas for Portuguese television.

15 Alto de Alges

This chapter is compiled from interviews with people in Lisbon: Abílio de Araújo, Anselmo Aparício, Luisa Pereira, Lídia Tilman, October 1992 and August 1997; Manuel Vilas-Boas, October 1992.

16 Christmas 1990

This chapter is compiled from interviews with Rogério Lobato and Lídia Tilman; and Manuel Vilas-Boas, 'Bispo de Timor-Leste morreu a fome' [Bishop of East Timor died of hunger], *O Jornal*, 8 March 1991.

230   OPERATIONS JOKE: *Seara*, 16 December 1972.

17 Hospital

Sources for this chapter are interviews with Sister Marina and Lídia Tilman, Lisbon, August 1997; and Manuel Vilas-Boas, 'Bispo de Timor-Leste morreu a fome' [Bishop of East Timor died of hunger], *O Jornal*, 8 March 1991; 'A carta que monsenhor não recebeu' [The letter that never reached Monsignor], *O Jornal*, 8 March 1991; 'A autopsia', *O Jornal*, 8 March 1991.

Index

East Timor cont.
increased protests from (1998)
xxi–xxiv
Indonesia-Portugal agreement
xx–xxiv
Indonesian invasion vii–viii, 110–15,
116–29
Indonesian language 162, 164
integration 129–57
international pressure builds
xx–xxi, 217
languages 15, 160, 164, *see also*
Galolen
loss of life 159
name adopted 94
political allegiances pre invasion
95–9
Popular Representative Assembly
129
post referendum violence (1999)
xxiv–xxvi
radio contact 122–3
resistance *see* Falintil; Fretilin
self-determination xv, 163
Smiling Policy 219
sterilisation program 186–8, 215
terror campaign by Indonesians
130–4, 137–43
UDT coup 101–8
unilateral declaration of independence 114–15
East, Roger 116, 125
Egas Moniz hospital (Lisbon) 230, 233
embassy occupations, East Timorese
protestors xviii
Estado Novo 17, 69, 84
see also Salazar
executions 125

Falintil xiii–xiv, 144, 150, 197, 208
see also Fretilin
Farano, Monsignor 134, 177
Fatima 203
Felgueiras, Father 127, 151
fence-of-legs operations 152–4, 176,
186
Fernandes, Father Francisco 73, 74, 77

Fernandes, Alarico 97, 122–3, 130,
143, 190
5 May Agreement (1999) xxi
Fiji 213–14
Filippo, Monsignor Ettore di 163
food shortages 153, 181–2
and overseas aid 112, 131, 139,
146–8, 176, 184, 185–6
Ford, Gerald xiii
Fraser, Malcolm 114
Freitas, Feliciano 17, 18, 33
Fretilin 91
amnesty offer 134
boycott of Macau talks (1975) 99
ceasefire and truce proposals (1983)
197–8, 205–6
coalition with UDT 94, 100
coalition renewed (CNRM) 218
communism scare tactics 99
control established (1975) 109
election campaigning (1975) 94–8
end of ceasefire (1983) 208
establishment of aid programs 88,
92, 99
guerilla strategy 129, 132, 150–1, 208
Indonesian invasion and 110–15,
116–29
popular support for 153
post civil war administration and
110–15
reorganisation 144–5, 190–1
setbacks (1978) 143
UDT coup and 101–8
unilateral declaration of independence 114–15
see also CNRM, CNRT, Falintil

Galolen (language) xi, 15, 133
Gerry, Bishop John 178, 180
Goa 90
Goulart, Dom Jaime Garcia 23, 24, 28,
32, 71
Gouveia, Maggiolo 102, 104
Great Rebellion (1912) 11–12
Grelléty, Dr Pascal 146, 148
Guinea Bissau 70–1, 79, 83–4, 135

INDEX

INDEX